Foreword

AS A LEADER in the animal health industry, Merial's mission is to provide products and solutions to enhance the health, performance and well-being of animals, which also benefits their owners and the veterinarians who prescribe and use our products. At Merial, we also aim to contribute to the growth of all aspects of animal health in the broadest sense of the term, and this is the reason we are proud to sponsor the first edition of *Essentials of Veterinary Practice: An introduction to the science of practice management*.

Thirty years ago, most vets did not worry too much about the way they managed their practice – indeed, the concept of a business was far removed from their day-to-day concerns. Clients would come in regularly, would keep coming back and income was sufficient to pay bills and salaries, keep some decent revenue and ensure a certain level of growth. Without any formalised management skills, veterinary practices were doing okay. However, that is no longer the case, and vets recognise they need to pay close attention to all those "other aspects of the profession" – not just the medical and surgical disciplines learned in vet school, but all the management science that is often not broached in the curriculum. Young veterinary graduates do not always perceive the need for, and importance of, a business-based approach to their chosen career, often because this is far removed from the initial vocation that led them to embrace the veterinary profession.

By reading *Essentials of Veterinary Practice* and keeping it close to hand for easy reference, we hope our young colleagues, future colleagues – and even experienced practitioners – will discover or rediscover some of the basic concepts relevant to running a veterinary practice as a business, working as a team with their staff and developing good relationships with their clients. In other words, all those aspects of the veterinary practice that are not directly related to the animal.

Our profession has changed and will continue to evolve over the next decade. Vets in practice are challenged both by new channels of competition (pharmacists, agronomists, other animal industry professions, e-commerce etc), as well as from within (more vets, corporate medicine etc). Our society is changing rapidly and so is the vet's approach to his or her work, aiming to maintain quality of life parallel with the profession.

Consumers' expectat[illegible] ever-increasing pace. There is now more choice than ever before – and what does that mean? The consumer expects easy, convenient, environmentally-friendly, high-quality services ensuring good value for money. To successfully meet these demands, personalised and carefully crafted communications and services will make all the difference.

At Merial, we are convinced that *Essentials of Veterinary Practice: An introduction to the science of practice management* will help you make that difference – the vital difference.

Jean-Louis Crosia DVM
Head of Business Operations
Merial Europe, Middle East and Africa

"This book will be of immense use and interest to all practitioners, irrespective of how long they have been in practice. The authors believe the main beneficiaries will not be decided by their length of service, but will be those who are willing to embrace the fact that practices – and their clients – continually evolve and, by following the book's advice and concepts, will find their practices become more successful and more enjoyable for the whole team.

Clients expect their vets to be good clinicians; so what makes a real difference to them – and the success of the practice – is its organisation. How you deal with clients, staff and the commercial aspects are all comprehensively covered within the text, providing the building blocks on which to grow the practice.

I have no doubt that *Essentials of Veterinary Practice* will prove to be an invaluable management tool and should be in the library of any practice aspiring to expand and improve."

John M Bower MBE, BVSc, MRCVS
Past-president BVA, BSAVA and VPMA

Essentials of Veterinary Practice

An introduction to the science of practice management

Philippe Moreau DVM, MS, DipECVIM- CA, DipECVN

Richard C Nap DVM, PhD, DipECVS, DipECVCN

Published by Henston

Designed and produced by Veterinary Business Development Ltd

Designer: Ian Clark BA(Hons)

Photography: Philippe Moureau, Richard C Nap and *The Veterinary Business Journal*

Printed and bound in the United Kingdom by Greenshires Group, Leicester

ISBN 978-1-85054-159-2

Contents

About the authors

Philippe Moreau

DVM, MS, DipECVIM-CA, DipECVN

PHILIPPE MOREAU graduated in 1978 from the University of Liège in Belgium. He specialised in internal medicine and neurology in the US, at Purdue University (internship) and at Texas A&M University (residency). He graduated from Texas A&M in 1982 with a Masters in Physiology and Pharmacology, and is a Diplomate of both the European College of Neurology (ECVN), and the European College of Internal Medicine (ECVIM-CA).

Returning to France in 1983, Philippe, together with partners, developed a referral small animal clinic in Limoges, with six veterinarians, 10 animal technicians and an internship programme, and a hospital manager.

In 1985, Philippe founded the marketing and communications company Medi-Productions. Since 1999, he has devoted most of his time to the company, providing consultancy services to the animal health industry, lecturing in practice management, and auditing and helping veterinarians with their vet clinic management. He created Vet'Kiosk (www.vetkiosk.com) – a digital signage service for veterinary practices – that has been translated into nine languages and distributed in several countries.

Philippe has delivered more than 200 lectures and training sessions on practice management topics throughout the world. He has been a major speaker at 14 WSAVA congresses and two Veterinary Practice Management Association (VPMA) conferences in the UK. He developed a veterinary management audit service in France, which contributed to the development of more than 150 practices.

He has written widely, including two practice management manuals: *Merchandising in the Vete rinary Clinic* and *Communication Tools for Veterinary Clinics.*

Philippe has been married since 1982 to Dr Jeanne Cook-Moreau and has two sons (Nicolas and Patrick), two dogs (Vickie and Pin-up), a cat (Spot), two horses (Funny and Calimero) and a sheep (Pickachu).

Richard C Nap

DVM, PhD, DipECVS, DipECVCN

RICHARD C NAP is a veterinarian from The Netherlands. He graduated from Utrecht University in 1979 and in 1993 attained his PhD from the same institution. He is a specialist and Diplomate of both the European College of Veterinary Surgery (ECVS) and European College of Veterinary Nutrition (ECVCN).

Richard has worked in private referral practice, as an associate professor in orthopaedics at Utrecht University, and as associate director external relations for Procter and Gamble, responsible for international academic affairs.

Since 2005, Richard has been involved in supporting private practitioners, veterinary organisations and the animal health industry as a private consultant (www.uppertunity.com).

He is the author of many peer-reviewed and other publications, is an invited speaker at meetings and courses around the world and has contributed to proceedings, books and book chapters.

Richard has a passion for supporting young colleagues and has initiated two international projects for graduating veterinary students to optimise their career start. These are: Vetstart (www.vetstart.org) an independent information exchange platform with animal health-related industries and organisations; and VetCoach (www.vetcoach.info) a not-for-profit book project. The latter collectively offers more than 3,000 years of experience from veterinarians from around the globe, which they believe will prove beneficial to the new cohort of veterinarians.

Three editions of VetCoach books were published within 12 months in Europe and Latin America; new editions for Europe, Brazil and North America are in preparation.

Richard currently holds residency in Punta del Este, Uruguay and with his wife Dra Betina Rama also spends a significant portion of his time in Buenos Aires, Argentina. Together they have four children (Mark, Franco, Olaf and Zoe), a dog (Nala) and a cat (Kudari).

Introduction

WE REALISED, AS practitioners and later as veterinary consultants working with colleagues, that scarcely any veterinary school teaching is devoted to a crucial aspect of veterinary practice – that is, practice management – which could be described as the profession's business side. *Essentials of Veterinary Practice* aims to fill that gap. It also offers us an opportunity to congratulate readers for joining such a great profession, and welcome them to the real world of veterinary practice.

Keeping in mind the veterinary student and the recent graduate, this book will focus on the essentials of practice management.

Our intention is not to cover all aspects of management, but to concentrate on the most important topics and introduce the major business concepts encountered in practice.

We are convinced that veterinary students are provided with adequate scientific knowledge and skills to make a good start as a practitioner; indeed, many leave veterinary school with an honours degree.

Unfortunately, the students who are best academically

It is now a well-appreciated notion that clients (pet owners) do not care how much you know, until they know how much you care.

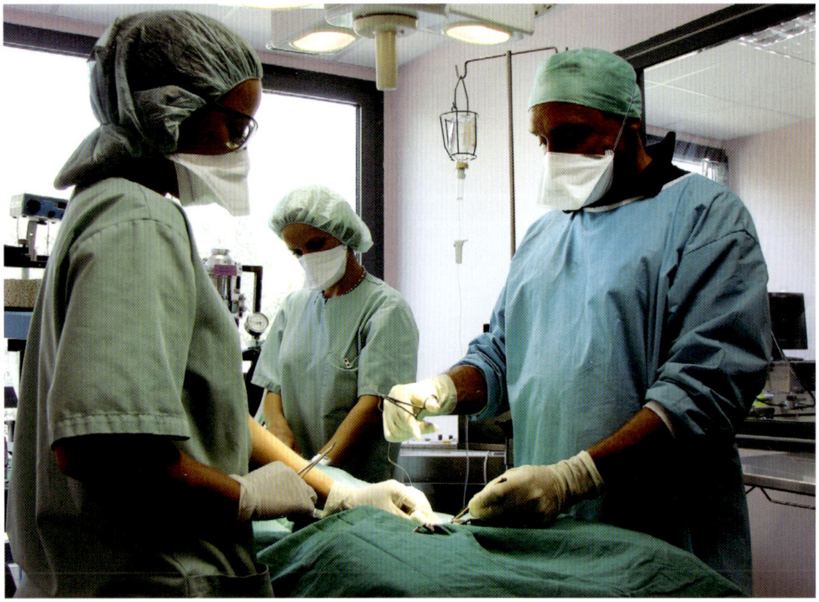

During veterinary studies, how much time was spent on communication and people skills?

are not necessarily successful in practice. More than likely, the new graduate will never be asked by a pet owner or colleague for details of academic success. Client (pet owner) surveys have shown that people trust the veterinary professional and assume the vet's level of knowledge and skill is more than adequate to diagnose and treat their pet. While it seemed critical

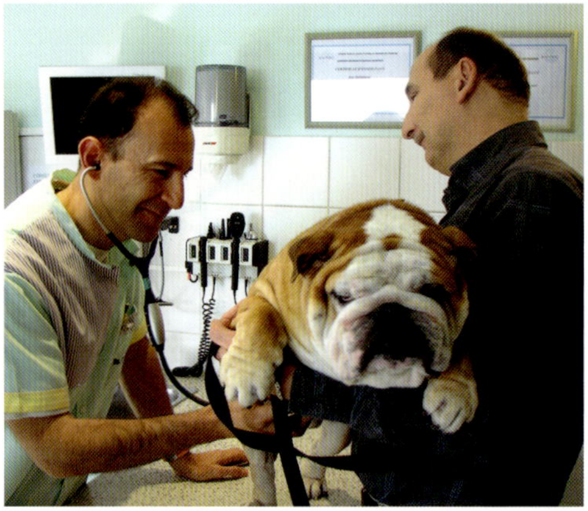

to attain a good degree grade when at university, this often assumes little importance in general practice. Even during job interviews, few senior veterinarians pay much attention to the applicant's marks and exams results.

This book is not about the classical veterinary sciences; it is about introducing the reader into the business environment of companion animal practice. The real world of the veterinary practitioner is that of a small business, which is subject to the realities, principles and laws of that world. Knowledge and skills in the area of practice management are highly scientific, and marketing and management studies form a whole new curriculum.

Veterinary practice is a mixture of services to clients, and of people and pet relationships. It is now a well-appreciated notion that pet owners "do not care how much you know, until they know how much you care".

During veterinary studies, how much time was spent on communication and people skills? Having focused on science, how much does the new graduate know about people interaction and communication? What about selling the services, and associated products?

In many companion animal practices, up to 50 per cent of the turnover is generated by product sales. Globally, this trend is increasing, although the percentage differs between countries and regions. This is an important part of our business, which differentiates us from our colleagues in human medicine who, for the most part, only prescribe.

The text presents the profession's historical background (to illustrate where we come from), and discusses changes that have taken place.

It will also deal with the basic professional and private questions that need to be answered before starting a career. These include: "What is my profile and what do I want? Where do I want to be in 10 years? What are my career objectives?"

Practice management principles will be discussed and the concept of the powerful human/pet bond will be introduced.

In the language of practice management, pet owners are "clients". Veterinarians need to know their client's expectations and how to meet and exceed them. Other topics include: How should we organise the practice, run a clinic and become used to working in a team? How do we learn to communicate with clients and staff, and how do we obtain a degree of client loyalty? Is the practice financially healthy? What are the financial indicators, and how should we interpret and influence them? Who are the competitors and how should we stay ahead of them?

The scope of the book would be incomplete without attention being given to the important topic of time management, to optimally balance professional and private lives.

The difference between success and failure in practice will depend on the extent to which the practitioner is compassionate when dealing with pets and people (both pet owners and clinic staff), while at the same time creating value for the practice. We believe this book will help new graduates be better prepared for their future professional and private life. It should also increase the quality of services tailored to the changing needs of clients and their pets.

Other questions for the new graduate include: "Am I eager to make the transfer from science to practice? Am I eager to learn about communication and people skills, about prioritising and time management and, of course, about marketing and sales programmes? Do I want to familiarise

Optimal veterinary healthcare can only be provided in an economically healthy clinic which allows continuous investments in human resources and equipment enabling ongoing improvements in quality.

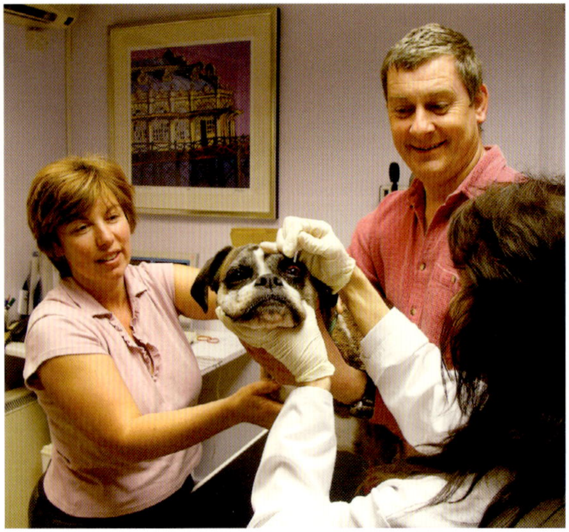

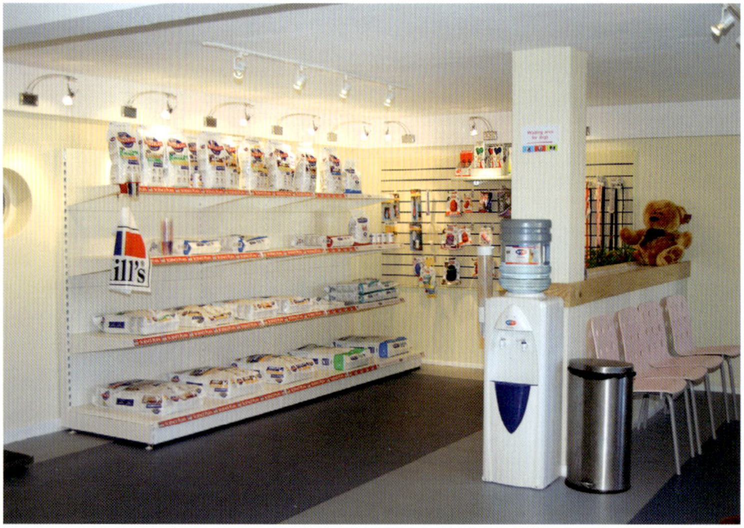

Solid science, quality medicine and surgery, and sound practice management are key factors that will enable a new graduate in practice to stay on track and attain his or her professional objectives.

myself with financial and organisational matters in the veterinary clinic?"

Optimal veterinary healthcare can only be provided in an economically healthy clinic that allows continuous investment in human resources and equipment, enabling ongoing improvements in quality. Working in such a practice, a graduate will have the best chance of long-term work enjoyment. A veterinary surgeon who is happy at work will enhance a happy working atmosphere.

We are confident that *Essentials of Veterinary Practice* will encourage students and recent graduates to study the subject in more depth to become better veterinary practitioners.

Solid science, quality medicine and surgery, and sound practice management are key factors that will enable a new graduate in practice to stay on track and attain his or her professional objectives. Progress will not be optimal if only one of these factors is in place; using them all, in a well-balanced manner, will enable the practitioner to keep ahead of the competition in the changing and fascinating world of companion animal practice.

Philippe Moreau DVM, MS, DipECVIM-CA, DipECVN
Richard C Nap DVM, PhD, DipECVS, DipECVCN

WE WOULD LIKE to take this opportunity to express our gratitude to Merial Europe (and in particular Jean-Louis Crosia, Jean-Luc Michel and Amanda Evans) for their support and for generously sponsoring a large number of copies our book's first edition, making it possible to reach out to the veterinary profession, including young and recently graduated colleagues.

1

Practice Management in Perspective

The evolution of the veterinary profession

1.1

THE FIRST VETERINARY school was established in Lyon, France, in 1762 by M. Claude Bourgelat, supported by King Louis XIV, with the principal aim of taking care of the royal horses. A second school was soon established in Maisons-Alfort, close to Paris. Following this initiative, vet schools were founded in Vienna, Austria and, subsequently, in many other countries.

The first veterinarians were essentially highly educated farriers. However, veterinary care expanded in earnest during the 19th and early 20th century, encompassing cows, sheep and other farm animals.

Despite 250 years of history, the global veterinary family is relatively small and is widely estimated to number some 300,000 veterinarians worldwide. Of these, about 90,000 work in Europe and approximately 50,000 in North America.

In the early years, the veterinarian, the pastor, the teacher and the doctor were the village intelligentsia – being the only people able to read. Vets were highly respected, were few and far between, and did not face any competition. Vets could prescribe (dictate) with no questions asked.

However, after the Second World War, farmers and people in nearby villages started to ask (often with some embarrassment), if the vet could have a look at the dog "while he was there". At the same time, equine and pet care medicine developed within cities. The design and organisation of many veterinary schools still reflects this predominantly large animal focus.

Veterinary care was initially developed to take care of farm animals and, in many countries, this is still the profession's main focus. This is probably one of the reasons many veterinary students still come from a rural environment. The horse was the "noble" animal used for most of the anatomy classes, and herd management and large animal medicine represented the greater part of the veterinary curriculum. In some countries, this phenomenon is still strongly embedded in the profession, and most veterinary school systems are still the responsibility of the ministries of agriculture.

The growing and significant trend towards companion animal care is changing the nature of the veterinary profession. Companion animal care is no longer based on economical factors, balancing the value of the animal with the expense of medical care. Today, when dealing with companion animals, we deal with emotions and affection; we recognise companion animal care is driven by the human/pet bond (see **Section 3.1**). People refer to the animal's sentimental value and, as a consequence, there is no limit on the amount that many pet owners pay for pet care.

As is often the case, history, education and culture all influence our professional behaviour. This includes, for example, the attitude of some veterinarians

In the early years, the veterinarian, the pastor, the teacher and the doctor were the village intelligentsia – being the only people able to read.

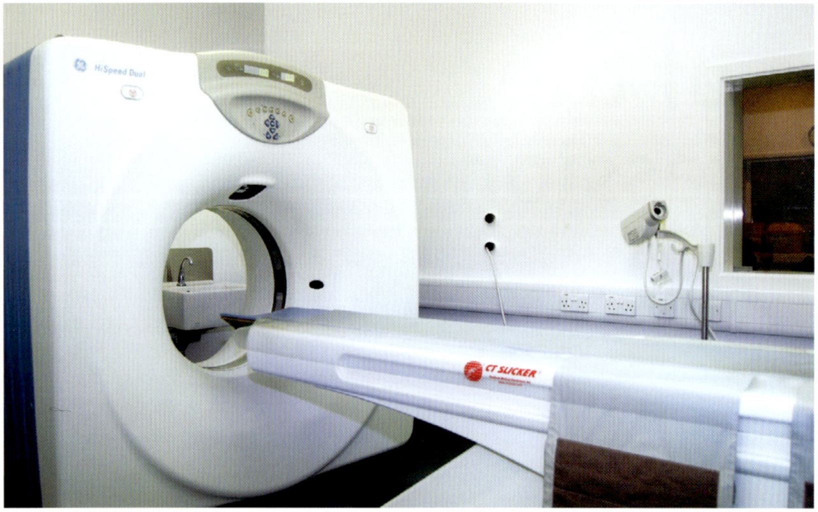

when facing the cost of pet care. We have to admit that veterinarians are increasingly involved in companion animal care. However, many vets are not mentally prepared for such an attitude change – because it was not part of their culture, background, education or even initial motivation when they joined the profession. Even the horse, once a working animal, is now a sport animal and considered by many as a companion animal.

It is important for young graduates to realise the veterinary profession has drastically changed with time. This is normal – as we are changing, so our society is changing.

It is clear that such a trend has influenced our practices, as well as the veterinary education system. The veterinary profession is also undergoing major transformations that will influence the veterinarian's future, with new curricula and modern, highly sophisticated diagnostic and therapeutic techniques.

However, some colleagues continue to regard an animal's market value as opposed to sentimental value and, therefore, advise clients that a treatment may not be justified. Euthanasia may be recommended because the expense of treatment is "not worth the economic value of the animal". Often, this advice is not what clients were expecting to hear. Of course, it is important to explain to pet owners the realities of the case – the chances of a cure, subsequent life expectancy, any pain and the cost of medical care – and then let the owners decide how they wish to proceed. Too many colleagues (particularly from the older generation) have a tendency to decide for the owner, because they were brought up and trained in that manner. As mentioned earlier, the background of vets with an agricultural link (a down-to-earth attitude) may be partially responsible for such service.

It is important for young graduates to realise the veterinary profession has drastically changed with time. This is normal – as we change, so our society changes.

In the past, clients were not as mobile, and did not consider asking an alternative veterinary opinion. Veterinarians visited their clients, and the veterinary practice was often a simple and basic place. Vets' main income was derived from animal husbandry, with no cash transactions as everything was invoiced, often only once every three months. No charge was made for time, as the fee was based only on results (many vets still find it very hard to charge when they feel nothing was done except to give advice).

The bulk of income was derived from large animal practice, often on herd medication sales. Dogs and cats were treated "on the side", often at no charge. Veterinarians were making a good living and there was no financial need to charge.

Historically, vets worked from home with their wife's help – vets were mostly men. Modern veterinary practices usually employ several veterinarians, some with specialist qualifications. Practices are well equipped, often with advanced technology.

Full consumer services are offered, with practice managers, receptionists, nurses, kennel and hospitalisation staff and, in some cases, grooming, boarding and retailing. Over the past 10 years, some countries have seen the growth of multiple-site practices, group practices, corporate practices, veterinary buyers' groups and franchises.

In the early years, special organisation was rarely needed; local young people were often asked to help. It is only recently that professional and educated staff, with dedicated veterinary nursing skills and degrees, have joined the animal health family. Our employees are very important to our success, and we need to spend time selecting and educating them, and demonstrating that we value their input.

Progressively, veterinarians were assimilated by society and are now regarded as pet family doctors. The "patients" are animals, the vets are "animal doctors" – and this title is important, particularly for those working in large animal practices. In general, veterinarians prescribed but, for the sake of convenience, in many countries they became "pharmacists" with the legal privilege to dispense drugs and, more recently, other animal goods such as pet food and hygiene products. The income generated from these sales gradually increased to significant levels, and is now often a necessity for the overall economic balance of a practice.

Work was charged and fiscally handled as undeclared income – no longer feasible with modern computerised systems. Previously, practice was a 24/7 occupation and the term "business" was not appropriate. It was a vocation, serving the community rather than a means of earning a livelihood. Many people still do not regard it as a commercial activity.

Our society is one of consumers and modern technology. We live in an age of computers and communication tools (television, telephone, fax, modems, internet, e-mails and cellular phones). This new technical environment is very demanding, with less time to relax and no room for inefficiency or error. Clients are more mobile, often changing homes and jobs, and trying different services. Many clients are happy to travel to reach their favourite vet, although one can no longer rely too much on client loyalty (see **Section 3.2**). As veterinarians, we have traditional professional obligations, but increasingly we are judged by clients only on results.

There are many reasons why veterinary medicine has made such progress in the science and art of disease prevention and animal care. The diagnostic and therapeutic methods we use are no longer empirical

The knowledge and skills acquired by veterinarians are such that our profession is still well respected. However, the veterinarian is no longer among the only people in town who can read.

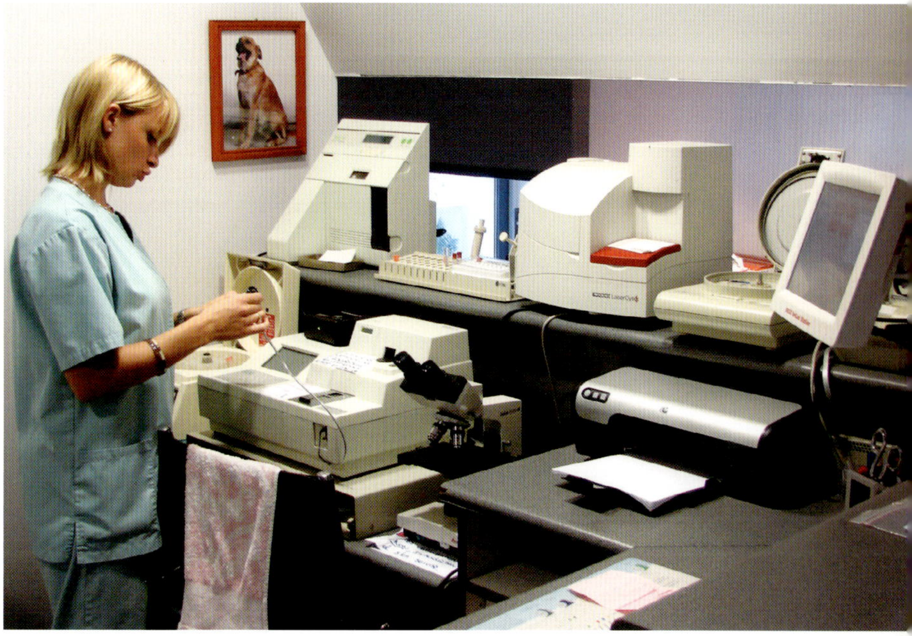

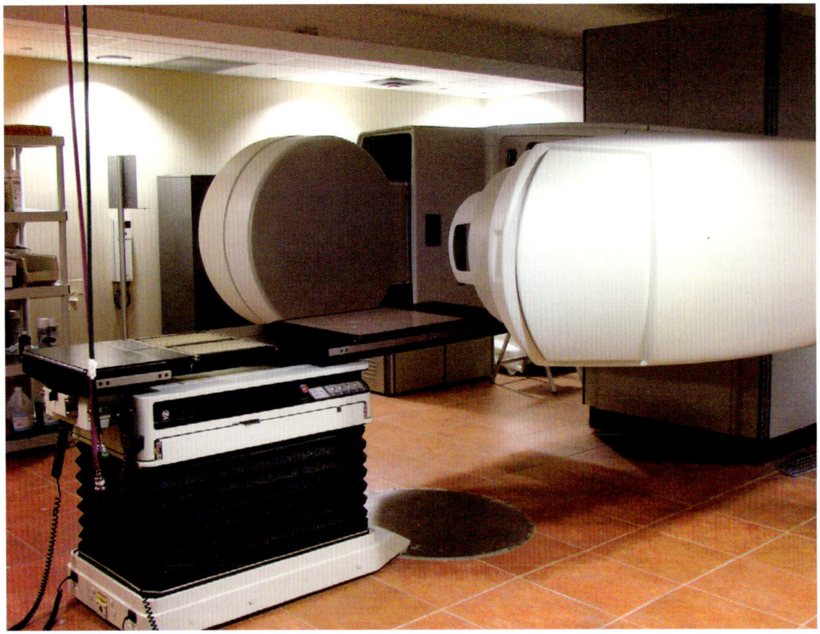

> Clients consume the services and products of veterinary practices and, therefore, react with a consumer's attitude.

in the management of either large or small animal disorders. These methods are often identical to those used in human medicine. The knowledge and skills acquired by veterinarians are such that our profession is still well respected. However, the veterinarian is no longer among the only people in town who can read, and clients are also better educated.

However, in the current selective and challenging professional environment, veterinarians have started to look at the management and marketing of their clinics and hospitals. The time of the family business veterinary practice is declining. The era no longer exists when vets were financially successful from day one, simply by placing their name and title on the door, and offering animal care for their neighbourhood. Competition is strengthening and the number of veterinarians is increasing, yet the number of animals is static in most countries. Farm animal veterinary activities have dropped significantly. Breeders and companion-animal clients are now well educated and expect a high-quality service, demanding better quality and more efficient services. In this consumer environment, clients expect veterinarians to comply with their own needs as well as those of their animals. Competition from other veterinarians, but possibly more significantly from other professions working with animals, is another reason why we must excel in our professional veterinary services.

For a veterinarian, it is no longer sufficient to be a good clinician and surgeon – it could be said that it is more important to be a good administrator, a good communicator and a person who is always available and concerned at all times with patients' needs and owners' requests. This new science is often not covered in the veterinary school curriculum. It is, however, a true science based on technical knowledge and theory, and for which exist numerous practical examples and applications. In this new competitive veterinary market, the use of good practice management and proper veterinary marketing techniques will allow veterinarians to develop their business and be successful entrepreneurs.

We also believe that: "Good practice management is good veterinary medicine" (Lord Soulsby of Swaffham Prior).

To achieve this requires basic knowledge of management, human resources, communication skills, computer and telecommunication technologies, sales techniques and finance. Above all, there needs to be a real desire to modify and change habits and methods. This is not easy. For some reason it is particularly difficult for the liberal professions – such as physicians, dentists, lawyers and veterinarians – to modify the way they have been practising for years, especially in countries where old traditions are part of national culture.

Mark Twain was right when he said: "The only one who likes change is the newborn with a wet diaper!"

Here, we are concerned with adapting our methods to fit the new environment of the future, making our daily work a more profitable venture for ourselves, our profession, our clients and their pets. Practice management is no longer the icing on the cake, but is an essential ingredient in a recipe for success. Veterinarians are now running small businesses and, in order to succeed, need to be aware and knowledgeable about the management aspects of the profession.

Veterinary practices offer both medical services and product sales. The latter is mainly medications, but the past 20 years has seen the development of non-medical product sales by veterinary practices. These include pet food and ancillary hygiene and healthcare products, such as non-medical shampoos, nutritional supplements, leashes and

Superstores have not replaced small retail shops – both coexist and satisfy different needs.

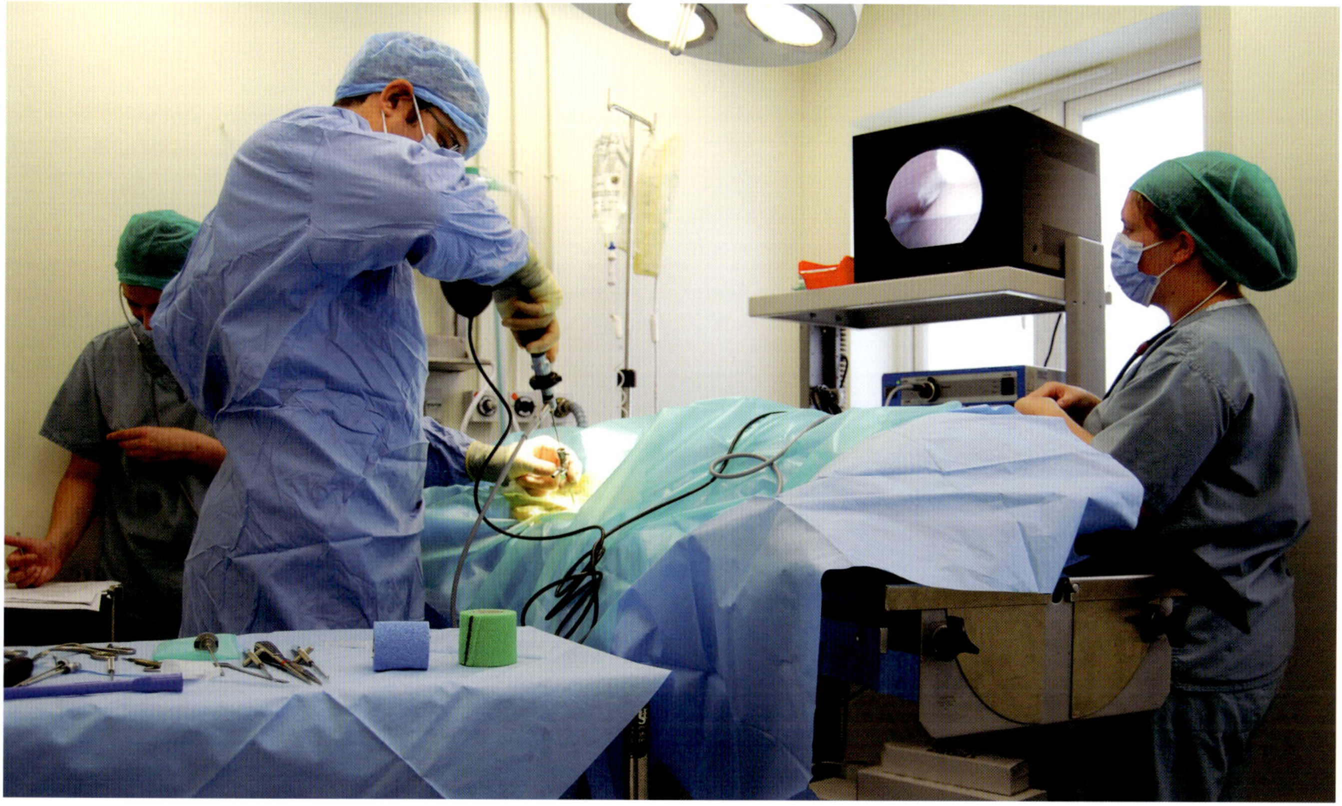

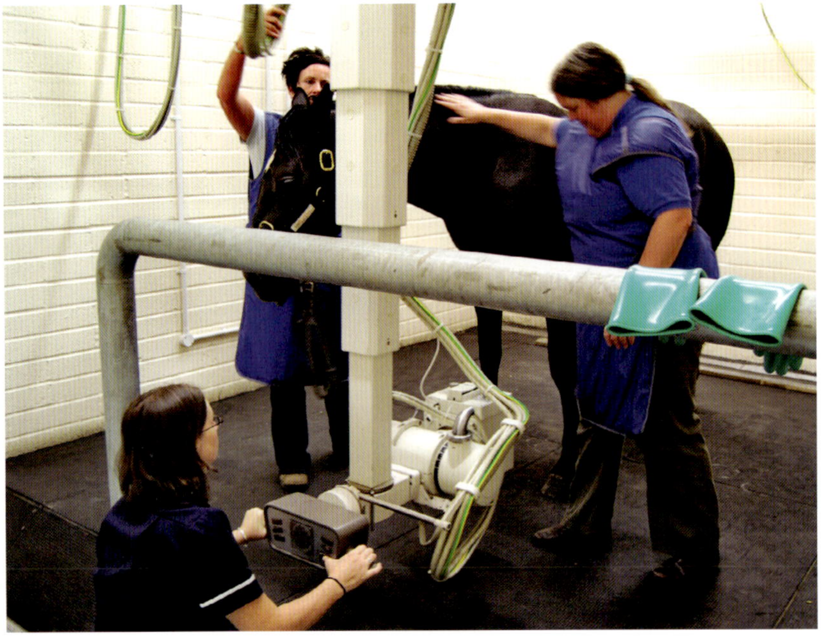

An increasing number of women are entering the veterinary profession.

collars. Preventive medicine has progressed, and the service is no longer limited to vaccinations. This is a key element of the modern veterinary profession: veterinarians are no longer limited to the care of the sick and injured animal, but are actively involved in the management of the healthy animal. Some refer now to "wellness" medicine, such as sending reminders for the annual medical checkups.

Clients consume the services and products of veterinary practices and, therefore, react with a consumer's attitude. This attitude encompasses demands for price comparisons; full service; single location shopping; and service value (not to be confused with cost).

Clients seek convenience and easily administered treatments, are concerned about environmental protection and product safety, and possible unwanted effects on their family and pets. Some years ago, veterinarians limited their actions to the medical care of animals. Today, there should be full integration of all preventive animal care including, in some cases, ancillary aspects such as grooming, boarding and dog training classes. Pet behaviour modification services have an increasing importance.

Sales of non-medical products, particularly pet foods, have grown significantly and, in many practices, represent a significant portion of total revenue. What used to be just an opportunity is often now an essential part of the practice income.

When starting a practice there is a choice of remaining a generic doctor (not retailing any products and letting others handle that business), or to embrace the idea and offer a retail service expected by the majority of clients. Needless to say, we encourage our young colleagues to produce a full-service practice, offering all the services and products needed by clients.

Comparing veterinarian incomes to those of other liberal professions – particularly taking into account the arduous and lengthy training needed to complete veterinary studies, and the massive capital investment required to practise – the clear conclusion is that other liberal professions generate better incomes.

An increasing number of women are entering the veterinary profession. Adolescent women are generally better students and perform better in professional examinations, which plays an important role when entering vet school is based on exam results. The decline of large animal medicine, which appealed more to men, may be another reason why more women are tempted to enter the profession. Working as a veterinary assistant can be undertaken as a part-time job and many women find this can fit in with raising a young family. Whatever the reasons, and they are probably multifactorial, women are taking a growing and crucial place in the profession. It is more than likely this trend will have an impact on the evolution of the veterinary profession.

Another professional trend is associated with the specialisation developing in veterinary medicine. An increasing number of specialists are well trained and offer specialised medical care. Generalist veterinarians can be compared to the family doctor in human medicine, who can refer their patients to specialists when this is justified and necessary.

We see a similar development with veterinary employees, such as veterinary nurses and veterinary technicians, who can also now specialise in fields such as anaesthesia, nutrition and behaviour. In the US and some European countries we see the growing presence of veterinary practice managers, specialised staff members responsible for all the non-medical aspects of practice administration. These include marketing, client communication and management, merchandising, negotiations with product and equipment providers, and human resource management.

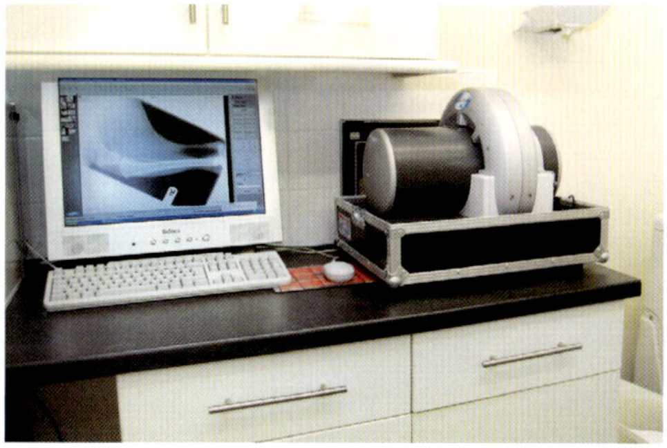

We need to be prepared for the challenges of tomorrow, adopting a positive attitude and looking at the best way to improve our professional life.

We see the growing presence of veterinary practice managers, specialised staff members responsible for all the non-medical aspects of practice administration.

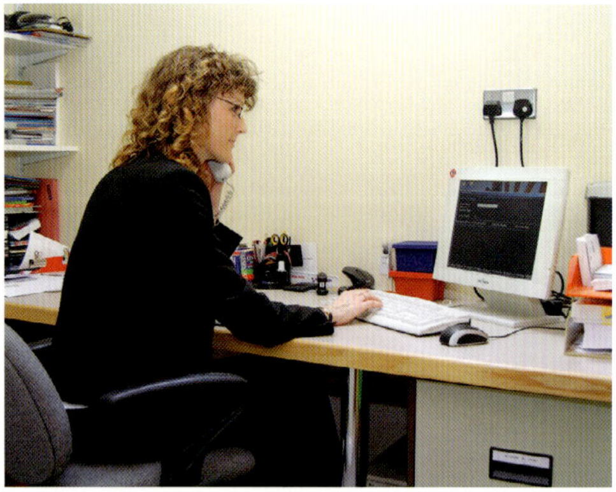

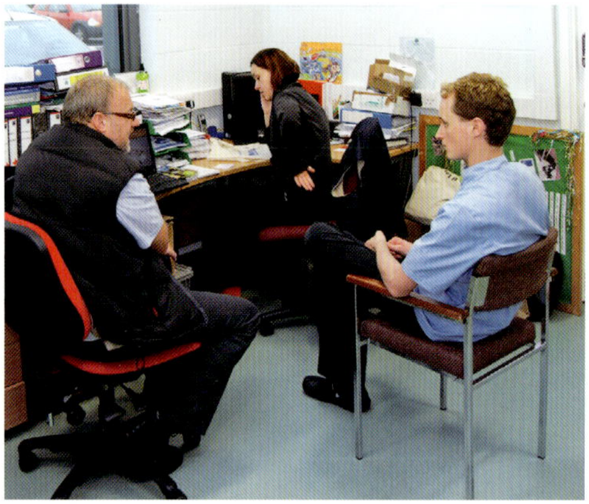

Just as pet medicine has evolved over the past 50 years, emerging new trends include new companion animals or "pocket pets", sometimes referred to as "exotic pets". New specialities, including animal behaviour and physiotherapy, are becoming increasingly important.

In the past, veterinarians sold their practices at the end of their career and retired comfortably with the proceeds from the sale. The value of practice assets, such as "goodwill" (veterinary client base), is now questionable, and many people feel value now relates only to the premises and equipment.

In some countries, corporate medical companies are growing in strength; these corporate models are emerging in the veterinary field and can include as many as 50 to 500 practices. Needless to say, work conditions in such practices are not comparable to that in the old family business. There is little room for improvisation or unsound economic decisions; everything has to be evaluated and based on the return on investment. In the veterinary profession, we will undoubtedly see the development of groups of practices, franchises and so-called corporate medicine. This should not mean the end of small practices. Superstores have not replaced small retail shops – both coexist and satisfy different needs.

Some of us may be nostalgic and look at the "good old days", but we must also be optimistic and recognise the exciting opportunities for the profession. We need to be prepared for the challenges of tomorrow, adopting a positive attitude and looking at the best way to improve our professional life.

We recognise a trend where owners are seeking veterinary advice and services to feel good about the level of healthcare they provide to their pets. The experience with their vet is partly based on facts, but is mainly based on emotions and perception. Veterinarians and their staff need to provide owners with an "optimal healthcare experience".

The evolution of the veterinary profession is well summed up in the words of Dr Michael Paul: "We must now develop communication skills, business skills, and innovative attitudes if we are to continue to have a vision of what we all want this profession to be... an opportunity to serve and provide service as we prosper."

What is practice management?

1.2

Definition

A SIMPLE DEFINITION of veterinary practice management would be: the science of managing clinical veterinary activity as a small business or enterprise. Practice management includes the planning, leading, managing, analysing, organising, executing and evaluating of all aspects related to selling products and services in a veterinary practice. It involves all aspects of running a business including products and service selection and production, marketing services, client communication, selling techniques and merchandising, human resources, accounting and finance, development and strategy, and future development.

Learning about practice management

Practice management is sometimes associated solely with the marketing aspects of veterinary practice, but this is only one facet of the discipline. It is a subject in its own right and there are dedicated educational programmes in veterinary practice management in the US (Purdue University's MBA in Veterinary Management), and in Europe (the CVPM from the Veterinary Practice Management Association in the UK, and the Veterinary MBA from the AVEPA in Spain). This speciality requires knowledge, skills and experience, and some veterinary schools have only recently included this important feature of veterinary clinical practice as part of their veterinary curriculum.

Specialists, marketers, managers, and merchandisers offer a vast choice of techniques to veterinary practices. Many veterinarians have devoted time and effort – learning through books, seminars, and personal experience – to become their clinic's practice managers. However, because of the level of knowledge necessary to complete all these tasks, a significant number have hired consultants or full-time practice managers to help them with this critical aspect of their profession. There are books, manuals, conferences, and other excellent sources of material related to these concepts. This manual should be considered as an introduction to the discipline.

Veterinarians should not limit themselves solely to operational management, but should look at the entire discipline as a part of their long-term business planning and strategy.

Guide through various sections

In planning *Essentials of Veterinary Practice*, we looked at some discipline divisions and we will refer you to these respective sections to facilitate your comprehension of the material.

Practice management is sometimes associated solely with the marketing aspects of veterinary practice, but this is only one facet of the discipline.

1.3 Getting started

This section aims to demonstrate to anyone newly joining the profession how to approach the early days of their career, thus hopefully avoiding the mistakes of their predecessors. From the outset, it is important to look at some basic concepts such as: "Who am I? Where do I want to go?" and "How do I get there?"

2.1 Veterinary services

Discussion includes veterinary services features, and how to best prepare and deliver them to clients for mutual satisfaction and benefit. This will also be examined from the client's (consumer's) perspective and will demonstrate that you neither sell nor consume (purchase) a service as you would a product.

2.2 Retailing and merchandising

Veterinarians not only sell medical and surgical services, but also associated products. For example, sales of medications, and also animal supplies such as veterinary diets, and/or health and hygiene products.

3.1 Family/pet bond

Our society has embraced the pet/family concept. In western civilisation, where life's basic needs are covered, pets are true companions and an integrated part of the home environment. Pets are family members. Treating them as such, and embracing this concept, should be an important part of the veterinary approach when dealing with pet animal care.

3.2 Knowing your clients

Pet owners seek veterinary services with the main objective of living a happy life with their pet; veterinarians should always focus on helping achieve this objective. Pet owners do not want to experience any problems with their animal. It is important to know clients' changing needs and expectations; this can be achieved through reviewing surveys and studies, and carrying out your own client surveys. This will improve knowledge of the services that clients are likely to buy from your practice.

4.1 General communication concepts

Quality is an assumed fact. You could be the best veterinarian, the best intern or surgeon, but if you fail in your client communication, they may not understand you and may not follow your advice. Communication is, therefore, the key to success, including skills and basic techniques applicable in daily work with clients, staff and colleagues. This chapter also covers handling different types of clients and telephone skills and techniques.

4.2 Marketing in the clinic

Most clients are unaware of the services available in your clinic. Client education and communication starts on the practice premises, educating them in all they need to know to live in happy and peaceful coexistence with their pet. This chapter also covers facets of compliance. If you offer the best quality veterinary care services and your clients are not buying them, you may be justifiably concerned. There are simple, yet important, concepts to improve significantly compliance and help you achieve better care of pets and, ultimately, further the development of your practice.

4.3 Communication tools to reach your clients

Communication starts outside your clinic. Tools range from roadside signs to *Yellow Pages* advertisements and websites. The objective is to make the people aware of your existence in an attractive way. Communication tools used within your premises can be as simple as a poster, or as sophisticated as a dynamic imaging system within reception and waiting area. Tools used to follow up with clients – such as reminders, e-mails and newsletters – are also valuable. All these tools should be selected and used appropriately to enhance practice development and client awareness of practice services and products.

5.1 Staff and team

Most practices, like most businesses, rely on the quality of their employees to reach an optimum level of activity. Selecting, training and keeping

We often wish the day had more than 24 hours – simply because we have not accomplished all the planned tasks.

your employees are integral aspects of any enterprise. In a veterinary clinic it is possibly even more crucial because, more often than not, it is your staff and your team that make the initial contact with clients. Managing human resources is often considered to be difficult, yet it is the most important part of any business management.

5.2 Time management

We often wish the day had more than 24 hours – simply because we have not accomplished all the planned tasks. We confuse urgency and priority and get distracted from major tasks. To achieve proper practice and personal organisation it is obviously important to use time efficiently and, ultimately, to include time slots for yourself and your family.

5.3 Organisation in your clinic

A good practice should run smoothly for everyone's benefit, including your staff and clients. This starts with your appointment system, but also includes all communication tools and their application. You can have the best lay staff and assistants, but if the delivery of services is not well organised, it may be badly perceived. The risk of client dissatisfaction will soon escalate.

6.1 Practice finances

This chapter deals with economics; initially, with basic fee setting. All services, including medical diagnostic, treatment and surgical services have a cost. Veterinary fees should be calculated on a simple and straightforward basis, taking into account all costs, including those of human resources, and finally adding a margin to reach a reasonable profit and make your services benefit the practice. It is not sufficient to call your friendly veterinarian on the other side of town and ask him how much he or she is charging for this or that procedure.
The second part of the chapter is devoted to financial indicators. From a business point of view, it is important to regularly assess performance and results, and to critically analyse the books; general accounting analysis is often insufficient. Some easy indicators allow measurement of certain practice criteria, such as dependency on vaccinations. Following these criteria, practitioners can critically and objectively analyse their practice performance and trends.

7.1 Epilogue and conclusion

This chapter concludes *Essentials of Veterinary Practice*. It elaborates on future challenges, how veterinarians should approach their strategy and their future, and integrate practice management into their next step.

Getting started 1.3

Introduction

GETTING STARTED AFTER graduation is easier said than done. Because of the relatively wide scope of most veterinary curricula, the new graduate has many options. For the purpose of this book and chapter, the focus will be on getting started in companion animal practice. Other options such as working for the government, research in industry or academia, and farm animal practice careers will not be discussed. Obviously, a new graduate needs to seriously consider whether these other areas offer opportunities that fit his or her requirements.

What, where, when and how

The first question the new graduate should ask is: "What do I want?" This includes the type of work and the location. This brings in the "where" question and, equally important, the "when" question. There are two aspects of timing: first is when to make the decision, and second is when to follow up. What first, what next? Be careful to make the right decision at the right time.

To answer the question "what?" it is very important to know the practical and theoretical options, but it is even more important to know what you want. To answer the "what?" question requires a clear picture of the options (objectives) and the way to achieve them. Also, consideration needs to be given to the various routes that may lead to the same end result, along with an

assessment their advantages and disadvantages. This leads to the "how?" question.

Most probably, the goal or objective considered immediately after graduation will not, in most cases, be the end-of-career target. It can be anticipated

Defining your objective needs ambition because "small dreams do not motivate nor move the soul".

that during the 30-plus years of professional life, there will be many changes (more than there would have been during the past 30 years) and it is wise to plan for a five or 10-year period, being aware of future alternatives. In general, it is advisable to keep open the options for career alternatives, providing this does not distract or hinder reaching the final objective. (If this is the case, it is better to close the doors that you don't choose and not to look back.) Also, defining your objective needs ambition because "small dreams do not motivate nor move the soul". Have the courage to be ambitious and set high targets. A business term for having ambitious targets is called the "stretch-objective", and these targets need effort to be achieved.

Consider what you really want to do or become in your professional life, and equally important, how does that fit in with your private life?

Objectives

The best objectives are those that are SMART: Specific, Measurable, Attractive (some prefer Achievable), Realistic and Time-framed. If any of these points are missing, the chance of failure increases. The time factor (deadline or due date) can be flexible, and reaching the final objective is the most important aim. However, in business planning and goal setting this approach is not realistic; for personal objectives it can be perfectly acceptable as long as the eventual aim is agreed beforehand, and does not reflect a "moving target" nor is the result of continual postponing of efforts.

Consider what you really want to do or become in your professional life, and equally important, how does that fit in with your private life? Life is more than just work, and with the increasing number of women in the veterinary profession, it is clear the stereotype practitioner, available around the clock and working together with his partner or spouse every day of the week, is a part of history. The work/life balance is an increasingly important issue. An excellent book on

this subject is *First Things First* by Stephen R Covey (Simon and Schuster). It describes important time management aspects, the different roles an individual has in his or her life, and how to optimally balance these roles. In our opinion this is a "must-read" book. Planning for the future should have goals classified as short term (one or two years) mid term (five to maybe 10 years) or long term (career). The most likely and attractive option is to decide on short and mid-term goals, at the same time having some idea regarding the longer term. There should be flexibility in the progressing of mid term and, certainly, long-term plans. Revision of plans on a regular (annual or biannual) basis is a must in this fast-changing world.

When the decision is made to go into companion animal practice, additional questions could include:

- at which level (first line or specialist);
- how; and
- where.

It is most important to address the first question at the time of graduation, as most specialist training leading to European (or North American) Specialist College membership (Diplomates) take place at university clinics. Relatively few (fewer in Europe than in the US) can be achieved by study in specialist clinics. Therefore, dreams of being a specialist mean starting an internship – and residency programme – soon after graduation from veterinary school. After working for several years in practice this route becomes virtually impossible, and the option no longer exists. It is equally important to decide the preferred area of specialisation. Several countries have certificates for national specialisation programmes that recognise additional post-graduate training in certain areas. When choosing to enter general practice, the decision is whether to start as an assistant or to immediately open one's own practice. Is a large multi-partner or a small practice preferred? There are pros and cons for each option, and a generic solution is impossible. We will not go deeper into this here, but obviously it is a critical decision. In most cases, the new graduate will benefit from working in several practices as an assistant before opening his or her own practice, or becoming a partner in an existing practice.

The "where?" question will depend both on private circumstances and on availability. Flexibility regarding location offers most options. To get a good overview of availabilities, it is in general advisable to look outside the "comfort zone", perhaps looking for opportunities abroad. This attitude will certainly provide a richer experience and afford better preparation for future choices and for starting a new clinic. It can often be an excellent decision to take specialist training at a foreign university. Applying for a position with a curriculum vitae that demonstrates personal initiatives and added value will put any job applicant in a preferential position.

In practice

The location of a practice is of critical importance to its success. It may be surprising – and even disappointing – to the new graduate, but it is widely accepted that location is the most important factor for success. A location with easy access and easy parking is preferred. For a specialist practice, location is less important, and it can be rural as clients come from a wider area. In this case, access to the motorway exits is important.

To choose the right location for a new practice, it is important to consider the level of services provided by existing clinics and hospitals, and then decide how to develop or use the market potential for the planned business. Will it be a mixed practice? Will it be just pets, including exotics? Will it be only exotics? Will it be only cats? Consider a market survey, looking at the local economy, local trends, area growth demographic factors, and the number of nearby vets, their ages and profiles. The local social environment and average income of the people living nearby (working class versus highly educated and high incomes) should be investigated. However, don't make the mistake of thinking that working-class owners spend less on their pets than do middle-class owners. The potential suppliers of products and services for your new practice might be willing to provide financial support.

Depending on the plans and the assessment of possibilities, the putting into practice of these ideas comes next. It is very important to have a strong drive to be successful. Do not let others decide your success. If this is what you want then go for it, and make it better than anybody else has made it and can make it. This will bring clients and will allow you to successfully compete with other practices in the area.

Working as an assistant in a practice prior to opening a new clinic provides observation and learning in veterinary technical knowledge and skills and, more importantly, experience in areas that received minimal attention in veterinary school. These areas include how to deal with clients and staff, and how

Clients, colleagues and team members need to trust your judgement, and know you will ask for help when you run out of options or solutions.

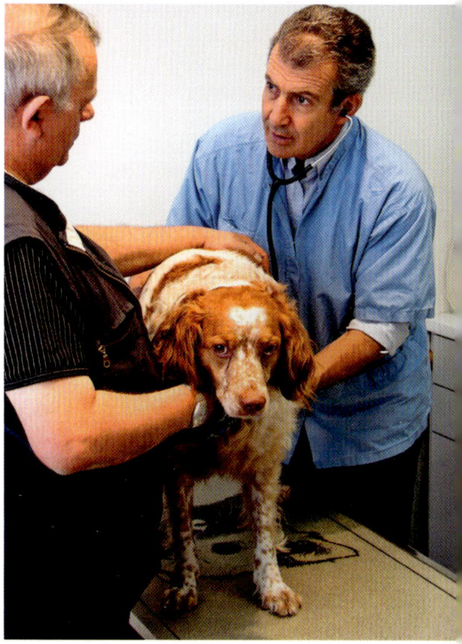

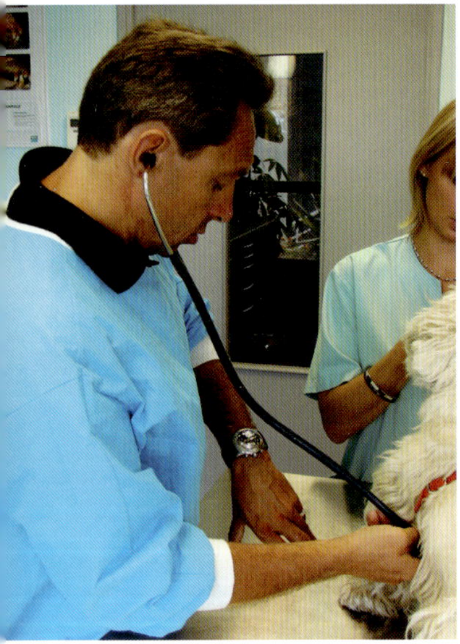

to work as a team member. It is important to develop these skills as they are of critical importance to career success. Working as an assistant also allows mistakes in a protected environment, and the ability to move on afterwards, avoiding the same mistakes.

The location of a general practice markedly influences the type of clients. In the middle of a big city, the practice is more likely to see many cats and the newer small pets and exotics, whereas a rural practice will, most probably, see more and larger dogs. The location and part of the country also influences the budget clients are likely to spend on their pets. If the objective is to provide upmarket, top-quality veterinary care, including higher-priced diagnostic and surgical procedures, this has to fit in with the region economics, and the prices charged by colleagues. In general, it is true that most of the financial turnover of a successful companion animal practice comes from product sales and basic procedures.

Confidence and trust

Clients consult a veterinarian to get peace of mind on a worrying pet-health issue. These do not always include complicated problems and can be very easy to solve. One of the most important skills of the general practitioner is to identify the routine and frequently seen cases that will quickly improve with simple treatment (sometimes with no treatment at all), as opposed to the less-common problems that need an additional diagnostic work-up and more specialised medical treatment or surgery.

When getting started, it is important to be confident and trust your observations and findings – without the supervision of the professor or senior clinician. To obtain such confidence, never compromise reality and never pretend to know or be able to do things when this is not the case. Clients (and senior clinicians) appreciate and recognise the need for a young colleague to gain experience. They have to trust you, and will only do this if they know you will never pretend to know a solution, and will ask for help (and refer a case) when it is beyond your knowledge and skills. To know, acknowledge and work within your limitations and experience is the best way to go forward. Building your reputation on pretence and suggestion is a dangerous strategy. Although it is understandable that one feels insecure as a result of a lack of experience, the most important value when starting in practice is personal confidence. Clients, colleagues and team members need to trust your judgement, and know you will ask for help when you run out of options or solutions.

Most important of all, knowing and respecting your limitations are of key importance when starting your career, in order to start trusting yourself as a veterinary professional. The next step after asking for advice is to study and work hard so you can do it yourself the next time a similar case comes in. ◘

2

Offering Customer Service

In this section:

Clinical veterinary services

Retailing and merchandising

Clinical veterinary services

2.1

"Offering excellent client services, adapted to their needs and expectations, is a major key to veterinary practice success."

PROVIDING CLINICAL SERVICES is the core and backbone of veterinary practice. Farmers and (increasingly) dog, cat and new companion animal owners have always valued the veterinarian's knowledge and skills. However, a significant new trend is the practice actively promoting the clinic's services, as opposed to passively waiting for clients to ask for them. Veterinarians realise many owners are unaware of clinic services that may be beneficial for pet family members and, therefore, will never ask for them. It is necessary to increase client awareness of the rapid developments in the diagnostic, preventive and therapeutic areas of veterinary medicine and surgery. Building this awareness is a key activity in practice development and growth.

Services have many characteristics. They are intangible, as they cannot be held in the same way as a product; their production is directly linked to consumption; they are heterogeneous (tailored to the receiver); and they are perishable (unsold agenda time slots are lost for ever).

Service importance and value

Offering excellent client services, adapted to their needs and expectations, is a major key to veterinary practice success.

Unlike a product, a service includes vet and staff time, and optimal healthcare can be provided only in a financially healthy practice. Service charges need to be based on staff time, and not primarily based on the products involved in the procedures.

Surveys show that people expect veterinarians to also provide preventive non-medical or surgical services. The veterinarian is expected to deal with both the

Remember: the perceived value is what people buy – they don't buy a price.

Quality perception and satisfaction are independent of price positioning, and apply to all market segments.

diseased animal and the healthy pet. For example, clients expect the veterinarian to advise them on the best vaccination and nutritional regime for their pet.

Based on client feedback, the expected services rank:

Health	74 per cent
Preventive medical care	63 per cent
Nutrition	60 per cent
Behaviour	44 per cent
Emergency services	30 per cent
Animal training	15 per cent

Development of services requires preparation, management, marketing and communications tools, training, internal set-up, and an effective launch. It is not enough to offer a service, it is necessary to study how it will be perceived and accepted by clients. It is crucial to study how the client will value the service, as well as the return on investment for the practice. For example, a senior check-up service will only satisfy client demand if it is well-documented and explained. In the same way, such a service will only be valuable if it generates sufficient revenue for the practice, making it worth the time and effort.

Offering quality services requires planning and appropriate team guidelines. In addition to a strong desire to do well, it is necessary to work and plan for it. Quality will be judged by the clients and not announced by its maker (in this case, the clinic staff). We are all consumers and, as such, we always want to receive value for money. This does not mean the cheapest possible product or service, but one that gives us our expected value. Usually, the highly satisfied client will feel he or she has received a high-quality service; the dissatisfied client will be disappointed by the service quality.

Quality perception and satisfaction are independent of price positioning, and apply to all market segments.

Marketing and education

Most of the classical marketing tools can promote services. Although some countries restrict public relations (PR) methods and client communication, a lot can be legally done to support business growth (see **Sections 4.2** and **4.3**). The internet has significantly increased available options, with YouTube and similar sites used by veterinarians around the world to promote their business at no cost, and to communicate with existing and potential clients.

Owner education is an important way to increase service sales. Many are unaware of the health risks involved in conditions such as dental and renal disease, dermatological problems, weight problems and osteoarthritis. Often, they do not realise the potential benefits of a preventive and therapeutic programme for their pets (and for themselves). In addition to straightforward advertisement, educational courses by veterinarians, or veterinary nurses or technicians, can bring an informative message to the target audience. Ideally, these educational programmes should take place in the practice, but can be held in a meeting room in the clinic neighbourhood.

Healthcare programmes support client loyalty by using reminder mailings and telephone calls for health checks. In general, owners do not consider reminders as a pushy way to promote the business, but more often appreciate them as a practice service to help keep pets in optimal condition. Don't you appreciate your dentist reminding you of the six-months check-up? The same thing applies for the pet-parent.

Clients' word-of-mouth promotion is a strong recommendation for a pet healthcare programme. Owners can be encouraged to exchange their positive experience with others who might be struggling with the same problem. There is no better or more cost-efficient method of promotion and advertisement than the positive endorsement by a happy client. Unfortunately, unhappy clients do the opposite; potential problems need to be avoided if possible.

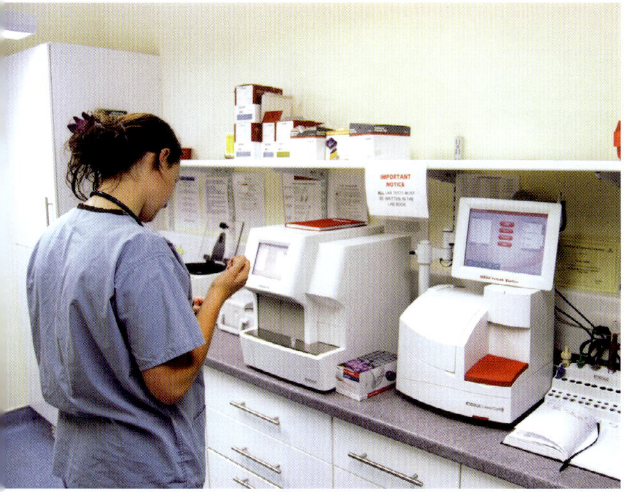

Client needs and satisfaction

Client satisfaction is important and should be constantly monitored, measured and evaluated by the clinic staff, adjusting protocols and techniques in case of conflicts. One method is the classic suggestion box for suggestions, ideas and comments placed in the reception or waiting area. The internet version on the clinic's website might be a modern way to do this. Well-trained staff who build client relationships will often receive information that owners do not necessarily share with the veterinarian. A clinic internet chat room might be a low-threshold way to allow owners to communicate with each other. These discussions should be monitored and

Depending on the nature of the procedure, the staff can make a standard follow-up call the day after the surgery to ask about the pets' condition. This procedure is highly appreciated by the owner.

Close monitoring of a senior pet is not only good medical practise; it is clear that such a preventive programme generates a positive financial return.

coached by clinic staff, thus managing the PR risk. Remember, an unhappy owner will communicate his or her emotions anyway, and you may as well know the content, and have the opportunity to become involved. The clinic (via a selected and educated employee) may start an internet blog, reporting on day-to-day issues and thereby promoting the clinic to the public, despite legal restrictions on advertising.

To evaluate client perception, it is recommended to create a panel (focus group) of clients who regularly meet. Such a group, of five to 10 pet owners, would typically consist of the most-appreciated clinic clients. Discussing strategies and healthcare programmes will provide an insight into the appreciation of such services, and can help tailor them to the local environment. New programmes can be tested and evaluated within the relatively safe environment of loyal customers, before being launched into the practice. Focus group members should be rewarded to stimulate long-term interaction and regular meetings.

Client satisfaction should be constantly monitored, measured and evaluated.

Another good way to evaluate performance is to keep a log of errors that resulted in unhappy clients, or worse, a conflict with a client or a referring veterinarian. Since conflicts have at least two sides, this process should also allow the employees involved to decompress, by debriefing and reporting their side of the story. Make sure staff members and practice owners are aware of any issue that occurs within the clinic. This also allows a personal apology by the hospital owner, which might help restore client relationships. Documentation should include the (perceived) reason for the conflict or error, the outcome, next steps and the staff members involved. It will provide a tool to evaluate current protocols, substantiate the need for adaptations and consequences, and be a great tool for training employees. Whenever possible, the pet owner's input is of great value; it is generally appreciated when the clinic has a procedure in place to hear the other side of the story.

Pricing a service

When it comes to pricing and selling services (and, to some extent, products) veterinarians should always emphasise the values and benefits for the pet and the owner, and not spend much time on the cost and price. What may be a lot of money for you as a new graduate, still comparing the price with your student budgets, may not be much for someone else. Veterinarians should not make decisions for the customers in "guesstimating" their

willingness and ability to pay. After you explain the benefits (pros and cons), let the client tell you: "It's too much and I don't want to spend that much on my animal," and ask: "Is there any alternative?"

It is often amazing how much time veterinarians spend being bothered by the terms expensive or cheap; it is better to leave the buying decision with the owner. Remember: the perceived value is what people buy – they don't buy a price. Present the options, benefits and value behind the cost, and close the sale naturally by giving at least two options that result in predictable, good and ethically sound results.

Maintaining a healthy client base

The best way to generate business is not to lose clients (or their pets), but the reality is that the practice will lose clients. Given dogs' and cats' life spans, 10 to 15 per cent of patients will be lost each year and need to be replaced by new ones. In addition, owners move and change veterinarians. It might be realistic to suggest about 20 to 25 per cent of new clients need to be recruited each year for the practice to maintain the number of services sold. Significant effort and cost will be needed to turn those numbers into reality. Therefore, every effort should be made by all staff members (from the cleaner to the owner) to maintain existing client levels.

Setting up a new service

People don't buy a service as they buy a product. It is necessary to point out the value of the service for the client (and for his or her pet). A product sale is easier because it is tangible, whereas a service has less objective value. This is the case for all services.

The example of a senior programme (including a check-up) is easy to understand. Veterinarians can be embarrassed when laboratory test results or diagnostic procedures are normal. It should be the opposite. We are taking care of a normal animal, not a sick or injured patient; it is a form of preventive medicine.

Detailing and listing features (various aspects of the check-up, including a complete physical examination, essential blood work that will allow most internal organ functions to be surveyed, thoracic radiographs, and so on) is the best way to present a service to a client. Explanation of each test's benefits is the next step – such as the benefits of the diagnosis of possible anomalies in an elderly patient.

In parallel to these explanations, it is always a good idea to show, through documents and images, the various aspects of the service. For example, show the documents, forms and folders that will accompany the service. These documents bring an important feature to the service, transforming an intangible and subjective subject into a tangible action – clients will look through the reports and documents you are handing to them. Even if the brochures and reports look basic to you, they add crucial value to the perception of the service. Imagine checking-out of your hotel without an itemised invoice detailing all the services you received during your stay.

It is also important to go over the material aspects of the service: how much it will cost, how the pet will be handled and what will be required from the owner. When approaching cost, it is our advice to present the price as a benefit, because of the package format of the service. Another important feature of a service (and a real value) is that all preventive diagnostics will detect abnormalities at an early stage and, therefore, allow treatment sooner, often better and for a reduced cost. Better results, better prices.

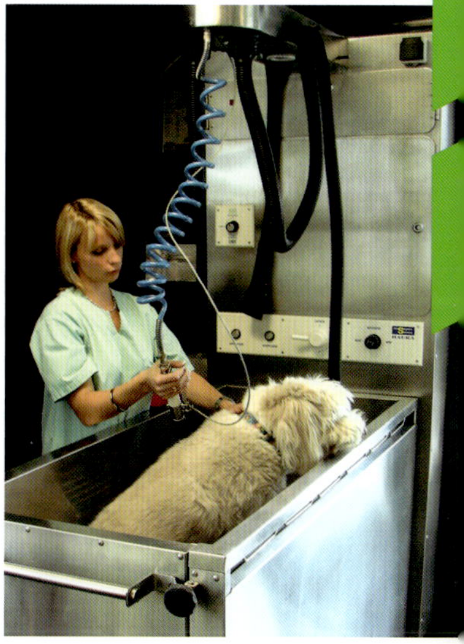

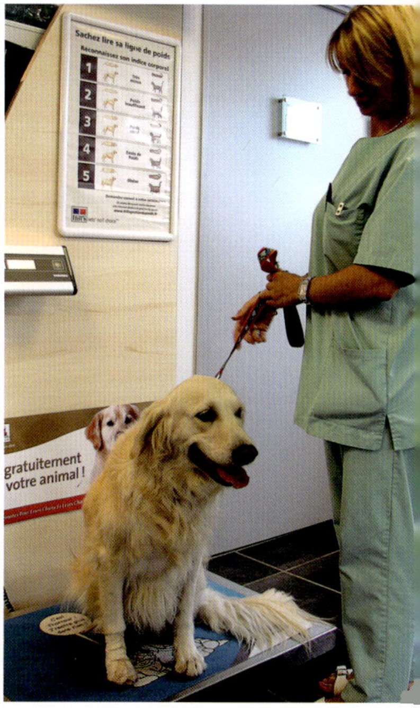

There are several services that would contribute to both better medicine and practice growth. Some of them would also correspond to clients' expectations, such as a senior pet management programme. The human/animal bond is such that there is a deeper affection for older pets, and a true need and demand from clients to keep them healthy and happy, with no pain or suffering, for as long as possible.

Senior pet management programme

A senior pet management programme is an important service to include in the practice routine. Once such a programme is started, it should be briefly mentioned to all clients, even those with young animals. As they become adult, and then senior pets, the programme will be a natural and normal step during the animal's annual health examination. Pet owners' efforts to help their older dog or cat feel better, and to have a happier and longer life, are often immense and, therefore, beyond veterinarians (and students) expectations. A 1997 Idexx survey showed US pet owners were spending $184 per year, on average, for their dog aged less than 10 years, and $277 for pets more than 10 years of age. Many people might still be surprised by these numbers, but they will have, no doubt, increased significantly in more than a decade. A study from the American Veterinary Medical Association (AVMA), showed the pet population was getting older and 25 per cent of pets were older than eight years.

> It might be realistic to suggest about 20 to 25 per cent of new clients need to be recruited each year for the practice to maintain the number of services sold.

Practical aspects

Once you plan to set up a senior pet management service, it is crucial that the entire clinic team, including veterinarians, technicians, staff and receptionists, become part of the service and adopt it. The clinic team should understand and communicate the value of the service for the owners and pets. Such communication should be part of

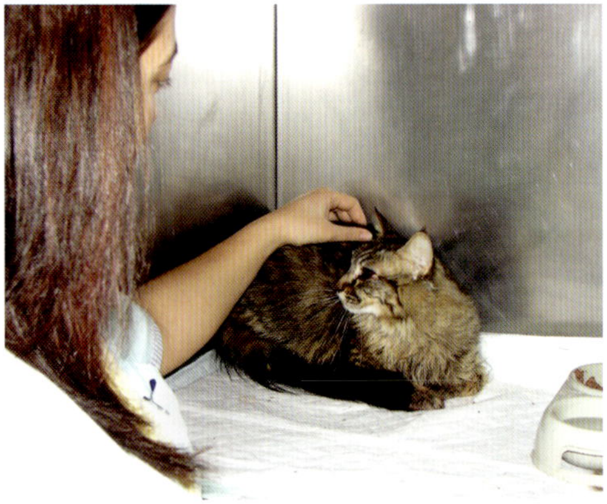

daily client messages and start before pets enter the senior category, because if clients understand that once their pet has reached a certain age, it will require a different sort of preventive management and check-up, it is natural for these services to be taken up, almost instinctively, at that time. Clients may even remind you the time has come for their pet to enter the senior pet management programme; the senior programme becomes a natural and normal step in the pet's lifetime follow-up. The programme's various check-ups and services no longer require detailed explanation and convincing communication. This is why it is important to communicate early about a service and, as a team, with the same energy and conviction.

Senior pet programme and annual health exam

An efficient method to set up a senior pet management programme is to start with the annual visit – often referred to as the annual vaccination – and try to reinvent such an examination.
Annual vaccine protocols are getting increasingly controversial, and these hitherto annual vaccines will change (read: reduce), with less boosting of immune protection in the future. This will be somewhat

compensated by new vaccines, protecting against diseases that were not part of the previous preventive programmes (such as babesiosis, Lyme's disease, leishmaniasis and feline immunodeficiency virus [FIV]). This is why it is important to present the pet's annual visit as the annual health check (during which some vaccines may be given as needed) instead of the annual vaccination. The entire communication should change – reinforcing and focusing on the pet's annual examination instead of on the vaccines. This includes reminder cards, letters or e-mails sent to clients, emphasising the clinical examination versus the vaccines only (change of focus from product to service). When the system is in place, with the annual examination placed in the centre of the service, focusing on the clinical examination and associated services, it is natural, when the pet becomes a senior, that the annual visit will include additional clinical tests associated with the pet's age. It is also logical to think that geriatric dogs (older than 12 years) and cats (older than 15 years) may require two visits each year.

● Financial return of a senior pet programme

Close monitoring of a senior pet is not only good medical practise; it is clear that such a preventive programme generates a positive financial return. Some would call it a good return on investment. Indeed, pets are often senior for several years, and these years are important to manage well, which is a significant difference from the services developed for pets during growth, which is a short period. Think of the time and effort put into client communication about pets' growth needs – nutritional, behavioural, external and internal parasites, and vaccines. All these pet care aspects during the first 10 to 12 months are important; however, the senior pet will need more follow-up services for a longer time, usually for several years.

Starting a new service, step by step

To set up a new service, for example a senior pet programme, one could adopt the following steps.

- Decide on the programme objectives, involving clinic owners and staff.
- Ensure the management team is convinced of the service, its added value for the pet, the client and the practice.
- Make sure the healthcare team is also convinced to ensure uniform communication about the service.
- Define the clients to be selected and targeted for the service.
- Develop appropriate communication tools to market the service.
- Prepare the launch or introduction of the service: date, practical details, logistic, tools and staff meeting.
- Initiate communication with your clients, starting with your fan club.
- Establish a development strategy for the service: where will it be in five years and what do you need to do to get there?

Unlike a product, a service includes vet and staff time, and optimal healthcare can be provided only in a financially healthy practice.

All components of procedures, and their contribution to the total invoice, should be itemised. As a result, clients will realise the service level and complexity, and understand the value and the price.

- Promote the service and try to bundle the offers into packages that add client value.
- Start the programme, making sure all details are covered prior to launch.
- Evaluate results against your objectives (client and employee surveys, as well as finances), according to schedule and make any necessary changes.

The role of support staff in client education is important, as they can reinforce the message during owner contact, and provide additional information. Staff members need to support the service programme and be fully trained on content. As they typically have more contact time with clients, staff members can contribute significantly to programme success by promoting boarding, grooming, health plans, senior management programmes, nutrition and weight-control management. In certain countries, staff members are also involved in providing services that may be considered para-veterinary, such as dental prophylactic treatment, behaviour and dog training.

New media, new services

A new type of client service would be owners scheduling appointments at their convenience, 24/7, via the internet. After receiving a reminder (perhaps via e-mail), clients log on to the practice appointment schedule at the clinic website and choose a date and time slot that fits best with their agenda. This also offers an opportunity to indicate how much time they will have and, when more time is needed, to schedule two time slots. This will help install time discipline, and the owner will not be surprised to be charged extra for a prolonged visit. We find this new service is highly appreciated by a segment of the clientele, saves staff involvement and frees up time for the reception staff's primary responsibility of paying attention to clients visiting the practice. A typical "everyone wins" outcome, which illustrates the new service's added value.

Payment: importance of a detailed invoice

Computers allow for specified and detailed invoices of all services; it is highly recommended that all components of procedures, and their contribution to the total invoice, are itemised. As a result, clients will realise the service level and complexity, and understand the value and the price. Presenting these details makes the service provided more tangible for the client. We will use the example of a feline ovariohysterectomy (OVH) for a fixed price of €130, compared to an OVH performed and priced with a detailed invoice according to the components listed here (**Figure 2.1.1**).

From this example, it can be seen that, by calculating an hourly fee for the veterinary surgeon and his involvement for 30 minutes, the total of the invoice is more than €172. It is

INTAKE CONSULTATION AND HEALTHCHECK	€ 0,00
• PRE-ANAESTHETIC EXAM AND SEDATION	€ 12,00
• INDUCTION AND MAINTENANCE OF ANAESTHESIA	€ 20,00
• VETERINARY SURGEON FEE (30 MIN)	€ 65,00
• USE OF OPERATING ROOM	€ 16,00
• HOSPITALISATION AND SURVEILLANCE DURING RECOVERY	€ 14,00
• MEDICATION, ANALGESIA AND ANTIBIOTICS	€ 5,00
• BANDAGE	€ 12,00
TOTAL	€ 144,00
VAT @ 19.6 %	€ 28,22
TOTAL	€ 172,22

Figure 2.1.1

also clear the pet owners received a free check-in examination, including the health check.

In most cases, it is advised that payment is handled by the clinic staff after the doctor has greeted the client in a friendly manner. The cash register staff member or receptionist explains the bill, highlighting the details of all the procedures, making sure (by asking if the client has any questions) the owner fully appreciates the complexity and professionalism of the treatment. After booking the follow-up appointment, staff can ask if there is anything else the client needs, or wants. Finally, assistance can be offered with taking the pet to the car. Depending on the nature of the procedure, the staff can make a standard follow-up call the day after the surgery to ask about the pet's condition and invite any questions. This procedure is highly appreciated by owners.

Compliance

Research by the American Animal Hospital Association (AAHA) has shown that owner compliance to veterinary advice is relatively low, with room for improvement. In some cases, only five per cent of owners follow through on the veterinarian's advice. Low owner compliance with follow-up recommendations has a significant negative impact on the veterinary business and the practice's financial health. Owners who understand the issues, health risks, and diagnostic, preventive and therapeutic opportunities for improvement, will demonstrate higher compliance and, therefore, support the practice. These are existing, motivated clients, with pets in need of medical support, to whom the practice has direct access. This is the ideal target group on which to focus, and should have a high likelihood of success when increasing the clinical services' (as well as product sales) business.

Suboptimal pet healthcare: the compliance gap

Compliance by pet owners to optimal veterinary care seems to be one of the biggest opportunities for pet healthcare improvements. A large AAHA study in the US clearly showed significant room and need for increased compliance by pet owners. The main references used for this chapter can be found in **Section 7.2.**

Delivering optimal healthcare to all creatures large and small from a veterinary and scientific viewpoint is what all veterinarians are trained to do. Practice realities can result in corners being cut, resulting in far from optimal care. Daily reality results in a significant gap between theory and practice – between the level of recommended optimal care and what is actually delivered to pets. The difference between full compliance and actual compliance is called

Low owner compliance with follow-up recommendations has a significant negative impact on the practice's financial health.

When a veterinarian estimates the compliance is 75 per cent, the actual value is probably closer to 50 per cent.

the compliance gap. In addition to suboptimal pet healthcare and suboptimal client service, this gap also has a significant impact on business results as the associated revenue opportunities remain untapped.

Compliance can be defined in various ways:

- the degree of client adherence to vet (and staff) recommendations and prescribed treatment protocols; and
- the activities associated with knowing and following laws, regulations, and professional codes or guidelines.

The gap between optimal and actual healthcare – independent from the question of why this gap exists – is the definition used by the authors, and is in line with the definition used for the AAHA study.

Compliance reality

Based on impressions that compliance was not optimal, and might be lower than most veterinarians estimate it to be, the KPMG megastudy commissioned by AAHA looked at six areas that have relevance to the US:

1. heartworm testing and prevention;
2. dental prophylaxis;
3. therapeutic diets;
4. senior screenings;
5. core vaccines; and
6. pre-anaesthetic testing.

With the exception of the first area, these are all relevant for healthcare programmes in other parts of the world.

The outcome of the study was impressive, with most room for improvement in compliance being in the areas of senior screening programmes (34 per cent), heartworm prevention (48 per cent), dental prophylaxis (35 per cent) and therapeutic diets (21 per cent). In all these areas, veterinarians estimated the compliance to be much higher (**Figure 2.1.2**). Although compliance was relatively high (and veterinarians estimated it to be lower), there is still significant room for improvement in the areas of heartworm testing (83 per cent), core vaccines (87 per cent) and pre-anaesthetic testing (69 per cent). In addition, these numbers are, most probably, too positive as the survey population consisted of pets that had visited the practice at least once in the past 12 months and can be qualified as active clients. Therefore, compliance values for the general pet population must be much lower.

CRAFT

Important factors influencing compliance are:

- recommendation;
- acceptance by the client; and
- follow-through by staff or practice.

Together, the first letters of these words (compliance, recommendation, acceptance and follow-through) make up the easy-to-remember acronym CRAFT.

Poor compliance is based on a mix of these influences. Improved practice compliance needs analysis and understanding of each influence. In general, veterinarians have a poor understanding of compliance in their practice, and most are happy with the current levels (78 per cent) – most probably because they have no idea of what the real values are because they don't measure them. In general, it was proven that when a veterinarian estimates the compliance is 75 per cent, the actual value is probably closer to 50 per cent.

Reasons for low compliance

There are multiple reasons why veterinary practice teams fail to make a recommendation for the care they believe is important. Number one, however, is that the recommendation is never made or does not reach the owner. Information overload during the visit might play an important role. Veterinarians (57 per cent) assume poor communication and inadequate client education to be important reasons for non-compliance.

The majority (80 per cent) of owners clearly indicate they prefer to receive information from the practice both verbally and in writing. During a visit, the content of communication gets lost for many reasons, including owner stress; in some cases, only 20 per cent (or less) of content was taken in by the client. Another important reason is clinic staff member being busy and not delivering the message in a quality fashion. A major (65 per cent) cause for veterinary care providers delivering less than optimal information is concern with the client's financial status and ability to pay, or misjudgment of a client's willingness to take action. According to surveys, veterinarians around the world are concerned about this – to an extent not found in other professions, such as doctors and especially lawyers. Because of this concern, veterinarians often fail to present optimal healthcare options and, instead, tailor the message to what they believe is appropriate for the owner. However, for most owners, the pet is a family member and they want to know (and have the right to know) the best healthcare option. The decision whether they choose that option is up to them, and not to members of the veterinary team. More than 90 per cent of pet owners want their veterinarian to present them with all options. The percentage of clients declining services or products due to cost is low: dental care seven per cent, therapeutic diets four per cent and senior care five per cent. The KPMG AAHA study concluded that while many factors contribute to low compliance, *"the cost of the procedure or recommended diet or treatment was not a significant factor in the client's decision to decline care"*.

Manage by measuring

An old management truth is worth repeating here: "One can only manage what can be measured". Although it may be difficult to be objective about some aspects of care, the practice's compliance gap can only be reduced after it has been identified and measured. Only 10 per cent of veterinary practices made the effort to measure compliance for healthcare programmes, and only measured it for a few services.

"One can only manage what can be measured".

There must be clear objectives and measurements of a specific healthcare programme, to determine success or failure – from both a veterinary healthcare and business point of view. Team members need to be clear about who will do what, and what will be measured, and how and by when. Objectives of compliance programmes – like all objectives – need to be SMART: Specific, Measurable, Achievable, Realistic, and Time-framed.

Figure 2.1.2

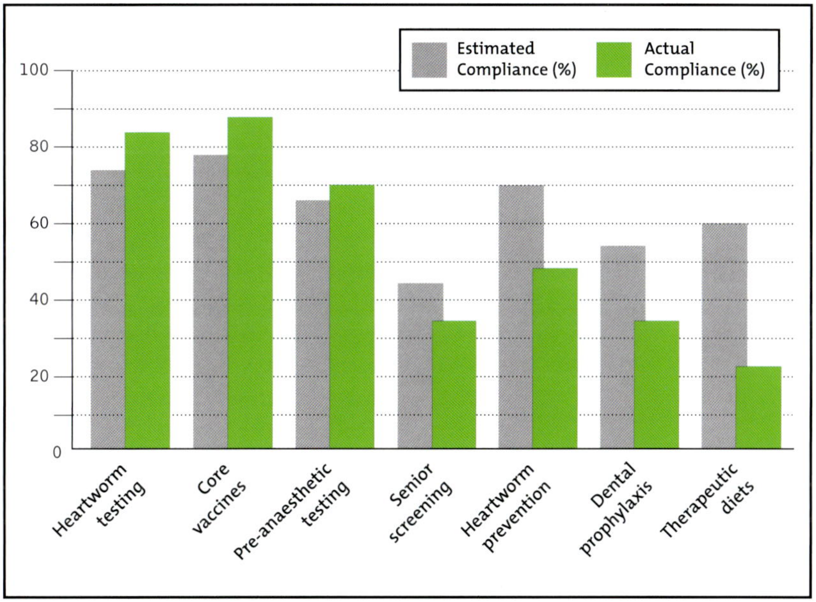

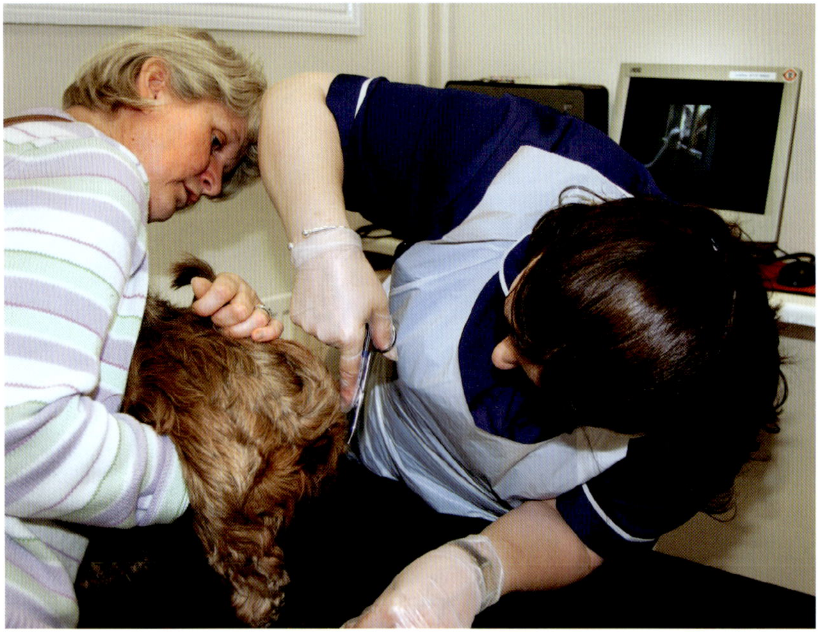

Improving compliance is a team effort

Improving compliance for existing healthcare programmes needs full support from all team members. In order to achieve team support and acceptance for the programme, team members need to understand the benefits of improved compliance. It has been shown that staff members can be optimally motivated to support the programmes when they understand the programmes' additional benefits for pets. Typically, staff are better motivated by non-financial arguments that directly benefit their patients. They may understand the additional financial benefits and revenue opportunities, and may accept these in their best career interests, but it is the benefits to pets that makes them act. This is, probably, because the job motivation is not primarily based on financial rewards but, rather, on helping pets. All staff training needs to be focused on pet health benefits, and staff input is important during the programme development.

> Typically, staff are better motivated by non-financial arguments that directly benefit their patients.

Improving compliance by improved follow-through

Clinic staff have a significant opportunity to improve compliance and healthcare by, first of all, making the recommendation. It is hard for owners to comply with a general recommendation they have never received (for whatever reason). In such cases, the only way for them to know what is available is by word of mouth from family, friends and other trusted sources, or via the internet. Other important opportunities for improvement are by scheduling a procedure at the time a recommendation is made and by providing clear instructions for at-home care and re-check exams. Most owners want instructions both verbally and in writing. There is little relevance in explaining all the possible options in great detail to owners and then leaving them wondering what to choose. If a big decision has to be made, one can allow owners some time, but a visit can be still be scheduled for the following day, to make the decision and schedule the next steps. This prevents owners from not taking action because they are confused or to go shopping for other (para) expert opinions. In some cases, a referral for a second opinion can be part of the diagnostic or treatment plan, and can be highly appreciated by the owner.

Sending reminders is another opportunity, and owners are happy to receive them. The same is true for follow-up phone calls. People appreciate it when the practice calls them about an overdue check-up. Almost 80 per cent of clients indicated they would like to receive such calls, but only slightly more than 50 per cent said that they had ever received such a call. This applies to services and products such as pet food. Helping owners to adjust from one product to another by follow-up phone calls is also highly appreciated. Of those owners who did not return for a recheck, 38 per cent indicated they would have done so if the veterinarian had contacted them as a follow-up.

Acceptance by the owner is an important factor in compliance. However, nothing in the AAHA study indicates that owners are a primary barrier to compliance. Veterinarians and their staff have more influence than they believe and could have a substantial impact on improving compliance.

Financial results of improved compliance

Performing one additional senior screening each day results in extra gross income per vet per year of $28,080, according to the KPMG study. According to the same study, 70 per cent of dog and 74 per cent of cat owners take up a senior care programme when one is recommended. Only five per cent declined such a recommendation because of costs. Additional services could be included in the calculations as a result of the increased compliance to a senior programme. The increase in the annual turnover is significantly higher:

- dental prophylaxis $76,320;
- therapeutic nutrition $33,013; and
- senior screenings $28,018.

This results in a total increased revenue of $137,413 per vet, per year. Based on AVMA data and results from the KPMG AAHA study, it is concluded that gross income per vet, per year, can increase by 43 per cent from $322,768 to $460,181.

The study also calculated the increased revenue in an average (2.2 veterinarian) practice that increased compliance by 10 per cent: $132,535 and by 25 per cent: $308,423; the biggest revenue opportunity is in the area of therapeutic diets: $48,587 and $121,469, respectively. With a 10 per cent compliance

Nothing in the AAHA study indicates that owners are a primary barrier to compliance.

increase, the gross profit is $81,364. When an additional staff member is hired, the practice still gains $55,364. This money can be invested in additional equipment, staff training, continuing education, higher wages or more benefits.

> All veterinary team members must support clients by providing optimal information, care and aftercare.

Summary and conclusion

Clinical services continue to be an essential part of the veterinary overall business with increasing emphasis on proactive and preventive attitudes towards clients and their pets. Although owners are highly educated and well informed, this does not mean they have optimal knowledge and understanding on how best to serve their pet's health interests. All veterinary team members must support clients by providing optimal information, care and aftercare.

New preventive and treatment opportunities become available on an ongoing basis, and owners are in constant need of the best possible services to support the health of their pet family members. The clinic should track the results of healthcare programmes and monitor, evaluate and adjust as needed.

Owners who are not compliant with the suggested healthcare protocols should be identified, contacted and trained to increase their understanding that optimal compliance supports their pets' interests as well as their personal interests. The ability to provide optimal healthcare to pets is closely linked to the profitability of the clinic. When investments have been made in staff, equipment and facilities to support healthcare programmes, suboptimal compliance creates risk. Sooner or later, that will result in a reduced level of pet care.

Retailing and merchandising

2.2

Introduction

RETAILING IS NOT part of the veterinary professional education programme, although many veterinarians sell services as well as products. In most countries, it is now generally accepted and appreciated by owners that the veterinary practice is the place to go for routine and emergency veterinary treatment, and to buy food and healthcare-related pet products. The change from services on request only, to proactive provision of services and products, has developed gradually and, in most cases, started in an unprofessional manner. Pet food and parasite control products make up the majority of sales, but depending on the veterinarian, a wide variety of pet-related products has been added to the product and service range.

Traditionally, most veterinarians, when initially confronted with the suggestion of retailing in the veterinary clinic, reacted negatively to the idea and referred clients to the nearest pet speciality shop. However, the market is changing. Globally, the general trend and direction are the same, although not to the same degree in all countries. Clients definitely appreciate quality pet products being available at the veterinary clinic, yet in many countries the veterinarian is often the last person to recognise it. This defensive approach toward retailing and the "I am a veterinarian, not a shopkeeper" attitude slows down the growth of veterinary professional business. In practices where retailing has been actively embraced, and veterinarians and their staff are fully exploiting the business opportunity, product sales can make up more than 60 per cent of practice turnover and profit. However, in some countries legislation limits the extent to which veterinarians can practise retailing. Belgium is an example of restrictive government legislation, and professional policy. Promotion and advertising of the veterinary practice, or its specific services, are forbidden, as is the selling of pet foods, with the exception of some diets. Owners are, therefore, referred to drugstores and pharmacies. As a result, professional development of Belgian veterinary practices is lagging behind most other western European countries, from a business point of view. In the UK, most products can only be sold via vets, while in Italy veterinarians cannot sell, but do prescribe, including diets to be picked up at specialist retail outlets. In other parts of the world, pet speciality stores hardly exist (or

In practices where retailing has been actively embraced, product sales can make up more than 60 per cent of practice turnover and profit.

A commercial business in a veterinary clinic: is it ethical?

Professional retailing is ethical, if it is done ethically. Always remember to satisfy the three major criteria within the veterinary practice scheme: first the pet, second the owner, third the veterinarian or the clinic. Selling high-quality products of benefit to animal health can only be right when it is equally beneficial to the pet and the owner, and the practice. If you are not convinced, ask your clients what they want. Would they like you to supply reliable, high-quality healthcare products for their pets, or would they prefer to purchase them from the supermarket or pet shop?

Is retailing a professional action?

The answer is obviously "yes". Through retailing, veterinarians help clients make informed and appropriate decisions about quality healthcare pet products. It is clear that, for owners, there is no better source than the animal care expert – the veterinarian. Owners expect products sold in veterinary clinics to form an integral part of preventive healthcare programmes.

Not only does selling quality healthcare products enhance the bond of trust between clients and veterinarians, but ultimately generates additional clinic revenues. Clients return more often to the practice for further purchases of products and services. An independent Royal Canin study (Biosat RC, 2002) of more than 30 veterinary clinics in France showed that clinics selling pet food also sold significantly more anti-flea medications, worming preparations and hygiene products such as shampoos. This is the ideal time and way to develop the loyal client base, which further enhances the client/practice bond. Everyone will benefit from such an innovation: pets are healthy and well managed, clients are happy to provide the best possible pet care, and the practice is more profitable and can provide a better and more complete professional service.

are owned by vets) and pet owners appear to be perfectly happy with the situation where the pet practice and retail outlet are in one location.

Retailing pet-related products increases clinic traffic (the number of visits, per client, per year). People like to shop at a place they trust, and the veterinarian is trusted as the pre-eminent pet professional. Moreover, these purchasing visits can also lead to additional clinical examinations, as the veterinary or reception staff may advise clients to bring their animal back to be seen by the veterinarian, following questions raised while shopping.

In a market where clients appreciate and expect convenience and competition among veterinarians and other pet professionals, veterinary clinics inevitably become more professional. In the future, it is likely that successful veterinary practices will offer the client a full range of services and products related to pet healthcare and well-being. Those practices that stick to the traditional concept of providing only therapeutic services will miss out on a significant revenue opportunity, and limit their professional development. Profits from the retail outlet can be used to invest in the clinic and allow the highly trained staff to work with state-of-the-art equipment in a high-class clinical environment. Insufficient resources, more often than not, result in price wars and excessive competition among veterinarians (not least by part-time practitioners), further eroding the profit margins and leading to a negative professional trend and a lowering of standards. This strategy results in a vicious downward spiral that inhibits the professional development in the market. Several European countries are examples of this (self) limiting or destructive model.

Company support for marketing and merchandising

Retailing also involves contact with company sales representatives who supply, or wish to supply, to the practice. Initial discussions and negotiations with the sales representatives will be by the person in charge of purchasing, be it a senior veterinarian and/or the practice manager. He or she will decide, most probably in conjunction with other staff members, which products are to be included in the practice stock range. Subsequently, the clinic support staff may be the first contact with the sales professionals, who will also advise on product merchandising. Pet food manufacturers and pharmaceutical companies may offer product display racks, usually at no charge, thereby guaranteeing a minimum amount of prominence and shelf space for the company's specialities. The racks and displays can be useful merchandising tools, but they tend to be bulky and cannot be used to display other companies' products.

From planning ...to selling

Success in retailing calls for careful planning by the veterinarian. It is not sufficient to have the will, you must give yourself the means to be successful. As an old traditional Chinese proverb goes: "If you wish to catch fish, it is not sufficient to go to the river, you also need to bring your fishing net."

One approach to planning would be initially to consider the following questions:

- **Why do we wish to retail?** Is it to improve our services to our clients? Is it to increase our profits? Is it to perform a better job and be more caring for animals? Or is it a combination of the above?
- **What do we wish to retail?** Professional healthcare products that have proven to be reliable and effective, such as premium-quality pet foods, general healthcare products or pet accessories (cat carriers, cat litter, nail clippers, leashes and collars etc), external parasite-related products, etc?
- **Who will do the retailing?** The veterinarians, the staff or the receptionists? Will further training be required, and who will provide it?
- **Where will I do the retailing?** Does it need some structural changes to the clinic? Do I have adequate space?

Having answered these questions (and any others specific to your practice), it is equally important to establish a timescale and plan for the launching of this new service, tailored to your needs and those of your clients. Ask your distributor to help you identify the initial selection of products and build a system that can be adapted to suit your individual practice requirements.

"If you wish to catch fish, it is not sufficient to go to the river, you also need to bring your fishing net..."

Product selection

Depending on the current national legislation there will be various categories of products that veterinarians may or may not sell to their clients. The European Commission will, in the future, probably make modifications to the rules of practising veterinary medicine in certain countries. Various categories of medications, food, nutritional supplements or pet accessories will be among the products that you will be permitted to purchase for retailing to pet owners that visit your practice.

As a rule, we suggest you initially select only those products that you feel confident about using and recommending. For example, those that you would probably use yourself. Do not forget that it is not economically viable to carry all possible products on the market. On the other hand, remember that clients will expect a certain degree of choice and selection.

It is important to pick products with a high-quality, professional image that match your standing in the market. Veterinarians work in a niche market where they need to select products that have a good reputation, offer value for money and are the result of sound scientific research. Ideally, these products should be proven as reliable, and should also have a strong veterinary or animal health image.

It is also important to make sure the product back-up service is adequate to help your practice develop the communication and the marketing aspects. This may necessitate some training seminars and potential daily contacts that you may need to maintain with the companies or their distributor. As will be the case for your clients, you will appreciate your suppliers being available to solve logistical problems and supply any necessary scientific product information. Sell only products that you know and trust, and that you will be of value and benefit to your clients and their pets.

Many veterinarians have successfully used small display posters to help clients choose items by self-selection from the range of goods on sale. These mini-posters can take the form of signs attached to the front of shelves, answering frequently asked questions.

For example, a premium puppy food poster could include statements such as:

"Puppy or Starter food"
"Veterinary recommended"
"Approximate cost per day is x.xx"
"Gives your puppy an ideal start"
"Available in 2kg, 5kg, and 10kg bags"

Sales

Retailing includes sales; it is well known that veterinarians are often not good sales people. They are excellent advisors and counsellors, but often fail to take the last step in the sales process, which is to "close the deal". This is business jargon for finishing the consultation with a purchase (product or service) by the client. The historical concept of the vet as the doctor, and not a salesman, only partly explains this attitude. The key attribute that distinguishes good sales people from mediocre is closing the deal. Frequently, staff and nurses are much better sales people than veterinarians.

The receptionists, technicians and nurses play a key role in the commercial success of selling non-prescription over-the-counter (OTC) products. They are usually the first contact between the client (consumer) and the practice. Also, they often face additional questions from owners seeking clarification regarding the advice or the prescription given during their consultation with the veterinarian. Such discussions, after the consultation, often easily lead on to further OTC sales. Therefore, sales of the recommended products may be enhanced by explanation and endorsement by the support staff. This product endorsement and advice (based on knowledge and experience) will increase client confidence in both the practice and the products.

Several factors influence the range of products offered for sale at a veterinary clinic.
These include:

- the positioning of the clinic;
- client profile; and
- the retail zone.

- **Clinic positioning**

Position does not refer to the geographic location of the clinic, but to the market segment and the clientele. The profile of a clinic develops from how it promotes itself and how it is perceived by the clients. The two are not always identical. Often, new assistant veterinarians have little influence in this area, and the clinic profile has evolved historically without any conscious input from the veterinarians. Obviously, it is better to develop the client perception based on a clear practice mission statement, the practice aims and strategy. The clinic owner, associates, practice manager and vets, as well as the support staff, should all be actively involved in such positioning, in terms of products, services and prices. Thus, the clinic's personality will directly affect the degree of client loyalty and satisfaction.

The clinic exists as an important part of the local community, and the vet should never underestimate this aspect of his or her practice. Clinics classified as general practices should endeavour to have a wide selection of products (large width of the line) while stocking small quantities of each (small depth of the line), thus aiming to satisfy a large cross-section of different clients. A specialist clinic, on the other hand, should concentrate on a small selection of specialised products (small width) with large quantities of each (large depth), corresponding to the needs of their chosen speciality.

However, it is important to remember that companion animal medicine is part of a consumer industry where the sentimental aspects of ownership (human/animal bond) play an important role, automatically defining the veterinary clinic, surgery or hospital (the term used varies per country) as a high-quality health centre for pets. This is one of the reasons the veterinary clinic should not look like a pharmacy, a drug store or a pet shop. If it is seen as such by clients, they will consider such places as having conflicting interests, which would be detrimental for veterinary clinic's image. This is where the principle of separating the sales from the clinical activities becomes important. Client expectations differ in various countries and, most probably, even in regions – such as city versus rural areas.

Sales of recommended products may be enhanced by explanation and endorsement by the support staff. This will increase client confidence in both the practice and the products.

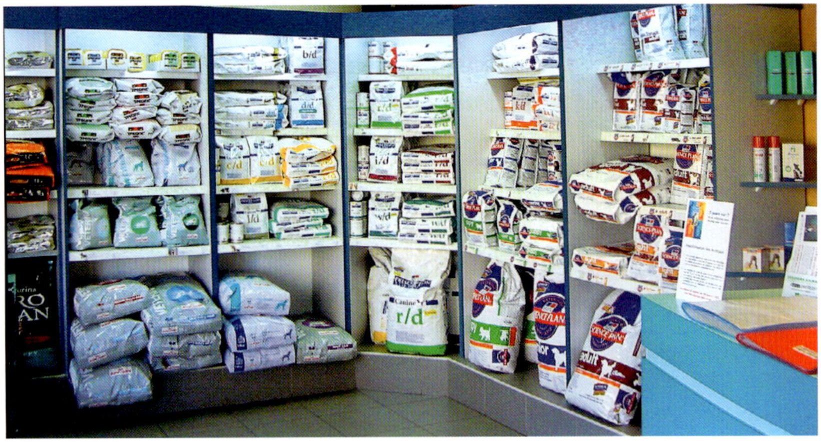

Frequently, staff and nurses are much better sales people than veterinarians.

- **Client profile**

This can be defined by the type of practice (companion animal, mixed and equine), by the client's socio-professional environment or the local trends, such as local market tendencies. Studies indicate that consumers have three major motivations for their purchases:

- product cost;
- product safety, and
- product matches the consumer's personality.

- Cost is essentially selection by price: "I am going to this clinic because their products and services are cheaper, therefore, I will pay less either because I cannot afford more, or because I manage my budget carefully."
- Security is a major concern for consumers: "I am a client in this veterinary hospital because it is the best, I trust the veterinarians." Another term is peace of mind.
- The client's image is not a well-known motivation, but it is a very powerful one for many pet owners: "I am a client in this brand-new, modern, expensive clinic, thus emphasising my own status in society, and demonstrating to my friends that I am part of an elite that uses only what is best."

Other motivating factors are innovation and product presentation.

- **Retail zone**

The retail zone is the sales/commercial area made up of clients and competitors. Marketing studies can assist in identifying the best locality prior to selecting a clinic site, and for assessing potential income. Important area factors include:

- the number of inhabitants;
- average income;
- projected neighbourhood growth;
- family lifestyles;
- number and type of pets; and
- the nature of the competition, including pet suppliers such as supermarkets and speciality shops – particularly important when considering sales of pet food and products.

Before establishing a veterinary clinic, it will be useful to identify the area's predominant people movement or potential client traffic. For example, in an area close to a commercial centre, it will be helpful to carry products of high necessity, such as food and cat litter. In a holiday area, small supplies of various items will satisfy the needs of potential clients who are short-term visitors. In an urban zone, it will be important to get to know the clientele well and adapt the selection of products accordingly.

Various types of sales

The veterinarian's strategic choice of clinic orientation and position, stock selection and services will impact subsequent sales techniques in the clinic.

- **Prescription selling**

In this mode of purchase, clients have a passive role as they rarely have free access to prescription products in the clinic retail area. This technique naturally

3

Building Relationships

In this section:

The family/pet bond

Knowing your clients

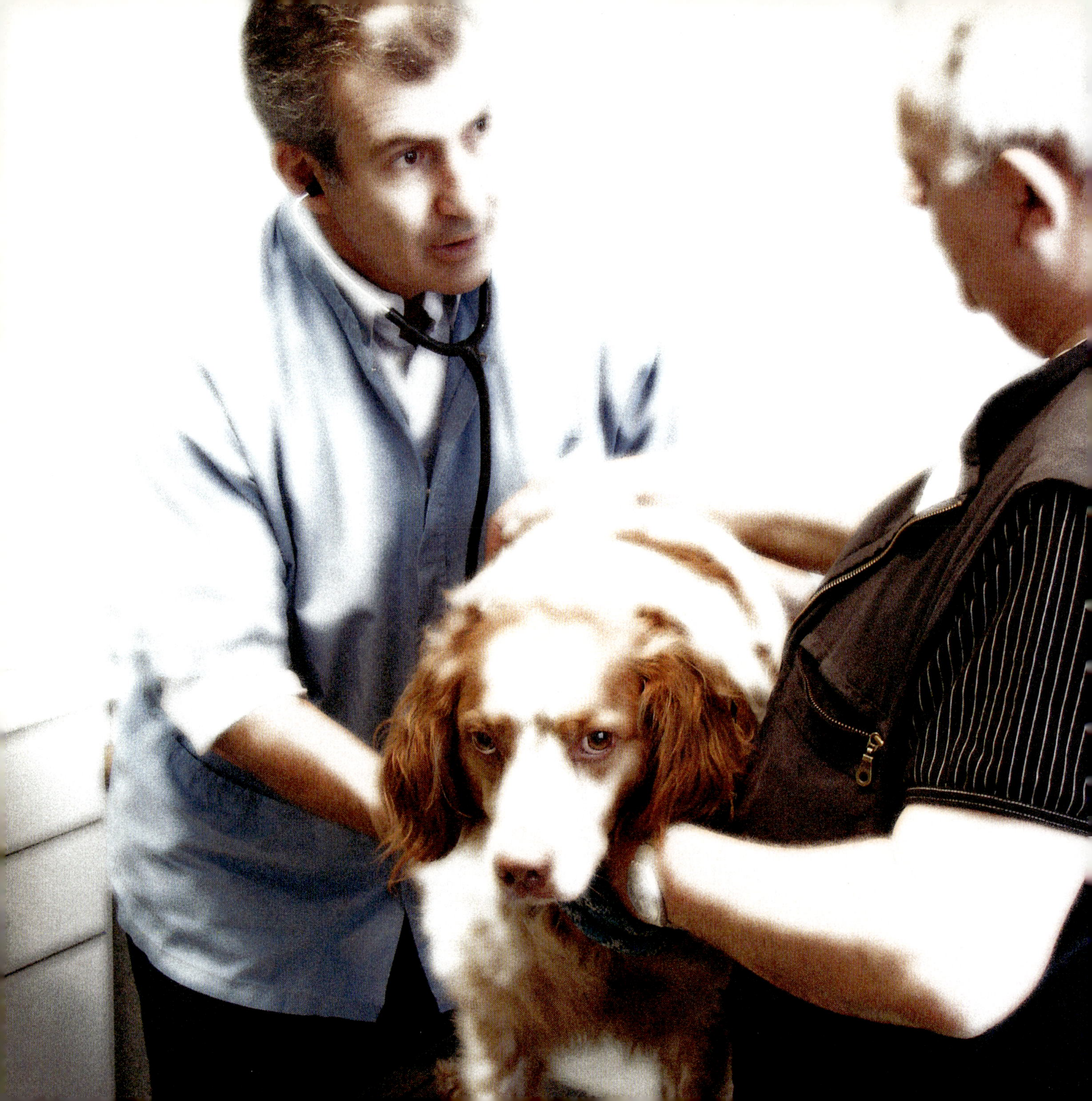

The family/pet bond

3.1

From animal to pet

THE RELATIONSHIP BETWEEN man and dogs started when the latter became early man's fellow hunters, which happened when our ancestors found out that dogs contributed to the hunt's success. Research shows that dogs understand human communication signals better than any other species, even monkeys. For these reasons, dogs became an important part of the community. In addition, young puppies have always been charming and attractive, and it is likely our forebears (particularly women and children) started playing with them. The relationship developed, but dogs were often treated with brutality and violence, in a similar way (and most probably worse) to disobedient servants.

Until the middle of the 20th century, dogs were considered animals and were kept outside the house, in barns or stables. At the same time, cats had proved to be valuable in protecting crops and grains from being eaten by rodents. Cats also lived in barns and storage areas. At some point, the charm of puppies and kittens must have become too hard to resist, the aggression of adult dogs was reduced by domestication, and they gradually moved into the house, although not to all parts of the house and, certainly, not the bedroom area. Most probably, they were allowed indoors for a limited amount of time, and maybe only for part of the year, such as the winter season.

Gradually, selective breeding resulted in different dog types. Selection was initially based on specific hunting needs, but later selection and breeding was based on beauty and other non-functional characteristics. The initial conscious breeding and selection was in the hands of aristocrats and landowners. On the farm, however, dogs continued to make the breeding decisions themselves.

Up to the 1960s, dogs were still used for pulling carts (the dog was harnessed into the small business cart), which gradually became non-appropriate animal use in western Europe. Despite ongoing discussions, sleds are still pulled with great enthusiasm for both work and racing competition purposes in northern Europe and North America. Significant cultural differences mean that, in some parts of the world, dogs and cats are on the menu.

In the western hemisphere, the industrial revolution created many middle-class families that were not farm-based, and wealth increased rapidly after 1960. Dogs and cats stayed with the people. The only reason for these non-farmers to have animals around, and even in the house, was companionship. The few exceptions included hunting and protection (guard dogs).

The cat had long proven to be a pleasant companion, but non-obedient and relatively resistant to domestication. Selection and breeding

I had three sons: they all left home... my dogs stayed.

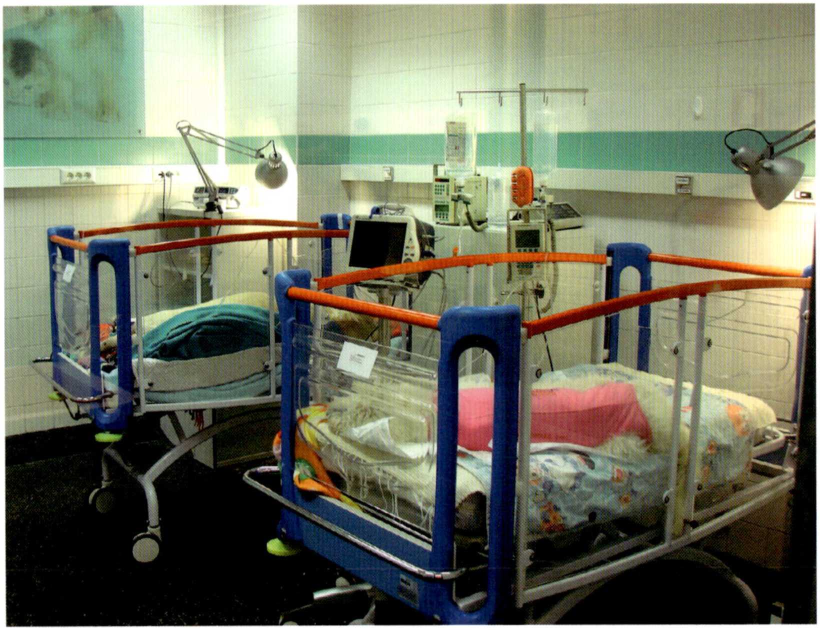

has resulted in hundreds of different breeds of cats and dogs, with key characteristics often based on non-functional, non-rational, and purely aesthetical and emotional criteria.

> Cost-based decisions are the owner's responsibility; the quality of preventive and curative healthcare is the responsibility of the veterinary profession.

Pets as family members

Cats, dogs and other pets can now be found in all parts of the house. They have even made it into the children's and owner's bedrooms, and sometimes even into the beds.

Obviously, differences occur in the level of this invasion, but the trend of pets becoming family members is generic and irreversible. Favourite pet names are listed in newspapers, and celebrity pets make it into news headlines. Small cats and dogs are allowed to enter passenger compartments of aeroplanes. In general, we can conclude that pets have gradually taken the role of children and companions. In a recent study by the American Kennel Club people were asked: is a person who is in a house on their own, with the sole presence of a dog, considered to be alone? Almost 80 per cent of pet owners responded that the person was not alone, and a remarkable 66 per cent of non-pet owners agreed. Pet owners are now referred to as "parents".

So, pets are no longer just animals, but are family members with a name and the owners expect them to be treated as such. Pets are loved, and owners are willing to go to great lengths for their "babies". Owners are considered the pet's "parents", and their behaviour towards their "children" is, more often than not, emotionally driven. As a result, pet illness causes similar emotions to such an occurrence in other family members. The death of a pet has significant impact on the "parents", and the mourning and grieving process is very similar to that of a human loved one. A pet cannot easily be replaced by another one, as used to occur. The pet is considered an "individual" with its own unique personality, just like a child.

The widely referenced US-published KPMG megastudy (1999) recognised the high commitment to pets, and the strength of the human/animal bond. Questions to pet owners revealed:

- 93 per cent would be upset if anything happened to their pet;
- 85 per cent believed people are more attached to their pets because pets are more like family members;
- owners would pay $688 for a 75 per cent chance of successfully treating their pet and $356 for a 10 per cent chance;
- owners would pay an average of $1,042 to keep their favourite pet dog from dying, or $657 to keep their favourite cat from dying; and
- owners would pay an average $92 per month to keep their pet healthy –$165 per month for horse owners.

This new pet status as a "family member" is an extremely powerful driver of owner behaviour. The maintenance of pet health is a high priority for both the owner and the veterinary healthcare team. Providing veterinary care and products to clients is more rewarding in the sense that the goods are provided to a "family member". An additional, important consequence is that we know implicitly that, when dealing with pets and family members, the financial aspects are not necessarily a major issue or primary concern. Therefore, the veterinarian and staff know they can treat the pet in the best way, and make every effort to manage the patient's health, with costs being a secondary priority.

Summary and conclusion

Preventive healthcare programmes for pets are appreciated just as much as they are for humans. Dental care, obesity prevention and management programmes have become accepted and supported. Most owners need professional pet support, as they have little or no animal-related background, and often only have experience with one pet. The veterinarian and his or her staff play a very important supportive role for this new family member, and owners place great trust in their veterinary practice

A dog is always happy when you come home and he will give you a feast, even if you return after only 10 minutes. Compare that to the welcome you get (if any) from other people in your household or family. Is this behaviour one of the reasons we love our pets?

Pets are no longer just animals, but are family members with a name – and the owners expect them to be treated as such.

to take optimal care of their "babies". The owners often want the best available treatment, and cost considerations are often in second place. Owners expect the same diagnostic and treatment options that are available for themselves. Many veterinarians either do not understand, or underestimate, the power of this new relationship between owner and pet, and fail to take responsibility for their new role as family healthcare professionals. Often, veterinarians and staff do not offer the optimal diagnostic and treatment options, because they assume these are too costly for the owner.

The powerful relationship between man and pets used to be called the human/animal bond. While we fully support the principle behind this term, we prefer to use the term family/pet bond, because it is the transition of status from animal to pet family member that is the basis for the power of this relationship. We consider it the responsibility of the veterinary professional to support this development, and to offer people the best available healthcare for pet family members. Cost-based decisions are the owner's responsibility; the quality of preventive and curative healthcare is the responsibility of the veterinary profession.

The veterinary/human/pet relationship offers significant business opportunities for veterinarians around the world. When offering products and services, all three parties must benefit from the transaction. As long as this condition is fulfilled, taking veterinary healthcare to the highest possible level will create a win-win-win situation for all parties – pet, owner and veterinarian.

Knowing your clients 3.2

Who are the clients?

CLIENTS OF MODERN practices are mobile and choose their veterinarian on the basis of their personal circumstances and preferences. In remote villages, the majority of clients may still come from the local community, especially when the practice is the only one in the area, but in most cases clients have a choice and take advantage of it.

The clientele will have developed over time and is based on the image and reputation that the clinic has with the clients. This is a long-term process and cannot be changed overnight. The modern client base is characterised by factors such as: demographics, lifestyles, (higher) expectations, more vocal attitude, being more knowledgeable, and placing a greater attention on personal experience.

Assuming you are not starting a new practice, but rather joining an existing practice team, you will have to be prepared to accept and adapt to the staff and clientele, in the same way as they will need to get used to you. It is, therefore, an important aspect of the job application processes to learn about the practice vision and mission, and to make sure there is sufficient overlap between the existing practice realities and your own ambitions, background, knowledge and skills.

The new veterinarian joining the practice staff needs to accept the realities of the clinic's style, its standards and protocols, and the clients and business it has already generated. When a newly recruited veterinarian finds out there is a mismatch between expectations and reality, the best move to make is to resign and move on. Don't expect practice realities to change short term because of the arrival of a new junior staff member, no matter how right and brilliant you think you are. The clinic clientele is

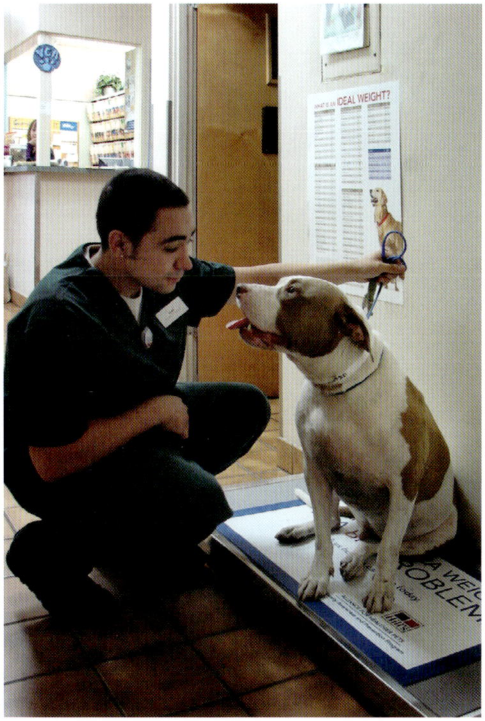

It is an important aspect of the job application processes to make sure there is sufficient overlap between the existing practice realities and your own ambitions, background, knowledge and skills.

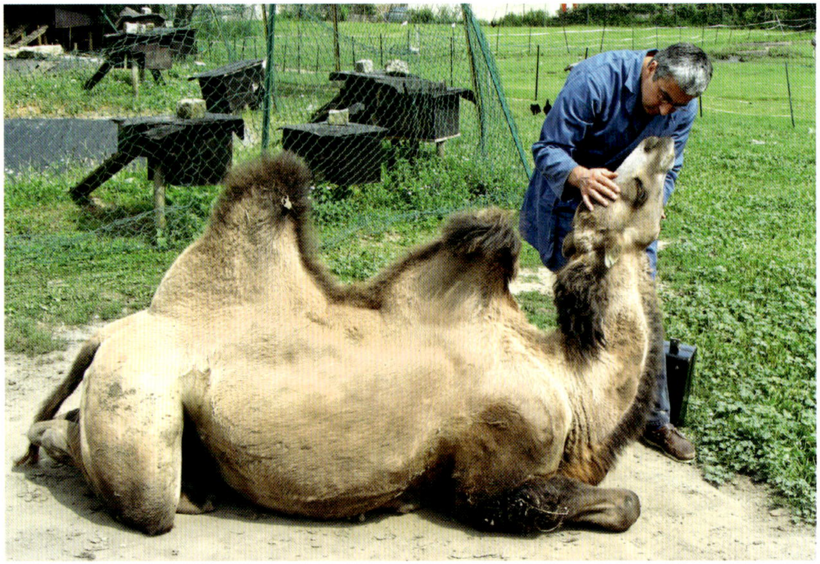

Who is my veterinarian?

How do clients choose their veterinarian? Location, visibility (of the premises as well as in the media) and word-of-mouth are key drivers for the first visit. The next important criterion is the initial and overall impression during the first visit. We know that "clients do not care how much you know, until they know how much you care" (Carolyn Bäck). Because of this, the clinic has to communicate the message of care about owners and pets – with CARE written in capitals when dealing with clients. Knowledge and skills alone are not sufficient to be successful. Care is communicated by everything the clinic does and does not do, including the design of the building (for example, separate dog and cat areas). Most important is veterinarian and staff attitudes, showing kindness and demonstrating active listening skills, genuine personal interest and empathy. When clinic staff impress pet owners with a level of care exceeding expectations, it is increases the probability they will come back and become loyal clients. When the perceived value provided by the practice during the visit exceeds the expected value, the client will be satisfied. Satisfied, happy clients play a very important role in generating new business. It has been proven many times that unhappy clients tell more than 10 people about their negative experience, whereas happy clients only tell an average of three – it's unfortunate there is such a gap when people share positive experiences versus the negative ones. The good news is that positive recommendations are very powerful drivers of new business.

based on the total package of services provided and products sold, as well as the location of the clinic, the opening hours, and the culture and atmosphere created by the staff. Also the quality:price ratio might be a reason for clients to prefer the practice, but in general, quality of care (perceived value) is far more important than the price.

Client expectations

Clients have high expectations, with the possibility of dissatisfaction if this expectation is no longer fulfilled. In other words, clients may be initially impressed because a service was beyond their expectations, but the ongoing challenge is maintaining the service level on subsequent visits. A lower standard will no longer be tolerated. A few years ago, a telephone call to a veterinary clinic, or any consumer service-oriented business, received a typical welcome such as "Good morning". A more appropriate welcome might now be: "Welcome to the Samaritan Animal Hospital, Jenny speaking, how may I help you?".

It has reached the point that when we don't receive such a personal greeting, we wonder if we have dialed the wrong number.

There are several kinds of expectations: expressed or "explicit" and non-expressed or "implicit". It is important to know the client's implicit expectations since, by definition, these will not be mentioned. An example is that, almost without exception, people expect the personnel and staff in a veterinary clinic to appear professional and medical, wearing white or a medical-type clothes. If it is not the case, people may be surprised or even upset. They will not mention it, because the expectation is implicit for them, but they will be disappointed. Veterinarians need to understand these expectations. Other classic implicit expectations include:

In touch with clients

In order for the practice to understand the existing clientele, service their needs optimally and develop new services, it is important to be in touch. Obviously, it is important to read the literature and observe trends in the markets at home and abroad, but the best way to know what your clients want, and how they would react to new initiatives, is ask and then test the ideas using a selected client group.

There are different ways to do this, and each one has advantages and disadvantages.

- You (or another staff member) can ask individual clients ad hoc during a consultation.
- You can install an "input box" (a real one in the clinic and/or a virtual one on your website) and encourage people to use it.
- You can hand out a survey to all clients visiting the clinic during a certain time period, or throughout the year on a fixed day of the week or month.
- You can create a client panel of trusted owners and meet with them to obtain ideas, comments and feedback on existing procedures and programmes as well as on new initiatives.

In order to make client feedback part of the regular strategic planning and evaluation processes, they can be invited to join a focus group to consider ideas and provide feedback in order to avoid personal bias. Finally, clients can be part of a representative group of owners who are part of the practice management, and meet regularly with practice staff and owners to discuss customer-related issues. Creating an atmosphere in which staff passes on information received or picked up (conversation in the reception and waiting area) guarantees valuable input. Owners often share comments and opinion with support staff that they don't communicate to the veterinarians.

Special attention should be given to those loyal customers who bring in the bulk of the business. A rule of thumb is that for any business a minority of good clients (20 per cent) bring in the majority of the business (up to 80 per cent). According to recent studies, these numbers might not be fully applicable to veterinary surgeries, where it is more in the region of 35 to 40 per cent, but the general principle that a minority bring in most of the revenue holds true. Obviously, this group is of utmost importance to the practice. They deserve special attention and should be treated as VIPs.

Existing clients can also help convince potential clients of the good value of the services provided by sharing their experience. A clinic that provides top-of-the-market, highly priced diagnostic and surgical procedures may consider asking some satisfied clients if they will consider sharing their feelings of satisfaction and act as experts-by-experience, sharing

Veterinarians, as service providers, must be equally concerned in managing the client's experience as in providing technical expertise.

testimonials on the website and answering questions from concerned new owners. Quality training of these ambassadors is essential for a successful project.

> "In the face of unprecedented competition, veterinarians and their teams must fight back with better skills, increased attention to detail, and a commitment to exceed client expectations."
>
> – Marty Becker

How to create a loyal client base

As Marty Becker from the US states: "In the face of unprecedented competition, veterinarians and their teams must fight back with better skills, increased attention to detail, and a commitment to exceed client expectations." Many veterinarians still value their business by evaluating their client base. Loyal clients are those pet owners who, when they think of animal health, products, care, service and advice, think of their veterinarian and not any other provider (such as the pharmacist, drugstore, supermarket, pet store, grooming or dog trainer). There will always be people who use other sources for certain services and products. However, in our society, time is so valuable that many customers are looking for a one-stop purchase (no need to travel somewhere else to get the quality reliable food or the flea product). Clients often look for specialised and customised services, and high-quality products – another reason why they select premium products and services provided by a healthcare professional, such as the family veterinarian. This is the basis for establishing a loyal and faithful clientele. The ideal clientele will use the practice services not only for the sick and injured pet, but also for the healthy one. The Americans have even created a new word – wellness – to cover this all-inclusive concept.

In order to establish loyal clients, veterinarians and their teams need to do everything to make people happy and convince them to return to the clinic as frequently as possible. This requires more than matching client's expectations; it is about exceeding client's expectations.

Marketing surveys show that the loyal client of a veterinary practice visits the clinic about 2.8 times and spends about €144 each year (excluding pet food). Loyalty, therefore, has a direct economical impact, but it is also an emotional one because it is rewarding and motivating to work with clients who follow your suggestions. We believe this is an important reward in

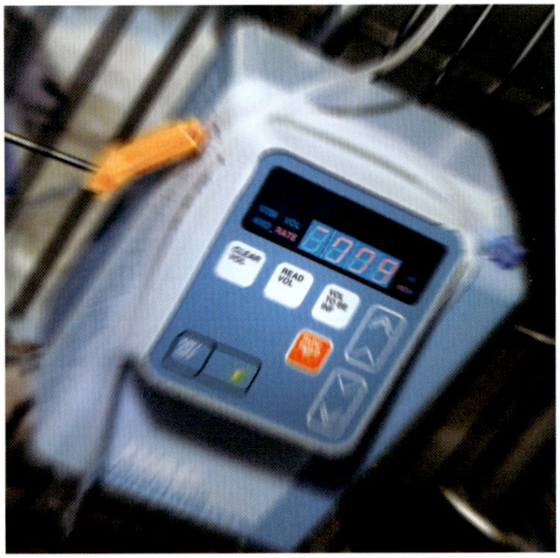

our busy work life. The statement by Walt Disney: "We will do what we do so well, that the people who see it, will want to see it again, and bring their friends", is an excellent way to summarise what veterinarians should achieve when creating a loyal client base.

Some common complaints from clients visiting veterinarians include:

- long waiting time;
- delayed appointments;
- too much information;
- not enough information;
- veterinarians and staff in a hurry;
- lack of listening;
- dirty premises;
- unpleasant and unfriendly staff;
- lack of concern and compassion;
- roughness and brutality with their pet;
- lack of courtesy;
- giving back a dirty or smelly animal;
- not knowing the pet's name or sex;
- neglecting to immediately take care of an emergency; and
- ignoring a client at the reception.

Referring clients

Clients are happy to accept referrals. If not all services are available in the first-line clinic and the general practitioner (GP) veterinarian advises clients to consult a specialist, this is usually

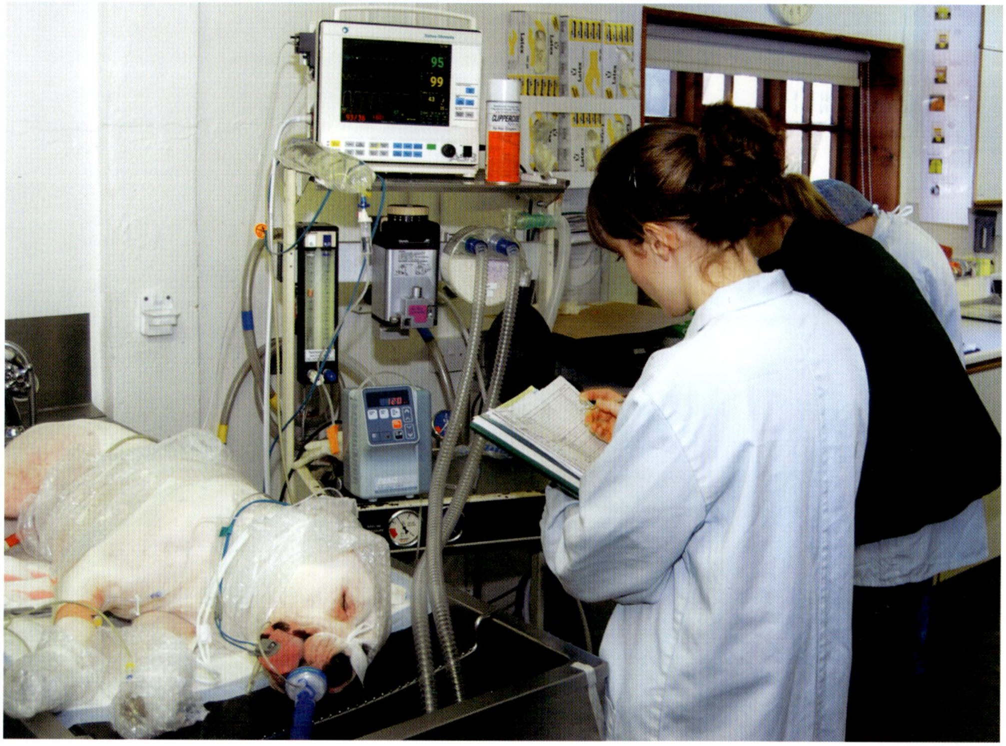

Owners are familiar with referrals in human medicine, and appreciate their vet referring in cases where he or she knows that better care will be available from a specialist hospital.

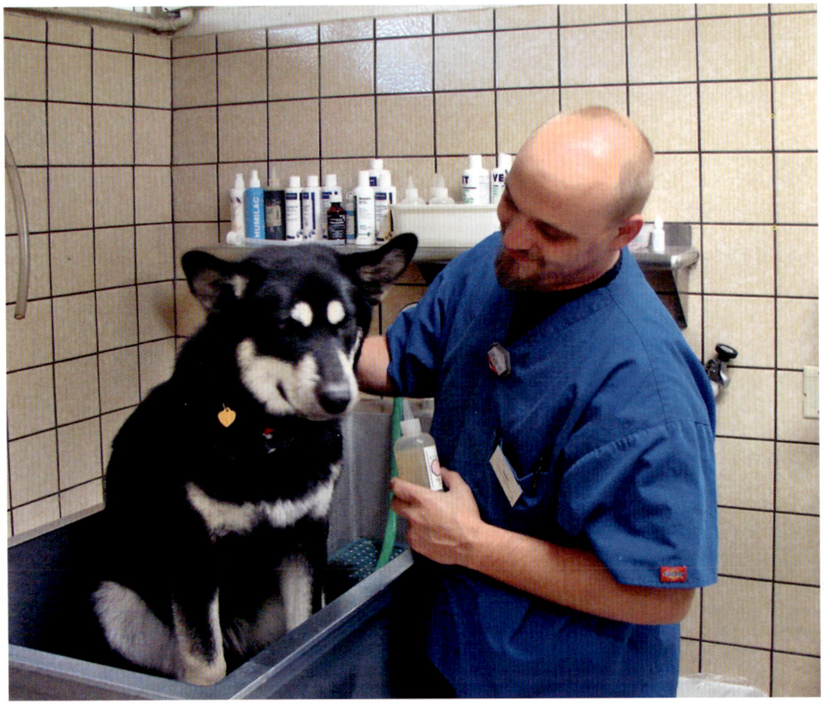

appreciated. Owners are familiar with referrals in human medicine, and appreciate their veterinarian referring in cases where he or she knows that better care will be available from a specialist hospital. This is not perceived by the owner as poor-quality veterinary care, but is highly appreciated when the veterinarian indicates the limits of general practice compared with the specialist facilities.

In the referral clinic, a team of specialists (maybe board certified and Diplomates of various specialist colleges in the US and/or Europe) and their staff will make sure the best diagnostic and therapeutic healthcare is provided for owners whose pets need specialist care. Fortunately, an increasing number of owners indicate they want and can afford specialist level pet healthcare. After treatment, the specialist informs the referring veterinarian of any necessary follow-up treatment, which, together with future everyday and preventive healthcare (so-called first line or basic care) continues to be undertaken by the practice.

The ideal clientele will use the practice services not only for the sick and injured pet, but also for the healthy one.

There is no competition between the two levels of veterinary care (generalist and specialist); rather they are complementary and together provide a synergy of optimal care. This is exactly what most clients expect from the veterinary profession.

Summary and conclusion

A healthy group of loyal clients is of the utmost importance for a healthy practice. Knowing clients' expectations, and making every effort to exceed them when clients visit the clinic, will result in continued client satisfaction. Clients are mobile, and although location is an important reason for people to select their vet, travelling some distance is not an issue when clients perceive the care suits them and their pet. A referral to a specialist is not interpreted by clients as a sign of incompetence. Rather, it is appreciated, as in human medicine, that the veterinarian is clearly indicating the limits of his or her competence.

4

Getting Your Message Across

In this section:

Basic communication concepts and techniques

Marketing in the clinic – communication tools

Communication tools outside the clinic

Basic communication concepts and techniques

4.1

Initial remarks

WE BELIEVE THAT communication in general, and communication tools in particular, have become essential integrated elements of veterinary practice development. This chapter focuses on the basic concepts of communication and techniques. Communication tools to reach your clients are detailed in **Section 4.3**.

Introduction and definition

Communication is a pillar of modern practice management for the new veterinary practitioner. The word communication comes from the Latin "communis" which means common, that which belongs to several. We know that communication represents much more than the simple linear relationship between two individuals. On the contrary, it relies on an inter-related system of reports and exchanges, a perpetually moving system that generates reactions (**Figure 4.1.1**). Communication is transmitting, revealing, and sharing knowledge and information. For some people, to communicate is also to please and to persuade.

Some clients will judge us on competency, experience and scientific knowledge, and others will judge on our personality. Some clients like us and some don't. We can conclude that, to be successful in practice and develop a strong client loyalty, one needs to be a person of communication. This is true with clients, staff and colleagues.

There are several modes of communication, including verbal and visual. In general, communication has to do with the five senses (including smell). The sense of contact and human relations is an important factor in communication; some inborn personality features will help us relate to other people and establish their confidence.

Communication includes an interchangeable exchange of messages between sender and receiver: answers, feedback, and comments. Communication is a two-way process of input and output, of action and reaction. One cannot communicate to a person or a target group, but only communicate with them.

In our case the sender is a veterinarian, or a veterinary practice, and the receiver is a diverse group of clients and potential clients, who have some things in common (such as their geographic location and pet ownership), and who differ in many other aspects (character, gender, hobbies, education, age, religion, nationality, social status and culture). When communicating with clients we always have to keep in mind the diversity and heterogeneity of the owner population.

Elements of inter-relational communication

It is essential to identify people's profile and react accordingly when talking with that person. Too often, we adopt the same speech and the same approach – to such a degree that clients think that manner

Communication represents much more than the simple linear relationship between two individuals.

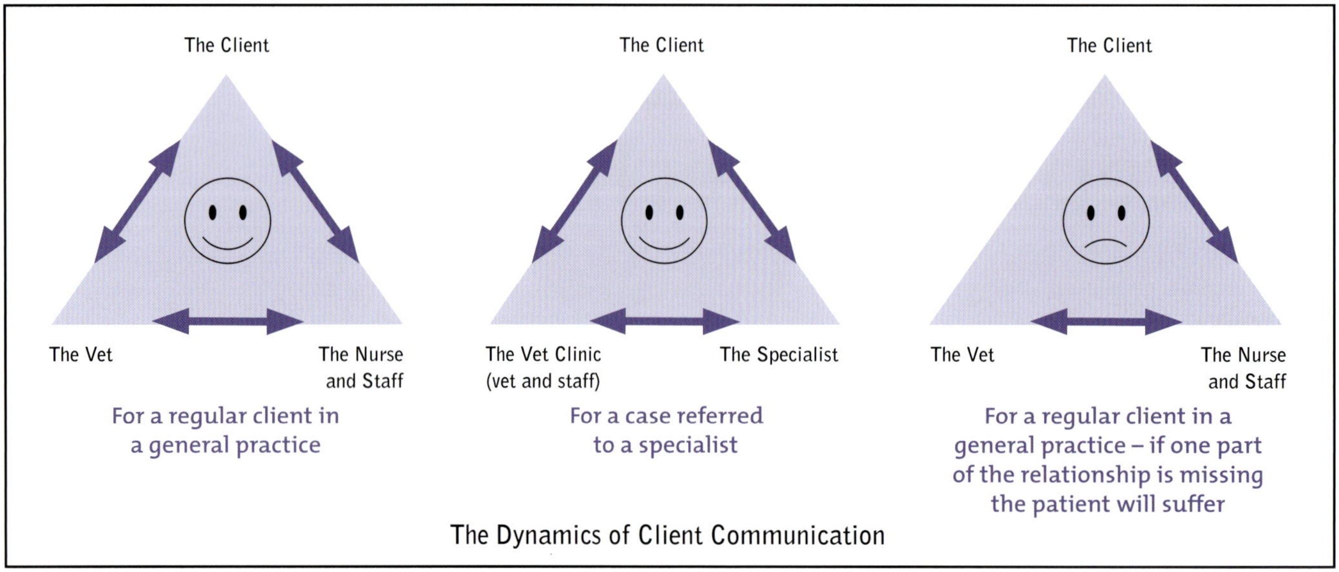

Figure 4.1.1

> You will need to react and, sometimes, modify your style of communication. If you don't, you may not be "in phase" with the person, and he or she will be unlikely to follow your recommendations.

is fixed, and unchangeable. This is a mistake. We need to accept people's differences and adapt our approach accordingly. In fact, there are two parts to this approach: understanding someone's emotions and behaviour (some people may use the word empathy), and the efficient use of adaptability.

Empathy is the ability to identify with someone else, to feel what that person feels. It is your aptitude to understand the person to whom you are talking. Adaptability is your aptitude to manage that person and their behaviour.

You will need to react and, sometimes, modify your style of communication. If you don't, you may not be in phase with the other person, and he or she will be unlikely to follow your recommendations. Empathy requires some psychology, where adaptability requires a will to change. We all know that sometimes it clicks and sometimes it doesn't. We all have an opinion, often based on impressions and, sometimes, very subjective features.

How to adapt communication to a person's profile

Every piece of information can help. Use common sense and all your senses. By looking at the way people move, talk and their body language, you can often obtain an initial understanding of their profile. Once you have formed your opinion, we suggest that you note it down somewhere, as a reference, and go back to it from time to time and see if you were right or not. This information is very useful. It will help you approach individual's according to their expectations. For example, a businessman who comes into your practice with his old Labrador dog may be immediately interested by the new diet to help with his pet's joints: he is a creative promoter. He does not need to know all the ingredients, and the pathogenesis of osteoarthritis (arthrosis), nor does he have the time to listen. For him, too much information will be negative. On the contrary, a high-school teacher or so-called technician confronting the same situation will need to study the facts and satisfy him or herself that this new diet is tested and proven to be good, safe, and efficacious. For him or her a full explanation will be needed and you will need to allow sufficient time. You may need to say: "We have just received this new food and would like to use on several dogs before we prescribe it for your pet. We will talk about it again in a few months when we have more information and experience with the product."

To summarise – the first impression is always important and often it will influence the entire client relationship. However, there are some potential pitfalls. You may judge and categorise your client with a high degree of subjectivity. For example, a person with ragged clothes may be wrongly classified as someone with financial problems. Don't judge without more information, and make sure you obtain all objective data from your client to avoid such potential errors. It is important to know more about your clients, to find out who they are (profession, social background) to be better placed to know their needs and expectations. Practically, a simple questionnaire filled in by new clients can help, with all additional information (gathered over time) added to the client record.

Active listening: the crucial step in communication

Speaking to a client on a one-to-one basis requires different communication techniques than communicating with a group of clients or a large audience in an auditorium. Written communication, via e-mail, internet or a newsletter, is different than oral communication. A one-to-one discussion in the examination room with a pet owner presents a completely different scenario than a conversation on neutral ground, talking about the health problems of pets in general. Obviously, we do not know what kind of people walk into the clinic for the first time, or contact us via the internet, and what will be the preferred communication style. However, a powerful communication technique to make sure we communicate with them in an optimal fashion is called active listening. This technique includes attentive listening to the owner with genuine interest, asking questions for further clarification, and then paraphrasing the conversation to confirm that we understand. Our attitude and actions during client conversations need to communicate that we care about them and their pet.

Remember the first lesson in communication is to listen, not to talk. As one communication expert once said: "This is the reason why we have two ears and only one mouth."

Communication by word or images – which works best?

This depends on monitoring the client's body language, and realising whether or not they are still with you or if you have lost them. If the latter, then you must go back and start again from the point where you lost them in your explanation. Documentation can support your verbal communication.

"Active listening" is a technique that includes attentive listening to the owner with genuine interest, asking questions for further clarification, and then paraphrasing the conversation, to confirm that we understand.

When discussing owners' highly emotional problems related to pet health, the likelihood of losing a significant part of the message is increased.

People remember only a small percentage (less than 20 per cent in most cases) of what they were told in the examination room by the vet. In some cases, it works well to have a nurse explain things again, outside the examination room, handing them a flyer that includes full details, and offering them an opportunity to telephone if they have further questions. Of course, this approach means the vet or a staff member is available to answer questions. It is well known that an image tells a thousand words, but some people can memorise words better whereas others prefer images, or relate to words that express movement and emotions. One method should not be assumed better than another, and in the clinic, it is a good idea to use different approaches. Don't assume that what you feel is the most efficacious method of communication is always the best for others. For example, some people love to illustrate by using metaphors, while others hate this method of explanation.

As with all products, both content and packaging is important to ensure full appreciation by the receiver. For a message, the packaging may include the environment in which the message is delivered or the communication (conversation) which took place. It can also include the layout, font, illustrations and the artwork of the flyer, brochure or website. A message delivered to a client during a hectic clinic, when rushing from one emergency to another crisis, is completely different from the one communicated in a quiet, well-furnished room in the clinic over a relaxing cup of tea or coffee. The communicative value of a handout using a boring font is completely different from a skilfully developed flyer that includes colours, pictures and photographs.

According to Mehrabin, more than 90 per cent of our communication during meetings is non-verbal, emphasising the importance of body language and facial expression (see **Figure 4.1.2**).

A smile (even when talking over the phone) can change the message perception. When a staff member listens carefully and responds actively and skilfully, the receiver's attitude can be changed from resistance to cooperation.

Modern communication technology

People are familiar with high-quality communication techniques, and media (television, multimedia publishing, internet, cell phone and SMS) and marketers (companies and institutions) compete for the attention of viewers, readers, clients and customers. Veterinarians' communication tools and skills are compared with these professional communicators. Very few people have the talent to fully comprehend and to practise optimal communication as second nature. It is, therefore, advisable to seek expert guidance when it comes to important aspects of client communication. There are courses and tools available to veterinarians and their staff, including generic, veterinary post-graduate or tailor-made courses for the individual clinic. Practice budget and size will be an important factor in deciding the method of choice.

Figure 4.1.2

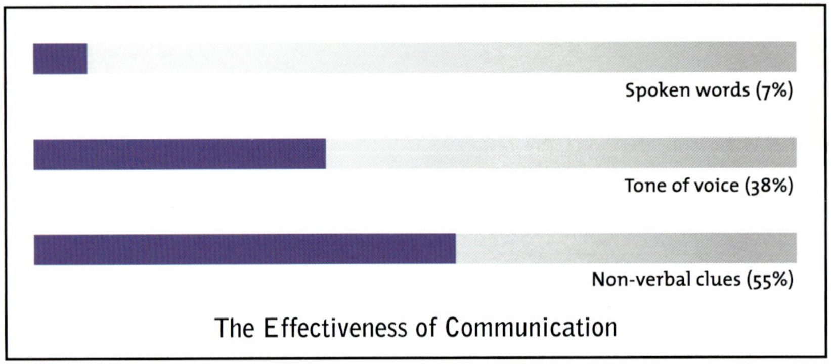

- availability – no waiting, flexible hours, easy access and parking, and sufficient stock;
- transparency – prices should be clearly labelled, invoices should be itemised;
- choice – various products and services, freedom of choice;
- environment – comfortable, neat, clean, odourless, friendly and modern;
- clarity of the offer – prices listed, estimates and badges; and
- services – various services adapted to various pet owners' needs.

Clients cannot easily judge the level of medical and surgical care, but they can and do judge the level of service they receive (read: perceive). In the clients' eyes, it is the only major factor that distinguishes you and makes you unique from other practices. Striving for excellence in client services is, therefore, essential.

Client surveys show that clients want the following from the veterinarian, in order of importance:

- kindness;
- availability; and
- capacity to listen.

Clients rank competency only after these three abilities. Why does competency only rank in fourth position? Simply because all veterinarians have the same diploma and, therefore, (in the clients' eyes) all have the same level of competency to treat their pet's common medical problems. Don't we react the same way with our family doctors?

A survey by the American Veterinary Medical Association (AVMA) revealed the factors that influenced people's choice in selecting their veterinarian:

• proximity	65 per cent
• recommendation	42 per cent
• prices	39 per cent
• hours and availability	31 per cent
• road signs	7 per cent

What is quite remarkable in this study is that proximity is the major factor, but recommendation has a very strong influence. We believe that pricing is always a sensitive issue in all areas of the world. However, in some countries and in some communities, it is more sensitive than in others. The survey was conducted in the US where pricing and teleshopping is, in general, a more sensitive issue and is part of the American culture. One should also take note of the paramount importance of recommendation. This is our best marketing tool. Everyone knows there are good and bad

Clients cannot easily judge the level of medical and surgical care, but they can and do judge the level of service they receive (read: perceive).

> Client satisfaction does not follow mathematical rules and is, by definition, associated with emotion, perception and personal opinion.

recommendations; they are both very powerful. With the rapidly increasing role of social media (internet networking) as a source of information and communication, the importance of recommendations (positive and negative) will further increase.

Client satisfaction

Client satisfaction does not follow mathematical rules and is, by definition, associated with emotions, perception and personal opinion. A pet owner's priority is to have peace of mind, live a happy life with their companion animal and avoid problems. Therefore, veterinarians and staff should focus on satisfying this number one requirement. The team should help pet owners with preventive medicine, nutrition advice, product selection, behaviour guidelines and pet insurance. We should not only be involved with medical and surgical procedures to treat the sick and the injured animal. It seems that satisfaction in the veterinary practice among client follows a bell-shaped curve. Most veterinarians can report from personal experience about a few clients

who were unhappy, are unhappy and will always be unhappy. Nothing can go right with these people and they can be classified as unreasonably unhappy. Everything is wrong. The good news is the practice also has a group of unreasonably happy clients; whatever you do, they are your fans and will always be your fans and remain loyal to you and the clinic. The important thing is to identify the median satisfaction level for the products and services provided by the practice. What is the perception of the majority of clients? Everyone needs a fan club, but their input does not provide direction and, while it should be enjoyed, it should not taken more seriously than the comments by unreasonably unhappy clients.

Measuring client satisfaction in a practice can help maintain a more stable, satisfied client base. Satisfaction is often a measure of the client's perception of quality. The highly satisfied client will feel they have received a high-quality service, whereas the dissatisfied client will be disappointed by the (perceived lack of) quality of service. Client service is the ability to meet client requirements. Veterinarians, as service providers, must be equally concerned in managing the client's experience as in providing technical expertise.

The first law of services concept was summarised by Maister as follows:
Satisfaction = Perception – Expectation.

In other words, if the client perceives services as better than expected, then satisfaction is positive and higher depending on the gap between the two values. This is the way all consumers analyse services. The aim of a veterinary team is that every client who comes to the practice goes away satisfied with the services received. This is the way business should be built.

applies to drugs and for specific technical products that require information and documentation, available only on a prescription from the veterinarian. In this form of selling, veterinary technicians and receptionists are only involved in the dispensing or renewal of the prescription. Clients have little involvement. Therefore, impulse purchases are very limited, and turnover relies heavily on veterinarians who prescribe. It is typical of a speciality referral clinic where merchandising is limited.

- **Self-service selling**

In this case, client have active roles in product selection: looking, touching, price checking and buying. This applies particularly to hygiene products, pet accessories, cosmetics and food treats. There is a tendency to use familiar products that give satisfaction. New products are often overlooked, and left on the shelves, unless attention is drawn to them and sales actively supported and encouraged by staff. This is a clinic model with an integrated pet shop or pet boutique zone.

- **Assisted selling**

This combination of the first two techniques is often considered the best type of sales approach, and is usually appropriate for veterinary diets and various anti-external parasite products. Clients appreciate support and advice from the staff, and new products are located close to the counter where staff and clients are in close proximity. Well-known, self-explanatory products, such as anti-flea products and pet foods currently being promoted by television or media advertising campaigns, are located in "cold spots". The assisted-selling technique is the best approach to keep clients regularly using the clinic, because personalising the sale and freely giving additional information and advice with each purchase provides added value. This brings clients back to

From advising... to selling

Professional retailing is an art

It consists of several phases. It would take a complete chapter in itself to detail all the basics and techniques of successful selling. This is not the objective in this context. However, we feel that some basic steps of successful retailing should be listed, including the following:

- identification of sales opportunity;
- identification of client needs through questions and answers;
- education about the features and benefits of using the products; and
- closing the deal.

Using such methods, veterinarians and staff can describe a product/service's important characteristics – those that are objective and technical. These characteristics – also called features – should, ideally, be differentiated from the product/service's benefits, which is the way it will help the animal or the owner. Features and benefits are linked, with the latter often derived from the product's characteristics, properties or technical details. An easy and practical way to differentiate between the two is by answering the question: so what? For example: this premium dog food contains moderate calcium levels and chondro-protective ingredients. These are the facts (characteristics); the benefits are these properties support healthy bone and joint development during large breed puppies' growth stages. By differentiating the characteristics properties (features) from the benefits, you will better inform, explain and also tailor recommendations to clients' individual needs.

It is important to listen carefully to client comments during the conversation.

- Overcoming client objections to convert negative responses into selling arguments.
  Most of the objections come from a lack of understanding of the products' benefits; countered by giving good information by skilled communication with the client. Communication tools are very useful here, such as brochures, videos and leaflets.
- Acknowledgment of the client's decision.
  Always make clients feel they have made a good decision – even if, in your opinion, that decision was not the best choice.

"By differentiating the features from the benefits, you will better inform, explain and also tailor recommendations to clients' individual needs"

the clinic for a product they can find elsewhere, but without the advice and service. For example, in the case of sales of flea and tick products, the veterinarian is perceived as by far the most competent advisor (86 per cent), compared to pharmacists (six per cent), groomers (three per cent), and breeders (two per cent).

Selling and merchandising products can create a client bond, resulting in repeat visits to purchase high-standard pet products, independent of medical consultations.

Successful selling

Communication means explaining product features and benefits, and personalising the sale. It requires a thorough knowledge of the product and of its use, preferably from personal experience. Ideally, the product has been used on the staff's own pet, employed in the clinic, or by someone known to the staff as this will inevitably increase client confidence. Personal reference or testimonial is always a great way to present a product in a friendly manner. This can be called "soft" marketing. Remember, more time spent on a sale translates to less profits, and also appears more commercial to clients. Three simple criteria for a successful sale:

- good for the pet;
- good for the owner; and
- good for the practice.

When these criteria are met, you can be confident of providing clients with good recommendations.

Summary and conclusion

Selling medical services and associated products is an integrated part of the veterinary surgeon's job. In order to excel in that role, vets should feel good and be convinced their services and products will help the animals' health and the owners' peace of mind. Selling products is different from selling services. It requires good selection, stocking, renewal, pricing, merchandising and marketing. Vets should also differentiate medications or drugs (that will be prescribed and are implicitly linked to the medical treatment) from para-medical products and accessories, including physiological diets, hygiene and OTC products. These products should be carefully selected to match the clinic profile. Product displays can be an issue simply because of space and logistics, particularly with pet foods. However, increasing growth in product sales has, in some instances, become a significant portion of practice revenues.

Selling and merchandising products can create a client bond, resulting in repeat visits to purchase high-standard pet products, independent of medical consultations. It is a part of healthy pet management, versus limiting clinic activities to medical and surgical services. Despite the growth of internet-based shopping and the trend for consumers to look for convenience, we believe there will always be a place for the sale of services and associated products in neighbourhoods. Vets should aim to differentiate themselves by selecting high-quality products and selling them in parallel to their medical services, aiming to best serve clients and pets.

The positive impact of first-rate advice and communication skills on overall business results justifies the investment of time and financial resources.

Communication when dealing with emotional issues

When discussing owners' highly emotional problems related to pet health (such as the pet diagnosed with a terminal illness), the likelihood of losing a significant part of the message is increased. The owner's emotional state might prevent him or her from picking up the essence of the message, and realising all eventual implications and ramifications. In such cases, it is often best to allow an owner some private time to consider and digest the first wave of information, and then continue the conversation when he or she is more receptive and open to discussion. Messages that include bad news need time to be absorbed and considered by the pet owner; often, all decision makers and family members are not present. It is very important that the final outcome of the discussion reaches the best conclusion whenever possible. When, for whatever reason, a decision needs to be taken quickly, and examination with family members in the privacy of the home is not possible, there should still be the opportunity for private time in a room in the clinic to enable consultation with loved ones over the phone.

Sometimes, veterinarians are upset by explosive and aggressive clients, destroying their day and even ruining their sleep. When unpleasant clients come to the practice, the overall atmosphere is affected. Employees are stressed, other clients are annoyed even if not involved, and the veterinarians often take these incidents personally and are sometimes deeply upset. It is not unusual for veterinarians to constantly re-think a particular incident that occurred during the week. Here are some ideas and suggestions on how to placate client anger and keep different types of difficult clients happy, allowing them to decompress without exploding. Most often, it is a matter of proper communication.

Types of difficult clients

There are many types of difficult clients. We have selected the four most common disruptive client types:

- the authoritarian or directive client;
- the explosive or angry client;
- the hesitant or undecided client; and
- the time consumer or compulsive talker.

● The authoritarian or directive client

This is not necessarily an angry or dissatisfied client, but, if not handled appropriately, could easily become one. Directive clients are demanding and usually use a tone of voice and verbal attitude that could be

The fact that more than 90 per cent of our communication during meetings is non-verbal emphasises the importance of body language and facial expression.

Unhappy clients and clinical costs

Unhappy clients are best prevented. Because the financial consequences of diagnostic procedures and treatment often top the list of reasons for client complaints, the practice needs sound protocols in place to inform and educate owners, in advance, on the costs of products and services.

Information regarding estimated costs need to be provided up front, as accurately as possible. For routine procedures, fees are best set at an average figure, providing a certain buffer to enable the clinic to cope with the ups and downs that occur when treating routine cases. It is important to communicate thoroughly regarding the total financial impact on the owner, and not only on the costs of the surgery. In general, owners do not understand that consultation costs, pre-anaesthetic work-up, radiographs, anaesthesia and hospitalisation are not usually included in the surgery fee. When told about these "extras" afterwards, it is obvious they are unhappy.

Many of them take the information home and may well be very happy with the result from the pet's health point of view, but unhappy with the overall management.

Clients need the best possible estimate of total costs involved in the procedure – from the first to the last handshake. These should include the total costs of follow-up and check-up visits (lab work, anaesthesia, medication and radiographs). This amount is what they will need to pay at the end of the day, and, in turn, will have an impact on their ability to pay all the other family bills.

It is a good idea to ask clients to sign a document approving the cost estimation; in many practices, it is routine procedure that the owner pays a percentage of the estimated total in advance. Electronic payments can be made 24 hours a day, seven days a week. When the people say that money is not an issue and that they will pay whatever it costs, but their bank balance does not allow an up-front payment, you may need to consider postponing treatment until finances have been secured.

In cases where the estimate is likely to be exceeded during the course of treatment, owners need to be informed immediately. They need to know why you are running over budget, they need to be provided with a new total, and they need to approve the increase in advance. You may want to have this agreement in writing; e-mail confirmation might be an excellent tool. All financially related information needs to be routinely and carefully documented as part of the patient's file. You may need it later. ◻

misinterpreted as aggressive or angry. This kind of person has a tendency to behave with authority and can, if staff are not prepared, place the veterinarian or employees in a difficult position.

It is crucial to differentiate remarks from actual objections. A remark does not necessarily require an answer; it is better to handle such a statement as simple opinion, and to remain neutral and respond with simple, objective facts. However, some questions are phrased as remarks and require answers; the answers should be straightforward and not require any complicated justification that may confuse the client and his or her interpretation of the question.

In contrast, and sometimes tricky to differentiate, an objection is fundamentally different from a remark. There is an obvious inference that the client does not agree with something. This requires an immediate response and the objection should be countered. It requires argument with objective information, delivered unemotionally and with a precise purpose. It should decrease or – even better – annul the level of objection.

The tone of voice, attitude and body language may help differentiate between the two forms of communication (remarks or objections), but sometimes this can be difficult.

For example, there are two ways to say: "It is expensive". One person would identify this as a remark (no need to object and counter with specific justification), whereas another person would perceive this statement as an objection that required a prompt response including a justification to diminish or alleviate associated negative feelings. In this case, after checking the details and objective data, it is important to first acknowledge and understand the objection, and ascertain the facts and not act on immediate impulse – which gives the impression of being defensive. One may then explain, for example, that procedures were complicated, required a lot of time and equipment, and so forth.

It can be difficult to remain neutral and avoid the possible confusion between remarks and objections. For example, if a client asks for a detailed and itemised invoice referring to his or her last financial statement, this could be because he or she does not agree with the total sum of the bill, or it could simply be because he or she wishes to understand better the nature of the expenses. In other words: is it a remark question or an objection question? The differentiation may sound pedantic, but is important, because a remark (or a question) is confused for an objection (or a possible source of conflict), then the nature, format and content of the answer will certainly sound different. Imagine a situation where a client asks for a detailed invoice and the employee interprets this as client dissatisfaction or even a reluctance to pay. In turn, this can result in the client changing their attitude to one of objection rather than remark.

As a rule, if you are not sure if the questions is a remark or an objection, respond as if it were a remark, not an objection. Provide the facts and answer in a precise way, with no additional arguments related to the interpretation of the question. An example of an answer in such case could be: "Of course, let me check the records and I'll give you the details right away" rather than: "Why? Is there something wrong with the invoice?"

As a rule, directive persons are authoritarian in their behaviour and in people handling, and they can be very difficult and disruptive. It is best to remain calm and not let these attitudes bother you. An authoritarian person responds better to someone equally directive. Therefore, remain precise and factual, and be directive and somewhat authoritarian yourself. There is no need for excuses, emotions and justifications of any sort.

- **The explosive or angry client**

These create the most difficult and stressful situations. Special attention and immediate action is required when it comes to communicating with this unhappy client.

For whatever reason, these people are not satisfied with the treatment by the clinic, doctor or staff member. In most cases, they have a tendency to be emotional and are likely to increase the volume of their voice during the conversation. It does not help either party to allow these angry exchanges to take place in the presence of other clients. The staff may be right in their factual opinion, but the classical yes/no exchange will not help the argument nor will it diffuse the situation. It is important to remember that facts seldom win over emotions. Furthermore, we should never blame owners for being emotional about their pets. The pet is a family member; the emotional bond with the pet was the reason for the clinic visit. In other words, these angry, unhappy emotions are, in a way, the other side of the same coin: the powerful, emotional human/pet bond.

As a rule, if you are not sure if the questions is a remark or an objection, respond as if it were a remark, not an objection.

If a pet owner doesn't respect your limitations, and all the other veterinarians and staff members agree that he or she isn't worth any more energy and time, it is probably time to fire the client.

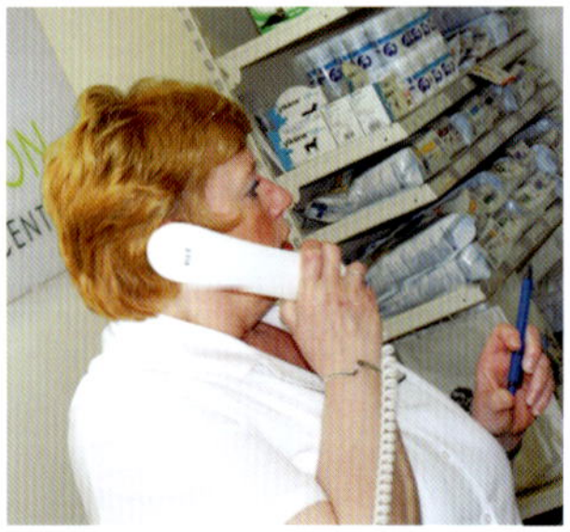

Because unhappy clients are always a poor advertisement for the practice, these conversations need to take place away from the presence of other clients. Immediate special attention (perhaps tea or coffee in a separate room) should be offered, showing you sincerely care about their concerns. These situations are best handled by one of the better prepared and trained veterinarians, practice manager or nurses. This person should take personal responsibility for the case and make sure it is handled as a priority. This category of complaint is always urgent and important according to the Covey classification (see **Section 5.2**).

- **The hesitant or undecided client**

Some people have difficulty in making decisions and need support and extra help. This is not necessarily critical, but it is often disruptive and it is better to identify those clients that need some help making their decisions.

If help is not given, they may hesitate, or end up not making any decision, and this can obviously be detrimental to pet health. In such cases, it is your responsibility to avoid any potential criticisms, such as: "You did not tell me that a decision was so vital".

When facing a person who hesitates, it is a good rule to give him or her two options and say there is a need for a choice on the spot (or within one hour). If the hesitation continues, the final option can be offered – in reality, corresponding to doing nothing – of "Wait and see", or "Go home and ask for the opinion of the family and come back or call back". Some people will appreciate the option to go home away from the clinic's stress and pressure, and will make a decision over a night's sleep. It is sometimes helpful to call the client next day to show you care, even if the decision is still to remain passive.

- **The time consumer or compulsive talker**

Some clients abuse your time and don't always realise this. Sometimes, when running behind with appointments you may have difficulty wrapping up the discussion in the examination room. This client lingers, long after the appointment time is over, to talk with staff members or other clients. These clients frequently want to chat even after your team members have answered all their questions. The way to deal with this problem is to establish a strategy and ensure that your team is aware of and adheres to it. Once this client has been identified, you should consider making a note on their record so the staff will know to adopt the agreed strategy. This mark on the record should be subject to review; it is best not to assume that the compulsive talker will remain one forever. Once you have finished a full examination and you feel the client is repeating some redundant issues, you could, for example, say you need to go because (and it's one advantage of clinic premises) there are other patients that need your immediate attention. If necessary, you can leave the area briefly and come back a few minutes later, using a wrapping-up phrase such as: "I'm sorry, but let me take you back to reception and Susan can go through things with you as I am getting behind".

Getting rid of a client: when there is no other choice

Occasionally, all one's efforts seem to produce no results. If a pet owner doesn't respect your limitations, and all the other veterinarians and staff members agree that he or she isn't worth any more energy and time, it is probably time to fire the client. If a client is repeatedly rude and never satisfied, then a time may arrive when you agree to disagree. One way to politely handle such a person would be make a copy of the pet(s) medical records and send it to the client with a polite, but firm, letter suggesting they seek care elsewhere, not recommending any specific alternative, but telling them there are several other practices close to their home. The terms could be expressed in such a way as: "We are concerned that our practice is not able to meet your needs. We are sorry, as we have tried hard over the years, but we now feel it is better for you to seek veterinary care elsewhere. To facilitate such a transfer we enclose copies of Fifi's medical records to make sure that appropriate medical care can continue without any interruption."

Specific telephone communication techniques

It is not difficult to comprehend the importance of the telephone. Think of the development of cell

The explosive client should be handled in four distinct phases

The Decompression Phase

The first part of the conversation with an unhappy client is to allow him or her to blow off steam and decompress, telling the story. Make sure the entire story has been detailed, and anger been expressed as fully as possible. This may take some time and you may need to give assistance: "Really? Please tell me in detail what happened? What were you told? How did you feel?"

Try to understand the client and see the situation from his or her point of view. Appear neutral and do not give non-verbal signals of agreement or disagreement before you have gathered all the information and understand both sides of the story. This active listening phase is critical and represents the true decompression phase. It is advisable to take notes and confirm full understanding of the issue. Making notes indicates to the client that you are taking charge of the case and will personally follow it up. It compels you to fully understand the problem, and provides documentation in case it subsequently develops into a court case. The complaint file can also serve as a valuable tool for new staff training and employee evaluations.

The Understanding Phase

This phase is sometimes described as one of agreement, implicitly telling the other person they are right, by saying "I agree" or "I understand". This empathy is important in, hopefully, leading to a final agreement. You can say these phrases even if you don't agree. In summary, once you have recorded the case and actively listened, make sure you tell the person that you understand why he or she is upset or angry. You may even say that you might feel the same way if something similar had happened to you.

The Action Phase

This is the time to take action and initiative, stating you will make inquiries, and will take appropriate actions. Ideally, you should add words such as: "I will take care of this personally". This process applies even if, in the end, you have to say there were no mistakes made and you do not feel responsible. Depending on the situation, it might be possible to resolve the issue on the spot, but in many cases other staff and colleagues need to be consulted first. Preferably this is not done in the presence of the upset owner, as it could recreate a pressure build-up. It is best to end the meeting thanking those concerned for bringing the matter to your attention, and giving them a clear indication of when they will be contacted for follow up.

The Follow-up Phase

It is not over. Make sure you follow-up. A client can never be satisfied if there is a failure to follow up a complaint. Show that you took care of the problem, came up with explanations, sometimes solutions, and that you handled the case completely and professionally.

When case examination shows mistakes (technical or communication aspects) were made by staff, causing suboptimal care and owner upset, it is advisable for the responsible manager to take the blame and try to settle the problem.

Taking the blame does not always mean accepting or admitting guilt. This is an important distinction when it comes to the responsibility of paying for the services and products provided during the treatment. ◻

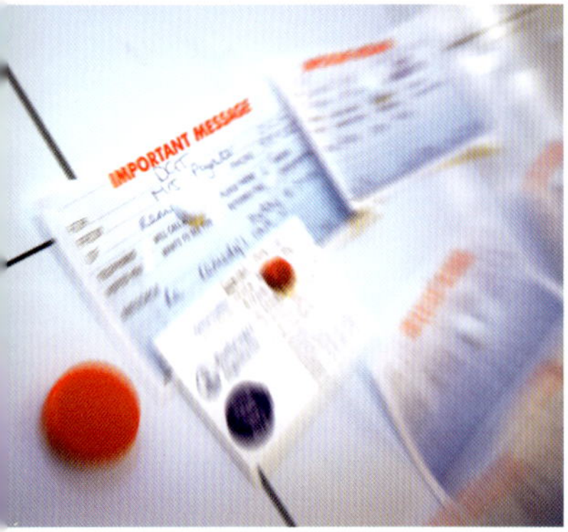

Consumers expect a personalised answer when they call a service company such as a veterinary clinic.

phones over the past five years or so. How much time do we spend on the phone every day? How phone dependent are we? We carry our mobile phones, and our e-mail connections can be wireless and we are, potentially, always available. This is a wonderful, but potentially difficult, situation. A recent report in the US business journal *Veterinary Economics* stated that veterinarians spend as much as 70 to 80 per cent of their time with clients on the telephone, and only 20 to 30 per cent in direct client contact. All employees who spend a significant portion of their time with clients should also be well trained in telephone use.

Basic telephone techniques

Most practices have a switchboard able to deal with various calls simultaneously, putting clients on hold and playing music or promotional messages. We all encounter, and sometimes suffer from, the menu system of some telephone systems. It is essential to know the basic functions and possibilities of the tool – don't wait to receive calls before becoming familiar with the system.

Some basic tricks and advice

- Place the telephone in an easily accessible and convenient spot in the clinic.
- Use all possible options to make the telephone more accessible – extension cords, wireless systems and headphone.
- Speak clearly, directly and with no distraction.
- Try to hold one conversation at a time (people deserve your devoted and entire attention).
- Use active listening techniques.
- Make sure people understand your messages by asking confirmation questions.
- Show your interest, smile and be aware that your attitude will be detected.
- If you wish to develop better techniques, tape your conversation; you will hear mistakes, appreciate a poor tone of voice, and discover the quality of your telephone techniques.
- Make sure you place a call on hold (including the musical background) before starting to talk to someone else in the clinic. Why? Because the person in front of you usually deserves priority, but you need to take care of the phone ringing and yet at the same time, tell the person on the line that you will be back soon to handle him or her.
- Never eat, smoke, chew, or drink while you are talking on the phone.
- Don't let the telephone keep ringing – allow a maximum of three consecutive rings.
- Ask people if they are willing to be placed on hold for a few moments before you do this, or alternatively say: "Could you hold, please?" or, even better: "Do you mind if I put you on hold as I have another call?" When you ask the question, do wait for their answer before putting them on hold.
- When returning calls, do so in the order they came in. Make sure you recognise that you talked to the person before and for what reason. To avoid mixing up cases, check the medical record before calling. Show enthusiasm, kindness, compassion and interest. Don't act as if you are in a hurry – even if you are. Never diagnose nor treat over the telephone.

The initial response to a call

Consumers expect a personalised answer when they call a service company such as a veterinary clinic. When clients do not receive such welcome answer, they may be disappointed, or surprised. Some may even think they dialled the wrong number. No longer is just "Hello" a sufficient response, but something more is needed, such as: "Dr Martin Veterinary Clinic, Christine speaking, how may I help you?" The way people answer the telephone, and welcome clients – in other words, the first contact – tells you a lot about the care given to clients and animals (Ross Clarke, 1995).

Rule one: be prepared

- Take notes.
- Have documents at hand, including prices, appointment book, message book, calendar of events, veterinarians' diary and news from the back office.
- Telephone contact numbers should be readily available. These can include animal shelter, local labs, referral clinics including veterinary school, vet's home and emergency numbers, including human doctors and hospitals.
- All client files, including the patient's profile, should be easily accessible.

Rule two: know and use the welcome formulas

- Greet the person accordingly – good evening, good morning.
- Use the clinic name.
- Introduce yourself: "Sonia speaking."
- Offer assistance: "How can I help you?"

Rule three: be attentive, enthusiastic, sympathetic, smiling

- Don't hesitate to use friendly words to show your desire to help and your kindness: "Thank you for calling" or "How are you today?" and if you know the pet's name (look in your computer files), ask: "How is Sissi doing?"

Filtering techniques for phone calls

Clients often ask to talk to the veterinarian and no one else. It is wise to use filtering techniques to satisfy clients without involving the veterinarian's time, particularly when answers can be given by other members of the practice's healthcare team. When the veterinarian is busy with a client, the rule is that he or she should not be disturbed. If it is not possible to avoid interrupting the vet, then at least make sure there is never more than one interruption during an examination. This rule is important, not only for the peace of mind and best use of the veterinarians' time, but is equally important for the pet owner in the examination room.

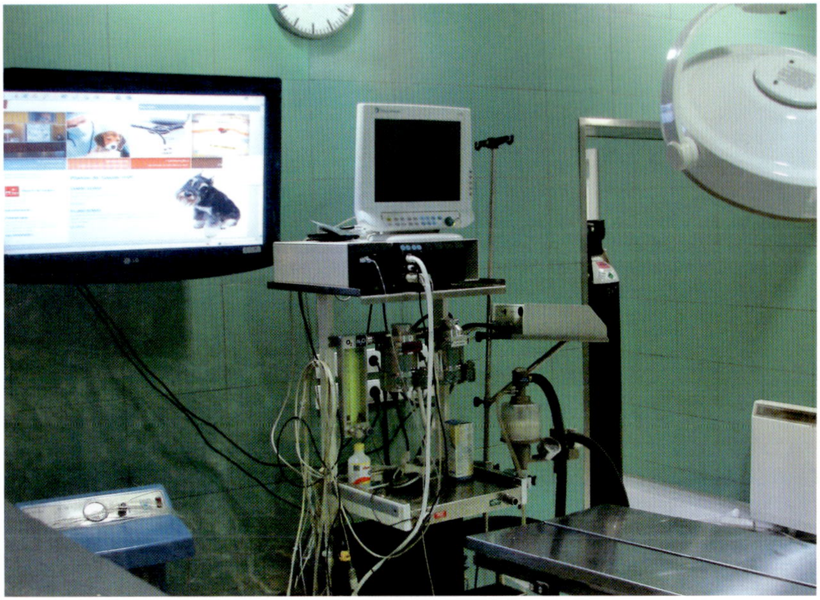

When the veterinarian is busy with a client, the rule is that he or she should not be disturbed.

It is best to use professional manners. For example, instead of saying: "Dr Smith can't take your call at the moment", it is better to say: "Dr Smith is unavailable at present". When trying to help people over the phone, always ask questions that show you are trying to help. This will also help you to be efficient and, possibly, enable you to answer the person's requests. Examples of questions are: "Is it urgent?" or "Can I help you?" or "Can someone else help you?" or "Can I take a message and we will call you back?" (if you use this excellent proactive method, make sure you follow-up and someone does call back). Don't assume that another staff member finds the post-it note that

> When people call and ask you the price, make sure you tell them about your services instead of just giving the price.

was put on his or her desk or mailbox and follows-up. To avoid forgetting these important recalls, use an aide-memoire, such as a phone bulletin board, either in a note book, or on the computer. This message bulletin board should, ideally, be placed near the phone, in a place where it is easily accessible to everyone. Make sure that the message you are writing down is complete, clear and comprehensive. It should include the date and time of the call, the person's and the patient's name, the phone number to call back – noting the preferred time, the purpose of the call and who needs to call back. Leave a space so the person who answers the message can check it out as complete. Such a message bulletin board is much better than multiple post-its or stickers placed on the wall.

When should you call people back?

It is better and more effective to take the initiative and be proactive, instead of waiting for clients to call. Consumers expect to receive such service. For example, instead of saying: "I am sorry, Mrs Smith, I don't have the lab results yet, call later today and hopefully we'll have them", try something else, such as: "Sorry, Mrs Smith, let me call you as soon as we receive the results. Where can I reach you and until what time? If you don't receive my phone call by the end of tomorrow afternoon, please call me back".

There are circumstances where it is necessary for the vet to call the client, including the following.

- Everything went wrong: you need to prevent any negative feelings and call before the client does.
- The client is annoyed or, discontented: when a client is unhappy, the last thing we want to do is to call and be confronted by him or her. It is normal to want to avoid conflict. However, taking the initiative is a very gratifying. Clients appreciate the effort and when you call, you lead the conversation.
- **A new client:** these are people you want to keep and to become loyal for life. Often, on a first visit, many questions remain unanswered simply because they were too numerous to deal with. Communication is not always ideal, at this first client-clinic experience. Call the new client and tell them that you want to make sure they understood everything, and that you answered all their questions. Show them you care.
- **A difficult case:** the case is not resolved and you are unsure of the outcome. Call and ask if Fifi is doing OK and is taking the treatment without problems. Don't be afraid to tell clients you want to recheck if the case is difficult. The same thing applies after sending a patient home after an important procedure or a long-term hospital stay.
- **An anxious client:** some people are consistently worried and anxious, often anticipating a negative outcome before one arrives. They will appreciate your call. Don't wait for their call – it's going to come anyway and may be at an inconvenient time. For

example, telephone and say: "Mrs Smith, Fifi's surgery went well and she is waking up normally. I know you are concerned and I thought you would like to know as soon as the operation was completed".

How to conclude a telephone conversation

The conclusion and correct ending of a conversation is sometimes as important as the introduction. Closing remarks are often the ones that people will hear and remember. Final perceptions will, therefore, be important in your relationship with clients. As a rule:

- ask people if there is something else you can do for them;
- thank people for their call;
- be courteous and gentle; and
- show people you take care of them professionally.

How to handle clients who shop around

Consumers call and shop around for the price of services and products. It is wrong to assume clients are looking for the cheapest price in town. This is not always the case. Most people ask the price to make sure that it is within the same range as others and that it is affordable. Clients will not necessary go for the cheapest. They look for convenience and for the right quality-to-money ratio. For this reason, when people call and ask you the price, make sure you tell them about your services instead of just giving the price. Make sure your explanation of the cost reveals the value of the services, not simply the price. These are two completely different considerations. Through good telemarketing, you can change a regular phone request into a presentation of the value of your services. Explain the differences and extra quality of the services you offer, and most people will be open to spend more for that extra value.

- **Rule one: don't give a simple price or a price list.**

Make sure you detail what services the client will receive before the price is quoted. If it is for a product, make sure you mention the fee includes a dedicated, personalised prescription, a demonstration of how to use the product and any questions (after sales service). People don't only buy what is in the bottle, but especially in a veterinary practice, what is around the bottle. Tell them about the value – not the cost.

- **Rule two: be on the client's side.**

It is always advisable to build confidence and give good, sound advice. Sometimes, this may mean prescribing something less expensive if that is the client's choice. This will build up trust and, in a long-term relationship, will retain client loyalty, ensuring that he or she will follow your advice and remain a long-term client.

- **Rule three: use testimonials.**

This technique is easy and quite helpful. You simply tell the client about your experience with products. You can also talk about other people

In order to communicate assertively, you first need to listen actively.

who have used the same services or products.

- **Rule four: always respect the client's decision.** Even if the client's decision implies that he or she decides not to buy the service or the product you suggested, don't be upset and do accept their decision with equanimity. It will build trust and confidence over the years.

Summary and conclusion

Communication is a critical part of daily relationship with clients, colleagues and staff. Handling people and clients requires talent, patience and communication skills. These attributes will help in most circumstances, even with the most difficult client. It is important to first identify the type of client and situation that requires special attention. After this has been done, then set goals for modifying the client's behaviour. Decide which of the client's attitudes are unacceptable and make sure that all team members know how to respond consistently. We encourage the use of in clinic interpersonal communication and conflict resolution techniques. These should follow well-established and efficient communication procedures. Many veterinary consultant agencies can assist with expert training. The last resort is to be prepared to ask a difficult client to seek veterinary care elsewhere. In order to communicate assertively, you first need to listen actively. This will be useful in most difficult situations.

An important aspect of handling problems is to try and avoid them occurring in the first place.

When handling medical issues, veterinarians must be able to demonstrate that all necessary measures were taken and all means available were used in an animal's treatment. This has nothing to do with results. There is no legal obligation to succeed in treatment. This is not always the client's perspective and opinion, particularly when there is an unexpected fatal outcome. From a legal point of view, in most countries the outcome of pet treatment cannot be guaranteed and, as such, complications and/or the death of a pet cannot be excluded, even if it happens during a routine procedure. On the other hand, routine is called routine for a reason. Complications during an ovariohysterectomy of a one-year-old healthy cat can happen, but how often is there a real veterinary reason, outside our control?

So, although you may be safe and protected from a legal point of view (by law, the veterinarian does not have to guarantee the outcome), circumstances require you to be pragmatic and service-minded. Owners have a tendency to compare your veterinary repair service to other repair services, and expect a quality outcome in the case of routine procedures.

An important aspect of handling problems is to try and avoid them occurring in the first place. For example, if you are really concerned about the outcome of a perceived routine procedure, then you and your team should be prepared to deal with a possible unexpected outcome before the treatment is undertaken. You should be able to handle the case, and any complications that may occur during the procedure. An example of this can be the heavily overweight female dog that comes in for spaying. The owners need to be told this is not routine, and there is an increased risk related to both anaesthesia and surgery. In addition, there may be financial implications – extra staff monitoring the anaesthesia, need to hospitalise the dog after the surgery, and/or provide additional medical support. The owner may pay a higher price for the extra monitoring and support staff during the procedure. Depending on the country, location or circumstances you may want owners to accept this extra risk when signing the pre-operative consent form.

Marketing in the clinic – communication tools

4.2

Communication tools overview

Definition and importance

PEOPLE ARE THE best vehicles for good communication. In a veterinary practice, the best communicators will be first the veterinarian and second, his or her assistant and staff. However, there is a limited time that veterinarians can reasonably devote to client communication. Employees also contribute effectively to practice production and to client communication, satisfaction and, therefore, loyalty. However, it is not always possible to have multiple employees because of human resources costs, which are limiting factors in staff numbers. This is a fundamental reason for using communication tools that will sometimes substitute for a person in relaying and supporting messages to clients. Documents and products will contribute to the practice image and will save a significant amount of time in client communication. Nevertheless, the communication or education tools are part of the communication process and require vet and staff involvement and an opportunity for input and feedback from the client.

A study published in France (*La Semaine Vétérinaire*, 2001) showed clients expect several types of attention (as described above) and veterinary services, including "an efficient, simple information and education service, showing the practice as a place where clients learn about pet care". Another client survey published in the UK (*Veterinary Review*, 2006) shows that one of the biggest limiting factors to providing proper client service is "the lack of time that vets and nurses spend on client communication".

In this section, we will focus on some communication and education tools that can be used, particularly within the practice.

Development of practical supports

In addition to general communication techniques and their applications, there are several tools that contribute to passing messages on to the client.

Clients expect "an efficient, simple information and education service, showing the practice as a place where clients learn about pet care".

– La Semaine Vétérinaire.

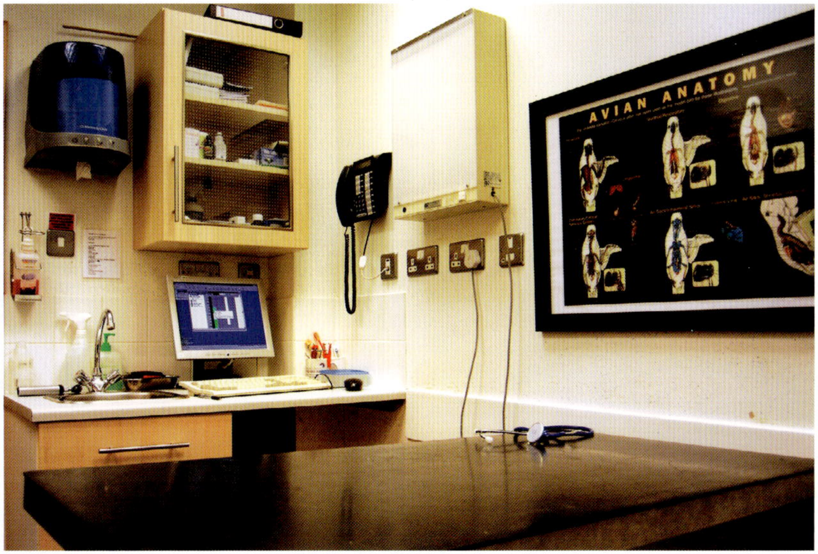

These support tools are essential for efficient communication. One of the primary principles for good communication is to make sure the same message is repeated in various ways. In addition, veterinarians and staff cannot afford the time to tell clients all they need to know at all times on all topics related to animal health, either over the phone, during an examination or before and after surgery. Human resource limitations emphasise the importance of communication tools.

Willingness to communicate directly with clients can vary with time and mood. As a colleague practitioner once put it: "My ability to communicate with clients will be significantly different depending on whether it is Monday morning and the appointment book is empty, or it is Friday evening and the waiting room is full." In addition, owners are not always receptive to messages due to their circumstances – private, work related or due to stress regarding the pet's condition.

How can we handle this dilemma concerning the occasional lack of availability and willingness to serve clients? First, by forcing adherence to the schedule and time devoted to each person. Second, by using tools to assist consistency, save time, and please clients. As a practice develops and grows, the need for high-quality services also increases – but usually with decreased human resources availability – leading to an increasing reliance on alternative client communication methods.

> The veterinarian is often the barrier; the owner, presented with the facts, should decide which one of these procedures he or she is willing to initiate.

Veterinary practice applications

Example one

A client brings in a 12-year-old dog for an annual check-up, plus vaccination. During the clinical examination, the dog shows some tartar on the teeth, a cardiac murmur and some fleas. This is not uncommon. Good clinical practise would recommend giving advice related to these clinical features, such as a dental cleaning and scaling. This would require a treatment prior to and after the procedure:

- a cardiac check-up (or senior dog check-up); and
- a treatment against fleas and deworming medication for *Dipylidium caninum.*

Some veterinarians might feel uneasy recommending all these procedures at once and might select only one or two, fearful of the client's negative reaction. The veterinarian is often the barrier; the owner, presented with the facts, should decide which one of these procedures he or she is willing to initiate.

Who is losing in this scenario? The animal will not benefit, the owner may have to spend more later on and be confronted with severe problems and, finally, the practice is limiting itself, via a form of self censoring, from performing veterinary procedures and developing the business.

It is interesting that, in general, a service business message used to trigger a sale would be stronger when given by a third party (therefore, the logical use of testimonial). This is even stronger when such an opinion is written – the strength of words and images. Active reliance on communication tools such as documents, brochures, flyers, and so forth, makes the message more independent, unbiased. When the client is asking, instead of being asked, is also a better situation for the veterinarian.

Using communication tools, one can expect to:

- add a written or visual support to verbal advice;
- consistently inform and educate clients;
- synergise messages (including team messages) via a neutral testimonial document;
- save time; and
- develop additional services and business.

Example two

An animal is presented with severe periodontal disease. The practitioner explains the condition and makes a recommendation. In addition to this, he or she illustrates the various stages of the disease and the potential complications using a special visual board with 3D images.

He or she also hands out a client education leaflet on dental disorders and management of dental problems. The client is asked to talk about all this at home with her partner. The leaflet provides a detailed, illustrated explanation of the potential results of periodontal disease.

The leaflet makes an impact on the owners, who call the practice the next day to make an appointment for the dental procedure. In this case, the leaflet was the vector and communication relay that participated in the overall service. However, handing out brochures does not replace the required follow-up and personal sale. ◘

Another interesting aspect is that communication tools will trigger decisions from clients about using the services. Veterinarians are often uneasy in soliciting a client to buy a service or a product; using a document that plays the role of selling the service or the product will make everything seem different. The client will also look at the documents as a testimonial and will not feel that he or she is forced to buy the offer; so the act of purchasing becomes easier. Veterinarians are usually comfortable in recommending a test or performing surgery (to manage the sick or the injured patient); they are much less comfortable when there is a need to sell a healthcare service or product (to manage the healthy pet). This is particularly true when the service or product is not related to the primary reason for the office call. But, when the client initiates the conversation about the service or product, the veterinarian becomes an excellent salesperson. This is a normal situation – veterinarians are used to responding to client's questions and are often not at ease when proposing additional services and products.

● The concept of message relay

To increase service value, tangible and accompanying objective features will substantiate and reinforce the message. Some practitioners are reluctant to spend time preparing these documents, because they feel it takes too much time, and is not necessary. It is important to understand these documents are very important as they increase the value of services, give a positive image and contribute to client loyalty. In addition, many pet-owner clients are avid information consumers and these documents will satisfy those needs. As clients are educated and become aware of their pet's health needs, the more they will use our services. Most professional veterinary organisations offer their members standard support forms that

◘ The client will also look at the documents as a testimonial and will not feel that he or she is forced to buy the offer; so the act of purchasing becomes easier.

> The shorter the distance from the clients, the better receptionist contact will be perceived.

can be tailored and personalised to the practice needs. These can often be found on the internet.

Communication tools in the reception area

● The reception area: the internal mirror

In a client relationship, the first impression is critical as this initial time will often determine perception of any future service: you only have one chance to make a good first impression. This initial feeling is subjective and could be revisited with time, but consumers will often make a judgement according to certain emotional elements. If these perceptions are not to their expected standard, they will categorise the entire service and possibly look elsewhere without pursuing further.

To make a memorable first impression there are several features to be considered. If people do not receive their expected service level, in their expected environment, we will not succeed – irrespective of skill levels. In practical terms, this means investing in highly qualified employees, trained and experienced in client services and communication, as well as in attractive premises and various tools to assist with internal and client relationships.

● Serving the client

It is helpful to put ourselves in the client's position: anxious, stressed and, possibly, in a hurry. It is essential to serve clients as soon as they come in. Ideally, this should be done by a person at the reception desk. If this is not possible, it is important to welcome clients (a simple smile and "Good day" greeting), acknowledging them instead of ignoring them. This seems very basic, but it is not uncommon to receive a negative welcome, where the receptionist is too busy to acknowledge clients. The worst-case scenario is using a mobile phone for private calls - in full client hearing. We have all experienced such

circumstances and know how it feels to receive such a welcome. Veterinary practices often provide services and also sell medications and health and nutritional products, which makes it difficult for staff to be available; increasing staff availability at the reception desk can alleviate the problem. Ideally, in addition to providing a welcome, clients and their pets should be personally acknowledged. Personal recognition makes the client feel an essential part of the practice. In a busy practice it is impossible to remember every client's name. Receptionists should, therefore, rely on the appointment book or computer file to identify clients before they are due to arrive. A basic list can provide the appointment schedule, client and pet's name and the treatment. This preparation takes a few minutes, but will be compensated for by the time saved when a client comes in. When clients feel they belong to the clinic community, they remain loyal.

● Reception counters

Any reception area needs a meeting point and the reception counter or desk is a crucial focus tool. Many different interactions take place at that level and the multipurpose role of this equipment should be emphasised. In line with an increasing trend to be closer to the client, reception counters are smaller, shorter and may be separated sections – breaking the

barrier that we used to see in the past. The shorter the distance from the clients, the better receptionist contact will be perceived. This phenomenon is observed in many service-oriented businesses, including hotels, banks, post offices, travel agencies, and pharmacies. Remember the old post office or

bank or train station desk with a (bulletproof) glass shield or metal bars and people talking through a small window or microphone/loudspeaker system? Some counters are designed to merchandise products such as food and healthcare items. The advantage of these furniture models is the efficient use of space, particularly in small urban practices where lack of room is a chronic problem; another important feature is in communicating products and services. This sort of counter display is essential, and can be where clients are reminded of common healthcare services and products. New products or a new promotion can also be advertised, and the counter can be partially used for direct communication with the client, either arriving or departing.

- **Entrance board or panel**

Despite all efforts, it is not always possible to be available to greet clients at the veterinary practice reception. A useful communication tool clients see in other environments and in certain clinics, is an entrance board that will immediately describe major features, services, and directions. This sign can also explain to clients how to proceed, such as: "Even if you have an appointment, please check-in with our next available receptionist at the reception", or: "In the absence of a receptionist at the desk, please press the service button of the speaker phone located on the desktop". These signs can also display and advertise special events such as: "Now it's summer, external parasites are back so make sure to protect your pet and ask us about it before leaving our clinic". It is also interesting to list the veterinarians and staff on duty. This sort of first communication impression is excellent and can be easily added in almost all practices. Ideally, the sign should be a ground-to-ceiling format, but desktop models could be used as alternatives. Messages should be simple and clear.

Fifty per cent of buying decisions are taken at the shopping destination – we should not neglect the impulse buy.

> Remember the principle taught in most business schools – an excess of information kills the information.

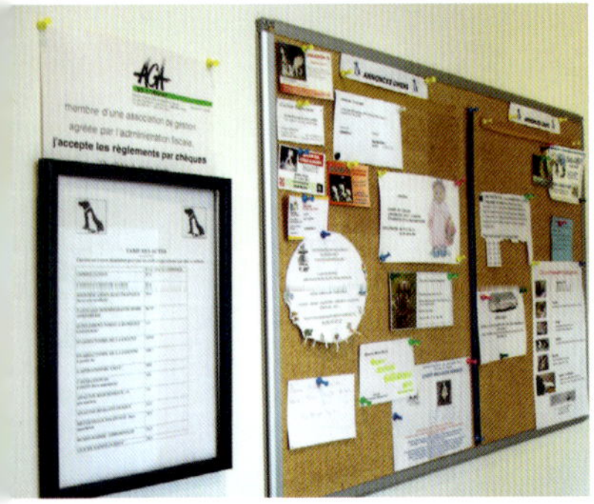

- **Warning devices**

In a world where people are increasingly concerned with security, several tools can be used to decrease the risk of damaging events, and to show clients that the clinic is taking care of security. Among these tools are the classic bell that sounds as people enter the door and a video camera – with a sign on the entrance door that the clinic is under constant electronic surveillance.
An internal telephone on the reception counter allows clients to call staff in the back office (in case no one is at the desk) and receive confirmation they will be attended to within a short time. However, avoid promising to show up after two minutes when it will be five or more – better to suggest a five minutes wait and show up after three. These basic communication tools are temporary replacements for the receptionist; there is nothing better than a friendly person at the reception desk. Small speaker phones can be placed in all rooms, corridors and kennels, and are extremely useful when a staff member is trying to locate a practitioner or another staff member within the premises. This is particularly true in large practices as people circulate around. This will avoid additional time spent away from the reception area locating people in the back office. Time is saved and efficient reception service is maintained.

- **Communication support at the reception desk**

Several small devices can be used to communicate with clients directly at the reception desk. These are usually small posters or panels. The messages should generally include promotional services (sales on certain products that month) or more generic information for hygiene, food or common healthcare products. These small panels are based on the principle of point of sale (POS) information or promotion. A survey on general consumer habits found 50 per cent of buying decisions are taken at the shopping destination – we should not neglect the impulse buy by making sure clients are reminded about the major features of pet health as they enter and, even more importantly, as they leave the premises.

We like to say that veterinarians are not selling, but helping clients buy the best possible pet products and services. This is a clear nuance and should help most practitioners who are sometimes reluctant to act in a commercial manner. Most promotional table posters or displays are provided by drug companies that are obviously interested in promoting their products on the practice counter, simply because it will increase their sales by at least 20 to 30 per cent.

The purpose of an POS display is three-fold.

- **To remind.** This is an endorsement of some communication elements given

Veterinary application
Point of Sale

For optimal results, the ideal communication message should be repeated in different locations while the client is in the practice. For example, the client will be informed about a message while waiting, either through the message boards or posters, or through visual animations (see main text for waiting zone communication tools).

The same message and technical details should be given during the examination or the client's visit, either by the practitioner or a qualified staff person. The POS sign is used to finalise the message, reminding and helping the client make the final decision.

elsewhere in the practice (such as the examination room or the waiting zone).

- **To inform.** Details about the specific product or service, and its features such as price or use (ie for old dogs).
- **To stimulate.** This is part of the impulse purchase concept.

According to a consumer buying habits study (*CB News* 407, 2002), 20 to 55 per cent of purchases in Europe ar e impulse purchases (65 per cent in the US). In that study, it was interesting to note the mean reading time of a consumer in front of a POS display is seven seconds – this is not long at all and yet is quite sufficient. This is why there is no need to have long messages on information message displays. Be concise and efficient.

It is essential for the practitioner to select which one or two displays to include on the reception desk. Ideally, it should be the clinic POS signs that prevail. As with wall posters, make sure that there is turnover at least once a month. Ultimate management includes measuring the return on promotions, which will help select the best one for the practice on certain occasions. POS tools are among the strongest and easiest communication tools that veterinarians can use. However, do not abuse the concept and transform your reception counter into a giant commercial display; it is a question of proportion. Remember, clients expect to be in a veterinary clinic, not in a pet shop. Also remember the principle taught in most business schools: An excess of information kills the information.

- **Merchandising displays**

Most clinics use part of their reception area to display products – mostly nutritional. There are specific techniques, dedicated furniture and an entire set of concepts, including specialised professionals (merchandisers) from a marketing division or speciality called merchandising. Merchandising is based on the optimised presentation of products and services with adapted supports (such as displays, racks, shelves). This product presentation is tailored to consumer's buying habits as well as to the premises' architecture. Instead of using standard displays proposed by drug or pet-food

Veterinary application

Segmenting Merchandise

The usual recommendation is to clearly identify communication areas within a display, using simple, clearly understood visual panels. For example, it is a good idea to identify the cat, exotic pets, or small pets areas. Displays should also be separated distinct purpose areas: fleas and ticks, shampoos or grooming, skin care, vitamins and dental hygiene.

The idea is to help the consumer by guiding him or her through the display using divisions or keywords. The concept of the product family can also be adapted, placing coat and skin management accessories (combs, brushes and nail clippers) close to skin products.

Point-of-sale tools are among the strongest communication tools that vets can use.

Veterinary application

Waiting time

It is good idea to distract and occupy clients while they are waiting. Ideally, the communication should be non-aggressive, informative or educational. The idea is to make the waiting time more pleasant for the client and, at the same time, useful for the practice.

Several methods can be applied. Staff (nurses, receptionists) should monitor any prolonged waiting time and prevent negative client reaction by paying attention to them, and explaining their waiting has been recorded and will be as short as possible: "We are sorry for this delay, we're doing everything we can" followed by such questions as: "Can I get you something?"; "Do you have an important meeting?"; "Do you need to use our clinic phone to contact someone about the delay?". Avoid lying about the delay, such as suggesting the vet has an emergency.

Visual supports (animation on television or LCD screens) are used to present several interesting features, for example the Vet'Kiosk concept developed in France. It runs short animation sequences on pet health topics, which entertain clients and, at the same time, inform them about the main clinic healthcare products and services. Basically, this powerful communication tool successfully fulfils two purposes:

- it decreases the negative perception of a prolonged waiting time through entertainment, and
- it triggers questions and, therefore, develops client's buying behaviour.

Criteria linked to the animal	
Species	(dog, cat, etc)
Age	(puppies/kittens, growth, senior, etc)
Level of activity	(sport dog, pregnancy, etc)
Criteria linked to the human/pet bond	
Health	
Beauty and wellness	
Highly technical / Innovation	
Criteria linked to taste and habits	
Bag vs can vs pouch	
Dry food vs canned food	
Flavour, speciality recipes	
Criteria linked to commercial advertisement	
Brands	

Table 4.2.1
Criteria to consider when organising veterinary merchandising.

companies, which rarely fit the practice environment, it is preferable to adopt a personalised solution, such as in pharmacies and beauty shops.

It is important to consider all functions of the displays that play a role selling products. Accessories include specific communication and information zones such as posters, panels, boards, brochures and stickers. These items participate in the entire product presentation and represent an integrated part of the concept. Cleanliness, lighting and neatness are also important components of such displays, and will contribute to positive and attractive product images. As clients will often use these displays for a self-service purchase, it is essential to place the proper documents and information on the displays to help in client choice and buying decision.

Depending on the situation (including legal and professional regulations) physiological diets (non-prescription) should be displayed and made freely available to clients. Medically-oriented diets should either be omitted from merchandising and only stocked in the back office, or displayed on separate racks located closer to the staff or veterinarian, and used on prescription in the course of follow-up treatment.

When organising the selling zone, it is important to follow certain criteria related to the client purchase decision, as clients respond to certain facts: some related to the species itself, others to the human/pet bond, and others to the type of animal (**Figure 4.2.1**).

- **Associated service with pet-food merchandising**

Weighing patients and registering body condition score (BCS) as part of the usual pet visit is an excellent routine and should be included in all examinations. The scales are, therefore, an integral part of merchandising, particularly for veterinarians who sell diets or any form of nutritional products. The pet's weight and BCS should be written in the medical record to document the service and give its entire value (internally for the veterinarian and staff as well as for the client). Information and communication related to objective dietary management should be placed close to the scale (for example, the age/weight relationship for overweight animals). In that sense, the scale becomes a communication tool related to several practice services and products.

The waiting area

- **The perception of waiting**

Prolonged wait time is one of the most common client complaints. This major objection is obviously stronger when clients have an appointment and arrived on time. In other words, part of the client contract is not respected and, therefore, justifiably criticised. It is essential to prevent these objections and to organise the practice so that waiting time is minimised. What is a reasonable waiting time? It varies from one individual to another, from one region to another. It is known to be shorter in a large city where people are traditionally more demanding than a small town or in the country. As a guideline, client dissatisfaction will quickly build after a 10 or 15 minutes wait. It is also interesting to note this objection will arise more quickly when the environment is less adapted for a waiting time (nothing to do while waiting, nobody to talk to the client during that period, too warm or cold room temperature and so on). In other words, improving the atmosphere and accommodating the waiting time will significantly reduce complaints.

ROYAL CANIN

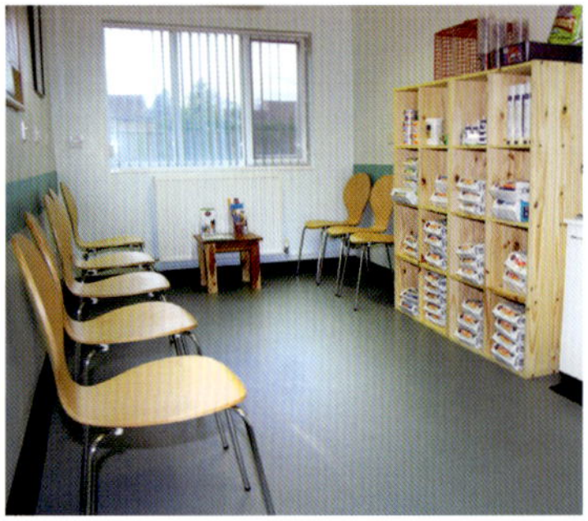

Veterinary application

Sample themes

Some examples of different themes selected for a certain period:

- in the waiting zone of the reception area, a multimedia communication on senior check-ups;
- in the intermediate zone (close to the laboratory or the radiology room), a frame of posters and documents emphasising pet identification (chip); and
- on the reception counter's exit side, a counter display or rigid desk poster reminding clients to protect their pets against external parasites such as fleas and ticks. ◘

● The waiting-room concept

One should no longer call it the waiting room. Who wants to wait nowadays? Waiting room implies, by definition, a waiting time – not optimal client service. Clients dislike waiting, so let's decrease the perception of a waiting time: reception area, welcome area, or client information lounge are all appropriate labels as long as it is implicitly noted there will be a certain waiting time, but the area is not dedicated to waiting. Once you have adopted this concept, it is important to make sure the premises match the idea of an open space, including reception, merchandising, information and seats. Clients no longer want to sit in a closed room – historically, the waiting room.

Clients should actively participate in the clinic service and feel part of the community that delivers it. This is the reason why walls and doors should be removed between clients and staff in the reception area. The waiting area should be integrated within the reception area, and people should be in contact with one another (staff versus clients). This environment is seen in many different businesses where clients see and participate in the action (for example, in restaurants where the kitchen and cooking area are an integrated part of the dining area). It is within that area that various services are delivered. Clients who see other clients using these services and purchasing products are inclined to adopt the same behaviour. There is a true synergy and the open space contributes to communication, as well as the development of practice activity. Many clinics have successfully adapted and transformed their reception area following this concept.

Clients may alternatively read, watch the multimedia animations on the screens, shop from the merchandising displays, talk to the staff, or other clients, or pet their dog and cat. People will usually try a little of each action. Remember, the client is there to see the veterinarian in the examination room, and time spent in the reception and waiting areas should be used appropriately, even if it is a transitional step towards the objective of the client's visit. This basic principle should be kept in mind when you plan to install some communication tools. For example, if you place a television screen on the wall to entertain and educate clients as they wait, make sure you place the screen within their natural field of vision, remembering the client's natural tendency will be to look towards the direction of the examination room.

◘ In theory, repetition of messages is a key concept to increase efficiency and return on client communication, but the total number of messages should be limited.

It is important to assign priorities and regularly change posters, such as selecting seasonal ones on parasites or by clinic focus, such as senior health management services.

Internal communication tools (placed and used within the practice itself)

It is helpful to differentiate communication tools that are available and consulted by clients within the waiting and reception area from those that clients may take home and use at distance. Some can play a dual role such as information leaflets and a "clinic journal" or "newsletter". Here we will refer only to communication tools or products that are used within the practice itself as opposed to those that can be actively given or mailed to clients and have great value as well. Both internal and external communication should be used concomitantly and be synergetic.

- **Printed documents**

Clients are consumers of paper and written documents, despite the era of electronic and multimedia communication. Clients like paper leaflets and other simple printed documents, and appreciate taking them home. Brochures and all written documents and information you and your staff can show or give to clients are essential parts of communication. Their value is immense when used appropriately and they are visual, well illustrated, handed to clients (versus taken freely by clients) and confirm information corresponding to the client's needs. Documents should be highly informative and yet simple (a minimum of complicated wording), attractive (colours and pictures) and laid out professionally. It is important to focus on drawings, illustrations, and other visual aids that are useful in explaining certain medical conditions. For example, post-operative reports should be simple and written as draft documents, reminding clients of the detailed and practical healthcare explanations that were given instead of describing at length the medical disease and pathophysiology of the pet's disorder.

- **Posters**

Veterinarians receive posters from drug and pet-food companies, wholesalers and other distributors. Some of these posters are generic (no products are mentioned) and some are directly linked to a product. Others present services such as the annual health check-up or dental healthcare. It is important to keep these posters neat and avoid a plethora of documents stuck to the walls with no strategy, order, and a minimum of judgement as to their relevance. It is important to assign priorities and regularly change the posters, such as selecting seasonal ones on parasites or by clinic focus, such as senior health management services. Remember that too much information, kills information. We like the technique of framing posters and producing dedicated collages from the documents you receive from multiple sources. The advantages are numerous :

- space dedicated to posters is predetermined and will not change (no risk of poster overexposure);
- posters are protected and remain clean and neatly fixed to the wall (no risk of crooked corners);
- frames have a constant standard size (no risk of marks on the walls left from different poster sizes);
- poster display is harmonised and aesthetically more pleasant than a patchwork of different illustrations; and
- communication can be personalised to the clinic (focusing on certain themes).

No matter which manner you adopt for poster use, the rule of regular renewal of messages applies. Consider that loyal clients come in to the clinic about three times a year, so these documents should be renewed and changed at least once every four months. A US survey on 31,000 clients and 412 practices showed that 38 per cent of the clients look at posters at least once during their stay at the practice. Compared to the visual impact of other media, posters come in second place after multimedia equipment (television screens) that is watched by 77 per cent of clients (*Firstline Veterinary Economics*, Jan 1999). A survey in France of 61 clinics equipped with a dedicated TV veterinary programme (Vet'Kiosk) revealed 87 per cent of clients mentioned watching the screen animation while they were in the clinic and 41 per cent mentioned looking at posters on the wall (*AJEV*, Jan 2004). The most successful posters are often those that display the various breeds of dogs or cats.

In theory, repetition of messages is a key concept to increase efficiency and return on client communication, but the total number of messages should be limited. Ideally, to optimise response, three different topics should be delivered in three different locations. When appropriate (a promotion campaign on a service or product) the use of a tripod or banner is a nice way to manage such temporary communication.

- **Brochures and leaflets**

Drug and pet-food companies inundate veterinarians with brochures and leaflets on products and services. The purpose of these documents is to inform and educate clients about their pets' needs, to contribute to veterinary communication and, of course, to support product sales. They are excellent, appreciated by clients and particularly effective when handed directly to clients by clinic staff (including the practitioner). Most brochures are produced by companies to leverage their products. Because these documents are mostly product advertisements, veterinarians are often reluctant to hand them to clients and, therefore, leave the brochures in a drawer, or display as free self-service documents on a counter or as a display in the reception area. However, to obtain optimum results, they should be handed out when a message concerning these products is initiated or when such a product is sold (to add to the product and give it additional value). Some practitioners use generic brochures, which they purchased, produced by veterinary associations or veterinary communication companies, because these documents carry a non-commercial message and, therefore, are easier to use as part of their examination, such as an illustrated prescription form, or in addition to the prescription.

These documents clearly contribute to client communication, as we described earlier, but also illustrate and complete veterinarian and staff explanations, often given in a limited amount of time. Often, veterinarians and staff members have these documents at hand, yet use them infrequently. The return on such documentation could be estimated as low and may vary from two to four per cent, but it is certainly much higher than the zero return when documents are not distributed. A survey published by *Firstline Veterinary Economics* (January, 1999) showed clients ranked brochures in third position among different communication tools. It goes without saying (but we mention it here for the sake of being complete) that clinic staff should be familiar with

For optimal results, the ideal communication message should be repeated in different locations while the client is in the practice.

Dedicated animations are the ideal form of multimedia programme for veterinary practices.

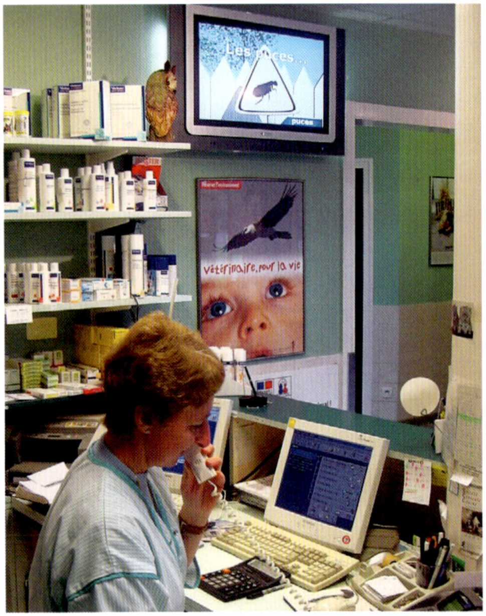

the content of brochures and leaflets. This requires adequate training by the vet and or the company sales representative. Don't expect the nurses to read these documents in their free time at home.

Magazines and newspapers

As a rule, clients will not read while in the practice. Should we have magazines and newsletters in the reception area? Some say no, suggesting clients will instead focus on the animated wall illustrations that deliver messages useful for them as well as for the practice. Others would say yes, and select magazines that are pet oriented and heavily illustrated – most people will flip pages and look at images. We do not recommend leaving magazines that illustrate the vet's leisure activities, such as travel, cars, sailing and outdoor sports. Whatever is available in the reception area should be relatively new, orderly and, of course, in line with clinic branding and core message.

Some veterinarians produce their own newsletters and vet magazines. This communication tool is excellent, but if it is produced internally, it requires a significant amount of work to bring it

Veterinary application

Small ads boards

Practical management of a client small ads board includes:

- provide a standard form for the ad, with pre-set information including the publication date;
- do not leave ads on the board for longer than six or eight weeks;
- limit board access to your clients;
- do not accept commercial ads (local pet groomer, pet-shop, dog trainer, breeder) unless there is a known synergy and active collaboration with these services;
- designate an employee who will be responsible for board management and maintenance;
- consider adding internal communications for your clients, such as schedules for puppy classes or clinic client education classes; and
- provide a permanent statement that the board is a service to promote client exchanges, and the practice has no control of content and cannot be considered responsible for product quality or health of pets exchanged or sold through the system.

to professional standards. We would recommend using a veterinary communication agency that will help produce the ideal format and appearance, but will also contribute and produce the content for at least three to four issues per year. A major use of such a clinic newsletter is in targeted mailing, regularly communicating with clients.

If you should decide to place a consumer publication in the practice, remember the most successful item remains the (local) daily newspaper. A newspaper rod insertion will ensure it stays orderly and does not leave the reception zone.

- **Small ads panel board**

Your clients belong to a community – your practice. A board where they can place small ads and announcements will help them communicate with each other. Such panels or boards contribute to the community bond and help clients identify with it. A standard form or card for these ads will make such boards practical and effective. Ads should be dated so that you can remove those that have passed a certain deadline, such as the expiration date or age.

- **Pictures of clinic staff**

A frame with pictures of the veterinarians and staff is a nice way to highlight the practice team. Ideally, you could include their speciality, graduation year, and any pertinent information you feel would be interesting to clients, of value to the practice or to the person's image. If you elect not to place these pictures on the wall, you can insert them in a clinic album or a practice brochure. This document can be handed to all new clients or remain at the reception, or the waiting area, available for clients to look at it. Just

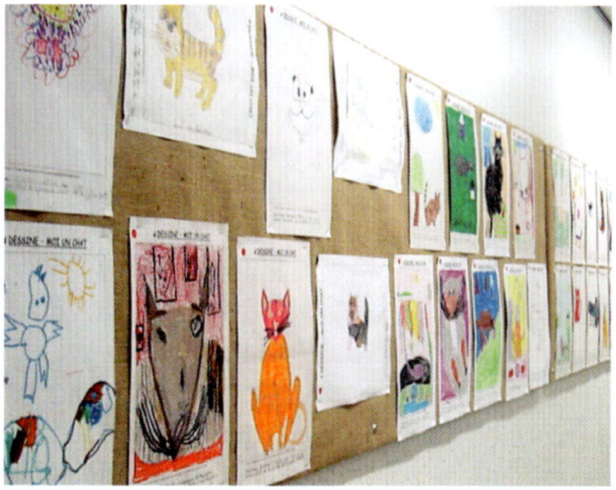

Practices should use soft marketing techniques and avoid any aggressive commercial communication.

as posters have a limited lifespan, veterinarian and staff photographs should be changed on a regular basis, and adjusted to staff changes. Some clinics include photos of the team members with their pet.

- **Guided picture tour of the clinic**

Most clients enjoy visiting behind the scenes of the practice. However, as this is not always possible, action photographs of the back office, showing staff using the equipment and services, are useful and informative. This type of communication contributes to the overall practice image and helps reassure clients when confronted with special procedures or ancillary diagnostic tests requiring their pet to be hospitalised. This is a perfect example of allowing clients access to your knowledge and expertise. The photographs can be framed and placed (as posters) on the wall within the waiting area. They will need to be changed regularly, which must be taken into consideration. It might be preferable to either keep these photographs for a practice brochure or album, or use them in conjunction with human resource photographs on a short video or DVD sequence, displayed on the screen used to inform and sell services to clients. In the Vet'Kiosk concept, this type of personalised practice presentation is included in the programme and can be updated regularly.

Clinic atmosphere is not a direct communication tool, but it is a concept that deals with client communication.

- **Practice photo album**

All veterinarians receive pictures and thank-you notes from happy clients. Most of the time, practitioners place these in a drawer (if they keep them at all). Why not use these testimonials from clients and place them in a practice photo album in which illustrations of human resources, equipment and various action images can be displayed? Pinning them on a message board is another way to display them to clients.

Multimedia concepts and products

- **General principles of visual display products**

Studies show new image technology, such as special effects, computer-generated animations and special videos, are used with optimal response by clients. Television and flat screens are used to entertain and to communicate services. This type of communication is referred to as narrow casting – as opposed to broadcasting (television), and is also a visual sales support. If the visual impact is strong and pertinent, sales follow accordingly.

In a veterinary practice, the environment is particularly favourable because clients have to wait for the appointment, they are sitting at least part of that time and they are concerned about their pet's health. The timing is also appropriate as most clients share a strong human/animal bond and, while in the practice, will be naturally tempted to buy products and services for their pets – if they are presented to them correctly. To match this client expectation, using the full potential of visual supports and yet not appearing overly commercial oriented, the practice should use soft marketing techniques and avoid any aggressive commercial communication. One objective of visual support is to entertain clients who are waiting for their appointment. Therefore, the programme should be attractive, amusing and yet informative. An audible sound system with multimedia systems in the reception zone and waiting area can be annoying and extremely negative for clients and staff. Ideally, there should not be any sound track as the images should speak for themselves, with captions contributing to the message. The more these programmes are animated, the less text is needed.

No matter which programme you select, make sure that you don't leave a monitor off, or a video tape running over its time leaving only a snowy screen for people to watch.

- **Video programmes and television movies**

Video programmes with a sound track can quickly became annoying, and movie length is important as clients will devote only a limited time to the screen. Topics or sequences should not be longer than three to four minutes. Ideally, the programme should be silent, possibly with low-volume background music and preferably one that provides a relaxing atmosphere (such as a nature, easy-listening style of music). Previously, most video cassettes used television-like programmes and sometimes veterinarians linked their television monitor to a pet or animal channel. These programmes produced only one objective: they entertained clients and decreased the negative perception of an extended waiting. They did not, however, produce any return on the activity and could not be considered as visual sales supports.

Dedicated animations are the ideal form of programme for veterinary practices. Clients prefer watching a cartoon instead of a movie with real animals, probably because the animal actors in these movies are always different from their own pets. In a cartoon this is not an issue.

- **Photo players on television screens**

These displays were used and distributed in some countries (US, France and the UK) in the late 1990s. The veterinary slide shows (for example, VisualVet) were based initially on Kodak technology; these products are now obsolete as people expect more sophisticated multimedia programmes. Some computer programs can provide the same sort of results (for example, Microsoft PowerPoint) and some practitioners have produced their own slide shows to display in practice. However, the impact of still images in a world of dynamic imaging could be questioned

- **Electronic letter billboards**

A few years ago, some practices installed electronic billboards (at great cost) that displayed written messages with illuminated red letters running across the board – similar to those found on streets, but made for internal use. These light screens are quite aggressive and not ideal for a practice, but

As consumers expect more information and assistance, a consumer-oriented communication must be more informative to be efficient.

are better utilised where clients pass by and there is a need to capture their attention. These products are no longer suggested for practice use –probably a good thing considering their prohibitive cost.

- **Multimedia DVD cartoons and programmes**

In some countries, various products fulfil most of the requirements for an ideal client multimedia programme within the practice (for example, Vet'Kiosk). These programmes are displayed on flat plasma or LCD screens placed directly on a wall. Some of these programmes include a presentation of the practice with all kind of visuals, such as movies and action pictures. The support is either on DVDs that are renewed every trimester or, more recently, with online streaming via fast broadband internet access, that links the screens via a central unit dedicated to these programmes. The animations run automatically all day. This type of communication tool is very powerful and certainly incites new behaviour from clients – asking more questions, using more services and buying more products from the practice.

The Vet'Kiosk concept is a success and veterinarians (and their sales results) testify to its efficacy. It entertains clients (most of them watch it) and builds a positive practice image while acting as a visual sales support. In a recent survey, 93 per cent of users expressed their satisfaction and agreed that it was an important vehicle to relay and deliver messages. In the future, it is likely this type of narrow-casting visual sales support will continue to develop and improve client communication. Most of these programmes also contain product information (where legally possible) and the product sales have been significantly increased by such media. Some veterinarians may react negatively, but in our changing society most clients expect to receive such types of information and support, as communication is delivered that way in most service-oriented activities.

> It is the proper use and synergy of all these media that will transform our clients into good and frequent users of our services.

- **Interactive programmes (touch-screen television monitors)**

In certain countries, such as France and the US, touch-screen television kiosks, with dedicated programmes for veterinary clients, were installed in clinics. It was hoped that people would spontaneously use the interactive system, however it was not always a success. Many reasons can explain this partial failure, but the main cause is simple: clients prefer to remain passive (in the presence of other people watching them) and use programmes that are automatically delivered. New programmes developed in the US, such as the Pet Ed Programme and Pet Tablets from Animal Care Technologies in Texas, have touchscreen information that are well suited for the examination room. In that context, these programmes and technologies are well adapted and accepted.

- **Computer with internet access**

Many veterinary practices and hospitals have a website for clients to learn about additional services; it would be logical to offer a computer station in the practice with internet access, including a direct presentation of the clinic website. Clinic websites now offer not only a presentation of the clinic services, but also a link to the patient record and medical information. Integration to the medical record and the practice management software and clinic database allows the client to obtain additional services on the clinic website, such as vaccination status and preventive care, appointments, reminders and product ordering. This powerful communication system has been developed by Vetinsite (now Vetstreet) in the US and is installed in several hundred clinics. Some clinics offer a log-in webcam service to monitor hospitalised or boarded pets in the clinic.

The overall atmosphere concept

Clinic atmosphere is not a direct communication tool, but it is a concept that deals with client communication. Offering practice services in a pleasant atmosphere can certainly make a difference. We all know that when we go to a restaurant it is not only the food that matters, but everything that comes with it. Certain accessories are useful and can be used to contribute to the clinic ambiance.

- **Musical background**

Music is often present in practices and is part of a background sound to soothe and calm people who are stressed and anxious – provided the musical programmes are well selected and don't generate a negative perception through being too loud, or having too fast a beat. It is essential the music does not drown out conversation as it's important to let clients interact and talk. We like to suggest music that gives a feeling of peace and nature, and there are many sorts of music that can be used. Remember to use music that can be played free of rights as, in certain countries, these property rights are quite costly. It is always a good idea to ask about the legislation on playing music in a public place such as the reception area.

- **An aquarium**

Some people think it is a good idea to place an aquarium in the practice as it may entertain and bring positive feedback in an animal clinic. If you decide to use such décor, you need to know about the numerous pitfalls. First, you will need to make sure the aquarium is clean and well managed at all times, which requires repeated and regular attention. We would not advise installing such a system unless you use an outside service to manage the aquarium, or there is someone within the practice who is designated and trained to take care of it and will enjoy doing it as part of his or her job. If not, it will quickly generate headaches. An aquarium seems most appropriate for a practice

Vaccination reminders are excellent and should be used, but they represent only a small part of the communication programme and different methods should be used for direct communication.

Clients come to the practice with their children to take care of the pets and, commonly, the children trigger that visit to the veterinarian.

that deals with tropical fish as a speciality. For a general practice without aqua focus, it seems out of place and may be even out of date. In addition, one might consider that a flat screen monitor can present the same image, without the hassle of maintenance.

- **Odours**

We communicate with all our senses, and the sense of smell is highly developed. It is important clients are not annoyed by odours that veterinarians and staff may not notice as the odours become part of their daily environment. Several devices, including automatic deodorisers can be used to prevent or mask some persistently foul odours. The best policy is to make sure the hospital is clean, including client and staff lavatory areas. You may consider asking an outsider to comment on the smell to avoid odours staying unnoticed by the insiders.

- **Kid's corner**

For most clients (between 80 and 90 per cent, according to recent studies), pets are part of the family. This phenomenon is intimately linked to the growth of companion animal medicine. Children are sensitised to this special relationship with pets and it is a known factor that family pets will contribute to child behaviour and development. Communication concerning this special relationship between children and pets can be done in many different ways. Clients come to the practice with their children to take care of the pets and, commonly, the children trigger that visit to the veterinarian. By including children in a child-friendly practice as much as possible, we please both the children and their parents. A natural way to tell clients we care about their children (because we believe they are part of the equation) is to offer a kids corner within the client information area, particularly for small children who

may have a hard time staying quiet for a long time. By the way, multimedia programmes such as those described above will also take care of that issue.

The principle of total communication

● Concept

It is essential to think of communication as a total service within the practice. Often, some initiatives have been taken, but not necessarily with a plan or a strategic vision. Sometimes, even the staff or veterinarians are not aware of the implications and certainly don't measure actions or follow-up the results of their communication efforts over time. It is, therefore, important to communicate internally and develop tools that are used and accepted by the entire practice team. All team levels should be happy with this principle to obtain an efficient and harmonised total communication.

As consumers expect more information and assistance, a consumer-oriented communication must be more informative to be efficient. As a rule, the more you transfer the information, the more you increase your credibility. The more you interest the client in his or her pet's care, the more you make him or her aware and part of this total communication related to pet management, including related services and products. For the client, there is no priority between the various communication channels. It is at the time of purchase that consumers see the overall offer. It will be very difficult for clients to make a decision if the information is spread out or, worse, if there are contradictions at one level or another. The frequency of information renewal is important and should be tailored to the number of annual visits (usually two to three per year). It would be a mistake to rely on an apparently effective vaccine reminder system to develop the practice activity and client communication. Reminders are excellent and should be used, but they represent only a small part of the communication programme and different methods should be used for direct communication.

Communication is an integral part of total customer management.

● Method

The method consists of transforming selling supports into buying supports. This can be done practically by transforming communication tools into information tools, using comparisons, consumer analysis, testimonials, drawings, animation and visual effects, and by replacing text with images, and phrases by interviews.

In summary, this corresponds to producing informative and educational communication that promotes take-up of practice services. The more personalised the tools (such as target marketing, personalised mailing, itemised invoices and presentation of personalised practice services) the more easily the method

The emergence of new technologies will influence communication and the tools associated with it.

will be accepted. What this means in reality is that the various internal and external supports should be coordinated, ensuring client communication becomes an integral part of the quality control approach to practice services.

This sort of approach should also ensure that clients can all the communication supports to their benefit. The practice can create a true synergy and increase the likelihood of clients adopting the messages.

Summary and conclusion

With regard to internal communication tools and, more precisely, those used in the reception and waiting areas, we can see that practices change as does society and clients. Communication will continue to evolve and will be a crucial part of future practice management.

Communication is an integral part of total customer management (TCM), which places the client as an actor in the service activity. The challenge is no longer to prescribe or sell a high-quality product and service (it is now an expected feature of veterinary medicine services), but to include products and services in global client management. This is where communication becomes essential and contributes to the client satisfaction that makes the difference.

The emergence of new technologies will influence communication and the tools associated with it. We see this already with the internet, personal digital assistants (PDAs) and cell phones with image and message transfer. The power and role of communication in marketing and managing services will, therefore, become increasingly important.

Many simple and practical communication tools are available and useful for veterinary practices. It is the proper use and synergy of all these media that will transform our clients into good and frequent users of our services – for their greatest satisfaction, for better animal health, and last, but not least, for prosperous veterinary activity.

Communication tools outside the clinic

4.3

Introduction

CLIENTS ARE FAMILIAR with new media and constant solicitations. E-mails and telemarketing can be a nuisance, but can, if properly done, be a convenience and service that generates satisfaction and results. It is crucial for vets to communicate regularly with their clients and be proactive, making sure pet owners remain aware of the services and products for pet health and safety. You should not consider such contacts as an intrusion in people's life, but as part of the vet's mission and a client service.

To the contrary, should you remain passive, your clients could react negatively and complain they were not properly informed. Communication is expected by clients, and it is helpful for the practice, informing pet owners about prevention and care to keep their pets healthy and family happy.

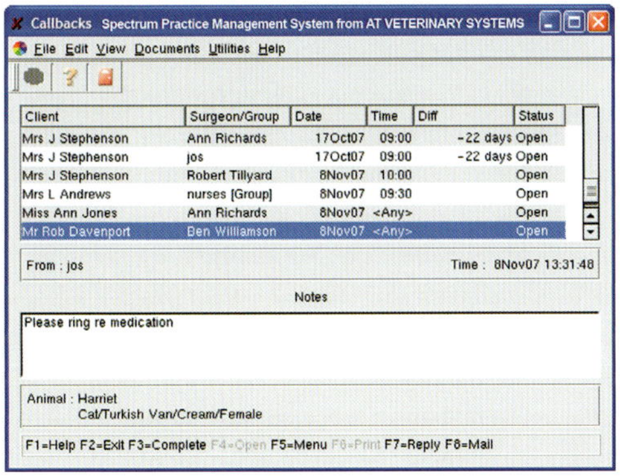

Vaccination reminder

About 25 years ago, veterinarians began the practice of sending client cards or letters as reminders of pet vaccination protection deadlines. This was initially related to the legal necessity of an annual vaccine to protect dogs and cats against rabies; however, this client service rapidly became a tremendous success. Clients were delighted to be reminded about their pet's vaccination booster, and veterinarians improved client satisfaction and the level of vaccination transactions and all other related sales. What was initially considered as a remote promotion action and, sometimes, an unnecessary push, became a true client expectation – to the point that some clients would be upset if, by accident, their reminder did not arrive.

Reminder cards sent to clients now include not only the annual vaccination dates, but also the annual medical check-up, during which, if necessary, some vaccines will be administered. This move from the annual vaccine to the annual medical check is a much better solution, and a better way to initiate the annual return of clients and pets to the vet practice. When one looks at the potential effect of long-acting vaccines (some protecting for more than two and even five years) and the tendency for some vet practices to be highly dependent on vaccinations for their annual turnover, it is clear that the emphasis (and communication) should be placed on annual check-ups and no longer on annual vaccines. The

Remember, it is a necessity to keep constant and regular contact with your customer base, to provide them with the service they expect as the guardian of their pet's health and well-being.

Veterinarians should consider the reminder concept as a true service for their clients, and use their imagination to make it more efficient.

recent development of internet pharmacies and client access to products and drugs, including vaccines, has accentuated the slow, but certain decline in classic pet vaccination transactions. However, to compensate for this negative effect on the number of annual client visits, there are more diseases that vets can vaccinate for, so the key is to improve the personalisation of each vaccination programme dedicated to each animal and communicate accordingly with the client. Again the annual check-up, during which the necessary vaccines for a pet will be prescribed, is the correct method for reminding clients about the need for a visit to the veterinarian for a medical examination. One can also mention that one year of a pet's life is the equivalent to seven years of a human life, adding implicitly that a person will certainly need to see a doctor for an examination once every seven years. The vaccination reminder service evolved over time, and several vet practices sent two or three client reminders, with slightly different messages for each reminder. Practice management software made the system and the logistics quite easy by automatically triggering edits of the reminders according to: client visits to the clinic, the animal's age, vaccines and their time line and possible death of the patient (never a good idea to send a reminder to a client when the animal is deceased).

Other reminders

As veterinarians saw the benefit of the reminder service and clients saw the reasons for such action and expected it, different reminders developed. Therefore, in addition to the annual check-up, other reminders could be sent for medical treatments such as contraceptive injections, or for some diagnostic follow-up such as control radiographs or ultrasounds or other controls related to many different medical or post-surgical conditions. Veterinarians should consider the reminder concept as a true service for their clients, and use their imagination to make it more efficient.

Electronic messages

The internet and e-mail message development has had an impact on the media that veterinarians can use to inform clients about services and medical care for pets. This includes vaccines and other preventive medical services, but also for a new diagnostic tool at the clinic, a new person on the staff or information about a medical threat in the region. Practice management software should have internet interfaces that allow the veterinarian to communicate with his or her client directly, automatically and with a high degree of personalisation. For example, if a pet is diagnosed with diabetes, the owner could automatically receive e-mail information about a new diet or a new form of treatment for pets affected by diabetes. Such a message would be sent to all clients owning a diabetic pet.

SMS or text messages

Several companies now offer a service to vets where messages are sent via the short messaging service (SMS) network. This is quite effective and adapted to a certain clients, such as mobile phone users. Some clients, particularly senior clients do not use mobile phones. The same principles apply to all these various communication media tools. Our recommendation is to use them all, and offer clients a selection of tools and ask them which one they would prefer the clinic to use in communicating with them.

Clinic newsletter

It is a good idea to tell clients about practice services, facilities, equipment and staff, but also about medical and preventive information for their pets. Producing a clinic newsletter is certainly a good way to accomplish such an objective. There are various forms of newsletters ranging from a simple, unsophisticated, one or two-page typed document that you produce every two to three months, to an eight-page, full-colour journal with images, produced for the clinic by a company specialising in such media that will also send the magazine to your clients every quarter. Budgets and time devoted to each of these media types vary. Our recommendation is to make sure you select a format and a budget that suits your and clients' needs.

Electronic mail systems have revolutionised these types of communication tools and also tremendously reduced costs. Using the electronic newsletter reduces two major cost factors – paper and the cost of mailing documents. The only drawback could be that some people (including you?) are bombarded with e-mails and newsletters and may not read them. Our recommendation is to make sure your clients select the media they prefer you to use. By doing so, you will increase the chances of clients reading your messages and news.

Clinic website

We believe a website is an excellent tool to encourage your clients (and future clients) to visit your premises and find out about the services. There are several rules that apply to a website: it should be attractive and the content should be dedicated to clients. Ideally, the information should be such that they want and need to revisit it – what would be the purpose if they only visit it once?

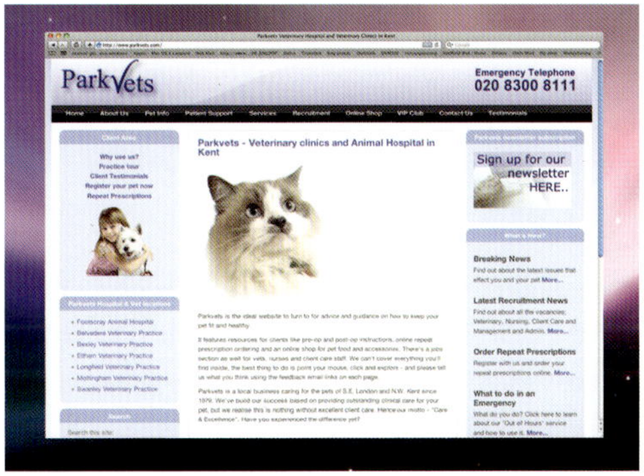

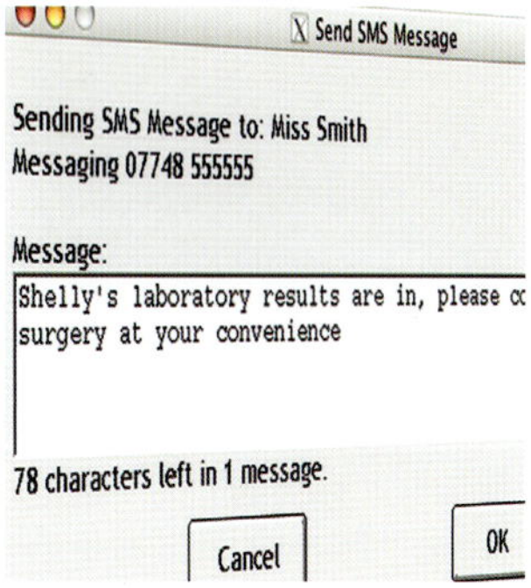

Ideally, the information on your website should be such that clients want and need to revisit it – what would be the purpose if they only visit it once?

In order to reach such a level of use, the website should link with the reminder system and, possibly, to each pet's medical record. These forms of websites already exist (Vetstreet in the US) and should develop over the next few years. Clients benefit from using the website because they can find information dedicated to their pet, via the medical record that accessed with their password. Clients should also be able to ask questions, order products and make an appointment. As with many marketing and communication tools, a website requires resources (time and budget) and ongoing attention, but it is certainly the ideal format, and one that will be used continuously. Other helpful features of a website include the possibility of asking animal health-related questions (and obtaining prompt answers, obviously), making direct appointments for examinations (and, therefore, there should be a link to the appointment book), and purchasing and/or ordering products including pet food (and possibly of having those delivered). All these additional services on the website require thought and proper logistics. They need to be well prepared and implemented to avoid any form of dissatisfaction related to poor delivery.

Target mailing and correspondence

Whether by regular mail or an electronic message system, the concept of target mailing is interesting and should be considered as part of your client communication. What is a target mail? As you probably guessed, it is a message dedicated to a certain type of client or pet. For example, a message can be sent to all clients with a dog or a cat, who live in a region affected by a certain form of contagious disease, or to all pets of a certain age, or type. Personalisation is a key factor in consumers opting to buy a service or a product. Our recommendation is to select the one or two target mail types that will be of most benefit to clients and to your practice. It is recommended to measure the response to all promotion and marketing actions against the agreed objectives. This will encourage you to repeat or delete such promotion action.

Special events cards

Some veterinarians will send a birthday card to their pet clients. Such an action may be considered as inappropriate or outrageous by some people, but these depend very much on the local culture and habits and will vary from one individual, region or country to another. It is best to keep your clients in mind. The birthday cards may seem inappropriate for some and totally natural for others.

The same applies to sympathy cards. Sending a letter or a card to a client because you understand and sympathise with the emotions related to the loss of a companion, a person's best friend, is considered as a very positive gesture by the vast majority of clients. Our recommendation is to send special events cards and letters based on client surveys and feedback for your practice – if you feel comfortable with such an interaction. You may also consider limiting such actions to clients that you know would appreciate this type of communication – clients that are part of your fan club, for example.

Thank-you cards

There are some situations where you should consider saying thank you and, even better, sending a thank-you note or card. Writing such a thank-you note makes much more impact than just saying it occasionally. When should you consider saying thank you? There are many occasions, but we would limit it to two major events.

- **The first visit of a new client to your clinic.**

A thank you card from the vet and staff for selecting your facilities and clinic, and at the same time reminding him or her that you and your staff are available to answer any questions. You can add something such as: "Please let us know if we have answered all your questions and don't hesitate to contact us, should you need any additional information."

- **The new client was sent by an existing client.**

The special client that recommends your clinic could receive a thank-you card. Simple words, preferably hand-written, could be added to this note with a message such as: "We recently saw Mrs Jones and her dog Sweet that you referred to our clinic. We would like to thank you very much for recommending us to your family and friends. It is because of such recommendations that we can hope to increase the level of our service and medical care. I would like to personally thank you for your contribution to the animal healthcare in our community. Kind regards, ... " To make such a thank-you note possible, you need to ask all new clients how they found out about your clinic – *Yellow Pages*, the internet or one of your clients. If the answer is "from one of your clients", simply ask for the client's name and the pet's name and you have the tool to express your gratitude to this special member of your fan club. Having used this thank-you system for many years, we can testify it is very well received by clients – many even keep the notes and bring them to the clinic to thank you.

Yellow Pages

Communication starts outside the practice. Clients looking for a vet will always try the closest location first. Many will search the internet, but another group will still use the phone book or the *Yellow Pages* to locate your clinic. It is, therefore, important to produce a complete, well designed and attractive advertisement within the directory.

E-mails and telemarketing, if properly done, can be a convenience and service that generates satisfaction and results.

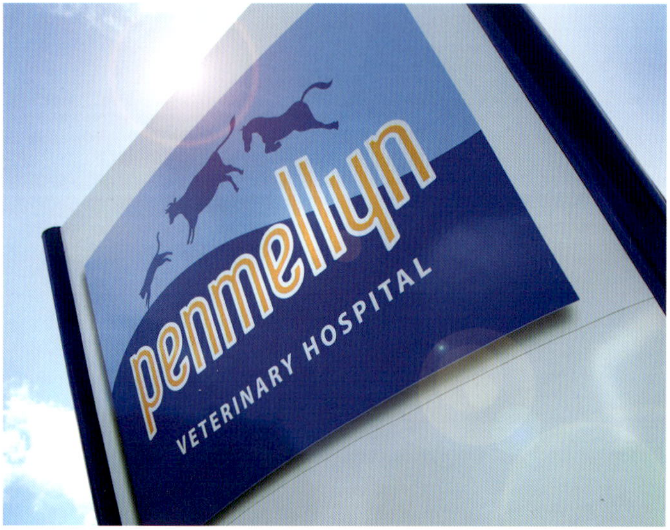

Offer clients a selection of communication media tools and ask them which one they would prefer the clinic to use.

Road and other signs

Clinic visibility is also an important factor for enabling people and potential clients to know about your existence within their neighbourhood. Placing some easily visible signs is obviously a good way to make clients aware of your veterinary clinic. Remember, however, there are several countries where restrictions exist for the size and design of the road signs you can use.

Invoices

Invoices could be considered as communication tools with clients. It is important to send invoices in a timely fashion and, should clients forget, to remind them (in a polite, but direct way) about the need to pay their bills. Our recommendation is to send one, two and then a final reminder with dedicated messages each time, before acting legally. A phone call will often avoid problems and solve most situations once you have reached a third reminder. We recommend you call the owner when the second reminder has not resulted in payment. The third reminder then spells out the legal steps when payment is still postponed. Practice management software allows you to automatically program and generate these mailings.

Summary and conclusion

The most important ways to communicate with your clients outside the clinics are reviewed and described in this chapter. Some are now classic, but still very efficient, such as reminder cards and newsletters, others are in line with rapidly evolving telecommunication technologies such as SMS, e-mails and other internet-based contacts. Ideally, a selection of these tools should be used, favouring those preferred by each client. Remember, it is a necessity to keep constant and regular contact with your customer base, to provide them with the service they expect as the guardian of their pet's health and well-being.

5

Working Effective as a Team

In this section:

Staff and team management

Time management

Organisation in your clinic

Staff and team management

5.1

The value of employees

ASK ANY MANAGER and he or she will tell you that the value of a company resides in its human resources. You can have the best products and services, but at the end of the day, if you don't have the right people to sell these products and deliver those services, you will fail. Some practitioners don't appreciate this and are unaware of the tremendous value of their staff, while others take it for granted. If you wish to motivate the team satisfactorily in the long term, you must recognise the efforts and energy of staff and be quick to acknowledge a job well done. Training employees, including veterinarians as well as technicians and receptionists, requires not only considerable personal time studying in advance, but also months, and sometimes years, of on-site continuing education. Long-term experience is extremely valuable and it is very costly to replace a trained person. Businesses estimate the cost of replacing a fully trained employee at about 1.5 times the annual salary. Training will have to start all over again with the new employee, consuming much time and effort. To summarise: value your staff, select them well, train and treat them well, and make sure you recognise and reward their efforts and their work. They are the people who contribute to your success.

Veterinary clinic team

Starting work at a clinic means joining an existing group of people. Depending on the size of the clinic, this group will most probably include a number of veterinarians (some of them partners), together with lay staff (nurses, technicians and ancillary staff) who work together for common objectives. We suggest any candidate seeking employment in a clinic should ask about his or her anticipated role and responsibilities within the organisation during his or her job interview. He or she should also ask about the clinic's (group's) objectives, the staff organisational chart and about the individual responsibilities of other employees.

Most veterinary clinics should be classified as: a small group of people working together with a common objective.

The owner or senior veterinarian is the leader of the group. In order to work together effectively the members of a working group need:

- a clear reason why they work together;
- effective and coordinated communication, involving all group members;
- clear roles and responsibilities;
- timely and efficient work routines minimising wandering discussions and wasted time; and
- a sense of accountability: each member helping the others to understand that individual contributions ensure group success.

When a small group works as a team, the results achieved are better than each individual result: there is synergy (1 + 1 = 3). Such well-organised groups do exist within the

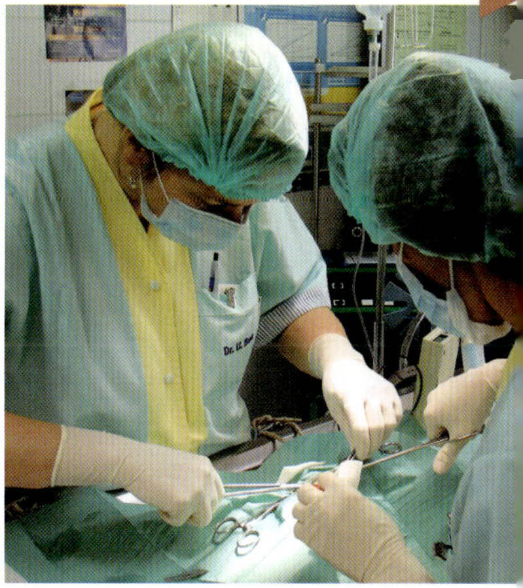

Businesses estimate the cost of replacing a fully trained employee at about 1.5 times the annual salary.

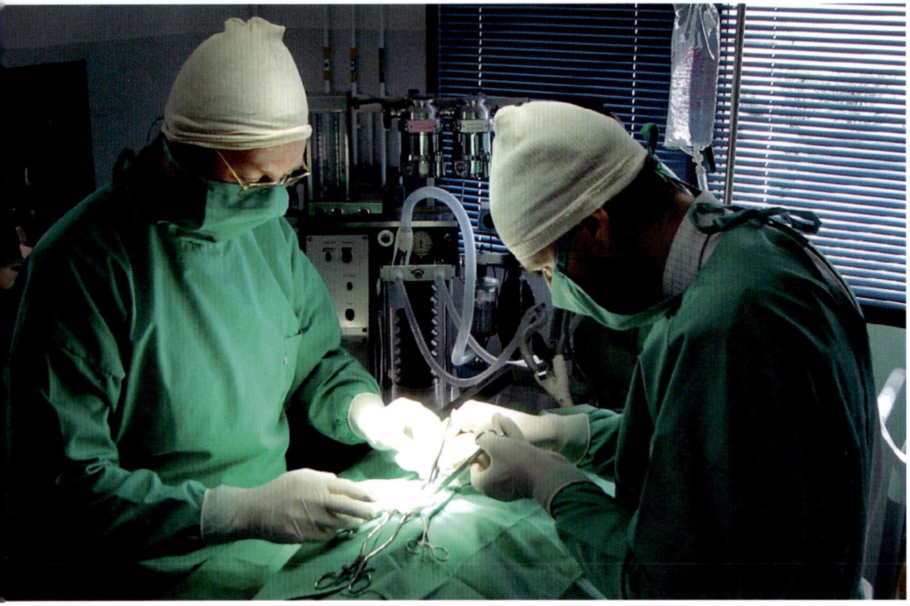

veterinary profession, but in many clinics there is room for much improvement in this area. Some clinics are strictly controlled by management, while others use a different managerial style with full delegation. Be aware that a rigorous management style can be repressive and may not reflect trust in and respect for the staff.

> The new graduate needs to walk a fine line between building on the wealth of experience available from the staff, without neglecting the responsibility that comes with his or her role.

When joining an existing clinic, a young veterinarian may feel lost in the reality of the practical world. However, the ancillary staff consider the new vet as one of their leaders, and expect his or her behaviour to reflect this. The new graduate needs to walk a fine line between building on the wealth of experience available from the staff, without neglecting the responsibility that comes with his or her role. This can sometimes be difficult.

In order to build a reputation of reliability with clients, staff – and, of course, employers – we recommend the new employee never makes up a story or pretends to have knowledge and experience when it is lacking. When a new graduate starts working in a clinic, this is clearly a time when mistakes will be made. That is what people expect from new team members and it is OK to make mistakes. New team members in every role are allowed to have a learning curve. Pretending to have knowledge that is not there will sooner or later become apparent and the new team member will lose the trust of colleagues, staff, and clients. It is much better to build up a track record of reliability, and to occasionally say: "I don't know", promising to get the answer soon. This will be accepted and appreciated. On the other hand, if team members and clients cannot trust you, they will avoid asking to see you again. This can be the beginning of the end. If one is afraid to say: "I don't know", simply because it is a negative answer, then there is a alternative in these situations which we encourage you and your staff to use. Instead of saying: "I don't know", we suggest you say: "I'm not sure and let me find out to confirm the answer to that question". By saying this, you implicitly mean that "you know", but "you want to make sure and confirm your initial answer".

Team performance and discipline

A common performance objective is far more motivating for an effective team than the desire to be a team member. The most important characteristic of a team is discipline – not bonding, togetherness, or empowerment. *Webster's Dictionary* defines the word team as: "orderly or prescribed conduct and patterns of behaviour". The discipline in a small working group or team is three dimensional. Obviously, there is the top-down aspect of it, but this might not be the most important of the three. Discipline is often associated with the words pain, unpleasant or unfriendly. However, a lack of discipline is also negative and is often considered by employees and staff members to result in chaos, lack of efficiency, and time wasting. On the contrary, good and fair discipline is linked to efficacy, and is a source of motivation because it helps reach practice and personal objectives. Peer discipline and self discipline are critically important to effective team success. Each member needs to know his or her role, and act accordingly. Everyone has an individual responsibility to do this, but constant effort and regular reminders are often needed by peers, and sometimes by management.

Practice vision and mission

It is the responsibility of the clinic leadership to develop a clear vision for the clinic. Such vision, however, needs to be developed with the input and involvement of the team members, otherwise it will not have the support of the team. This vision communicates what the future holds, and where the leadership eventually wants to go. It is part of the long-term planning process. Based on this vision, the mission statement can be developed. This will indicate how the practice will achieve the vision. To make the process tangible for all employees, annual overall goals and objectives will need to be defined. We believe it is also a good idea to spend time thinking and writing down a mission statement, preferably in carefully constructed, short sentences. Once established, it can be openly displayed to the team members and clients. If done correctly, it is good practice to regularly remind all team members of the practice's vision and mission, and to discuss the need for revision on a regular basis.

Sharing success as well as failure

By definition, team members cannot have individual success. It is important to thank other staff members and colleagues for help, and to share successes. The flowers, chocolates and the bottles of wine should not all end up with the veterinarians. Each team member contributes his or her unique

The most important characteristic of a team is discipline – not bonding, togetherness, or empowerment.

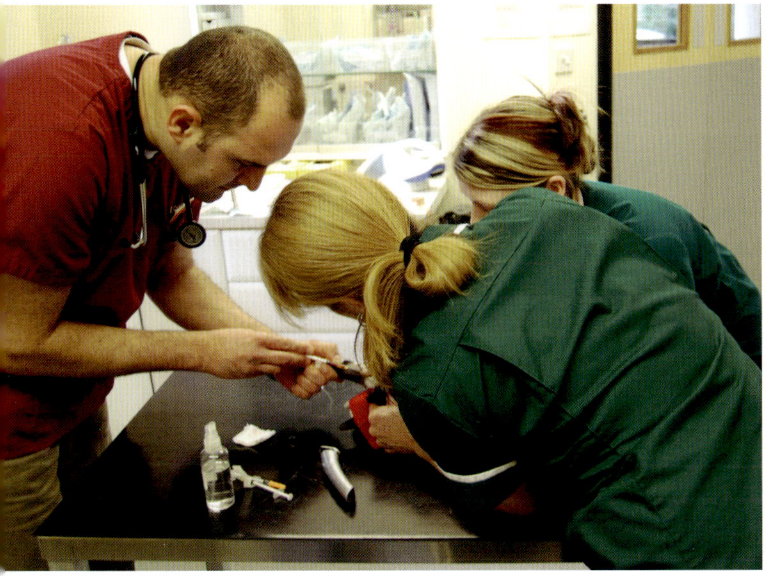

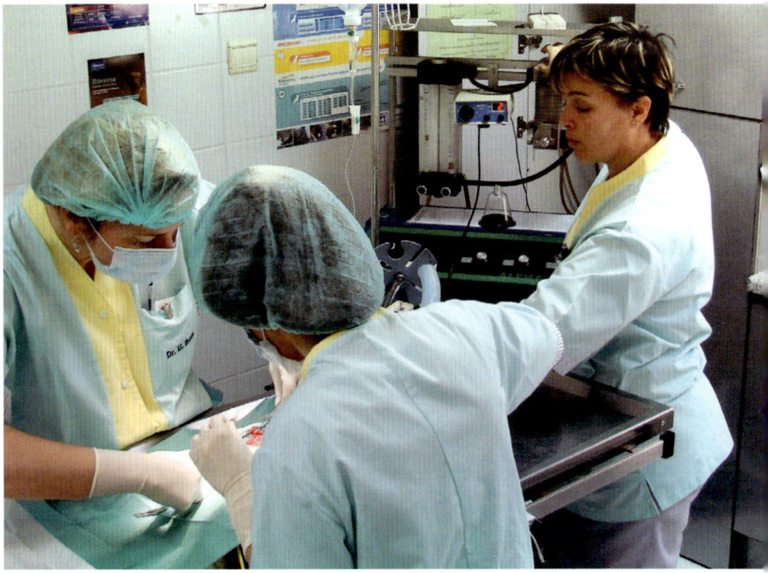

Team: the employee's perspective

Your first days in the practice, your work

After graduation, a veterinarian is taken on as the newest member of a practice. It is important to make an immediate good impression and make others notice you. This will, potentially, result in the development a long-term, fruitful and mutually beneficial relationship. When starting a new job, there are some basic rules.

- **Remain modest and open to learning from other people.** Rather than saying: "This is the way we've been told" or: "This the way I do it", it is always better to say: "Please, show me the way you do it, as I wish to learn the way you and the practice usually handle it."
- **Look after yourself.** A common mistake of young graduates is to consider that cleaning up dog mess, or a cage, or a table is not a task for an educated veterinarian. Such an attitude may upset and alienate the staff who could, potentially, make your life miserable, or at least limit their involvement in helping your integration.
- **Avoid adding workload to your teammates.** The same thing applies to the workload. When it is 5pm and you have a patient that needs some treatment, make sure you do it yourself and don't assume that others will do it for you. It will not be appreciated if you leave work undone, particularly if it becomes a regular occurrence. Be a team member and act as such.
- **Be pleasant, open and friendly.** Hopefully, this will be natural and should not require any effort. However, stress and shyness may initially make it less easy. Don't neglect person-to-person friendly contact.
- **Listen and think before you talk.** Never forget that you still have a lot to learn, even if you feel that you know more than some of the people around you. The listening aspect of communication is crucial and will allow you to adapt more easily to each individual and each situation. You will avoid many mistakes, and people will appreciate it if they feel that you are interested.
- **Smile, show a little humour and have fun.** Life is too short; we should always try to enjoy our work and have fun whenever possible. You will be surprised how much people enjoy socialising with people who are happy.
- **Share and care.** Show your colleagues, the staff and your boss that you care about them and about your work – and not only about yourself. It is always helpful and appreciated when you express empathy. Make sure you understand, care, and if possible agree, with the other person's concerns and opinions. This should be done with everyone, not only with the persons above you in the hierarchy.
- **Make extra efforts and don't hesitate to go out of your way to help.** When people realise you make extra efforts and try hard, then mistakes and imperfections are often excused and allowed for because of your inexperience.
- **Learn and know the rules, policies and procedures.** Make sure you ask about various practical aspects of the practice organisation, such as working schedules and dress code. This will help you to adapt automatically and rapidly, and to adopt the normal practice rules of conduct and daily operational protocols. It will avoid potential criticisms from your teammates or your employer.
- **Remain calm and avoid conflicts.** In the case of a problem with another person in the team, remain calm and listen. Learn to take personal remarks, attacks and criticisms ina calm manner. This does not mean you should acquiesce to and accept unfair judgment, but the best way is to talk openly and in a friendly manner about potential conflicts and how problems can be best solved.
- **Help the incoming members of the team.** Remember how it was for you when you started and make sure you help out the newcomers just as you were helped or as you would have liked to have been helped. Ask them how they want to be supported, and you are likely to make a new friend and someone that may help you in the future.

Handling various people

- **The person with the most experience and knowledge.** This should be the individual you learn the most from; it may or may not be your boss. Try to get as much training and educational experience from him or her. Tell him or her that you wish to learn, and ask if this is possible, and if he or she would be prepared to share knowledge and spend some time to assist your training.
- **Your boss.** Treat him or her as you do everyone else – nicely and with dedication and attention. Don't go overboard to the

extent that you appear to be someone who is trying to obtain special favours from the boss by being abnormally attentive.That attitude will actually often be rejected by the boss and also may alienate you from of the rest of the team. If you have a problem, go and talk to him or her. Be honest and open, and don't hide things. If problems are hidden, then your work and your life will be jeopardised. Other team members will also be affected. When you have good ideas, share them with your teammates and then suggest them to the management. In general, never bypass your boss if you have an issue as, in most cases, this is a recipe for professional suicide.

- **Your teammates.** These should be your best work friends and you should treat them as such. Share, talk, listen, work hard and have fun with them.
- **The technicians and ancillary staff.** Make sure you respect all employees, especially those who are below you in the hierarchy, particularly if they have been in the practice for a long time. If you show interest and care about them, then they will help you and teach you many practical and inside tips relating to your work. On the contrary, if you neglect them and don't listen their opinions, and if you give them additional work instead of making their life easier, then watch out because they can make your life miserable. Make sure, however, that you adopt a clear line of conduct and don't be overly friendly if you will need to show authority later on. There is a happy medium, and it is our advice to exercise careful judgment regarding the personal relations you have with other employees, staff and teammates. Avoid favouring one of the team members. In general, personal or private relationships with team members complicate the team performance. ◻

characteristics to the team, and team members do not all have the same apparent role or position.

The same is true in the clinic as it is in sports. Scoring goals is more than just the contribution of number 10 – the striker. Although critical, in order to perform optimally, this player needs support from many others in the field during, before and after the match. Many of these support roles are invisible, but still essential to the team's success.

The same is true in a clinic. Team members correct fellow team members' mistakes, and keep the dirty laundry confidential. Team members gossiping on the phone, or talking loudly in the reception area where clients can hear or see, can break team confidentiality and destroy the image of the team and the clinic. It is a general rule to praise in public, and punish in private – no matter what the reason is and no matter how right one may be. Internal conflict and gossip are never good advertisements for a business.

◻ Praise in public, and punish in private – no matter what the reason is and no matter how right one may be.

When veterinarians and their teammates are experiencing internal conflicts, practitioners do not always realise that clients soon feel the ambiance and relationship between staff members has deteriorated. This sort of situation has strong negative consequences on clients' overall perception of the practice.

Adding a new team member

From the clinic owners (team coach) point of view, adding new members to the team is a critical process. Adding the right person can lift the team to higher levels, while hiring the wrong person can break the team. This can be compared to introducing a rotten apple into a basket – it will have an impact on other apples that were originally healthy. Adding the wrong person to a team can have the same effect as the rotten apple.

Knowledge and trust are intimately related.

The best indicator of future behaviour is past behaviour. Asking for past evidence to support statements during an interview is more informative than asking for examples of how the applicant would act in the future. Current employees (potential colleagues) should be involved in the process of hiring new members. Employees that were hired, but who do not fit into the team, for whatever reason, need to be informed and given the supported opportunity to change their behaviour. This advice should be documented. If their attitude improves, everyone benefits, but if not, they should leave the team.

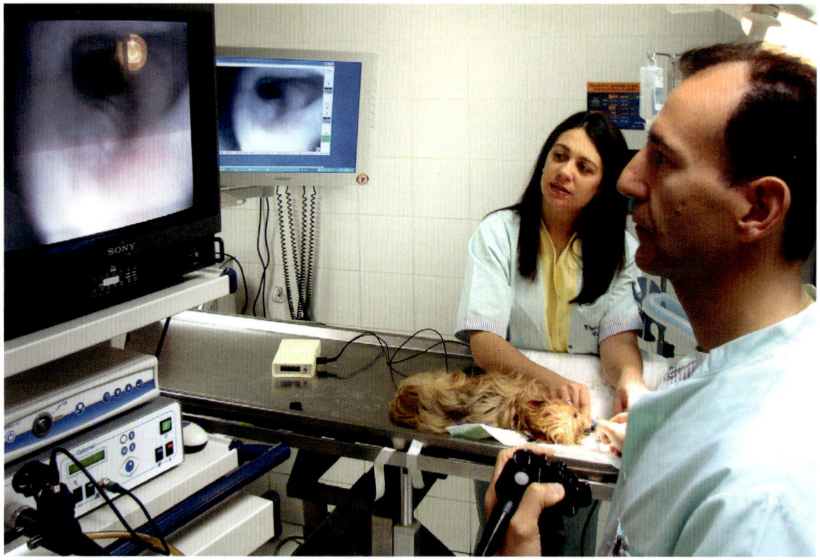

Each member adds his or her specific contributions to the team and delegation of responsibility is crucial in order to ensure optimal performance. Team members need to rely upon others. New team members need to be trained effectively. This means existing staff must allow new members more time to learn and complete tasks during the training period. Often under a heavy workload there is a temptation to do it yourself, because training others takes longer. To have an impatient attitude is a short-term strategy. Veterinarians, like many small business owners and entrepreneurs, find it hard to delegate. Those who allow new team members time to learn, will benefit from delegation and see their business grow. In an ideal world, the veterinarian should only do those tasks in the clinic that can be done only by a vet. The rest should be done by support staff.

Who is the best trainer?

If you wish your staff to practise in your image and under your rules and methods, it is clear the best teacher is you. This is one of the reasons why we believe that veterinarians should spend time in employee training and education. Once you have shown how you place a catheter, or a Robert Jones bandage as you like to see it done, then you will trust the person and are more likely to delegate some tasks to that individual. There is truth in the protocol: see

Team: the manager's perspective

Empowering your team

Team members need to feel they are part of the team and that they belong. This is the main reason why management needs to communicate with staff, allowing everyone to participate in various ways in the organisation, and welcoming new ideas. The more involvement that staff have in the decision process, the more they will implement directives and accept decisions. To achieve this:

- delegate;
- communicate;
- organise staff meetings; and
- empower your employee, vets or nurses.

Delegating to staff. Delegated responsibility, trust and additional training are among the most powerful rewards for clinic staff. When meeting with nurses and veterinary technicians, we often hear complaints that employees are frustrated by limited responsibility and the lack of confidence their employers are showing in them. Some staff, who have undertaken extensive training, are not allowed to use their newly acquired skills. Delegation of responsibility and information is vital to the success of a team. As Mr Carlson (the head of SAS – Scandinavian Airlines) once said: "A person without information cannot take initiatives, and a person with the information cannot avoid taking initiatives." Why is it that vets have a tendency to want to do it all themselves and do not delegate to their staff?

There are some legal issues associated with delegating some veterinary actions to lay staff and allowing non-veterinarians to handle medical care to animals, such as injections, anaesthesia and dental procedures. If you don't know for sure what can and cannot be done, check with the national veterinary board (in the UK, it's the RCVS) for delegation limitations regarding nurses and technical staff. You will often be surprised that most places allow more procedures than veterinarians believe. There are several reasons.

- **They don't trust their staff –** *"my staff doesn't know how to do it... it takes me two seconds and it takes them 10 minutes... I'd rather do it... I know it will be done faster and probably better".* Trust comes with time and with training. The best trainer is the person who will eventually delegate. Therefore, we encourage vets to devote time every week to employee training, and then they will trust and eventually delegate.
- **They like to do it –** *"I like to place the catheter and do the Robert Jones bandages."* If this is the reason, then you should continue to do it because you like it. However, allowing your staff the fun may be a powerful incentive.
- **They think it is more cost efficient –** *"it takes my staff 10 minutes to place the catheter or to run a blood sample, and often they use three catheters when I use only one".*

We believe vets should concentrate on the diagnostic and intellectual features of their profession, or on higher technical procedures, and leave the nursing and basic patient care to other people. To devote their time to brainstorming, to think, to use their talent and time at other tasks – those tasks that staff will never be able to achieve.

If you don't trust your staff, it is unlikely you will delegate.
This is a good reason for providing proper training, year after year, and investing in continuing education of your personnel. Learning new techniques is also a source of motivation for the employees... and, when well adapted and provided, it is expected and appreciated by the staff. Actually you should question yourself about an employee that is not interested in his or her continuing education! We believe that it would not be a good sign. □

"Knowledge and trust are intimately related."

one, do one, teach one. However, for many veterinary procedures, seeing and doing one is not enough to be master the procedure and be a good teacher. However, the principle is valid. How can a student learn, when a teacher does not allow him or her to practise?

Make work an enjoyable daily event

Another aspect of working in a team environment has to do with fun and pleasure. People working in an enjoyable place will be happy to arrive at work, to stay at work for long hours, and will generate happiness

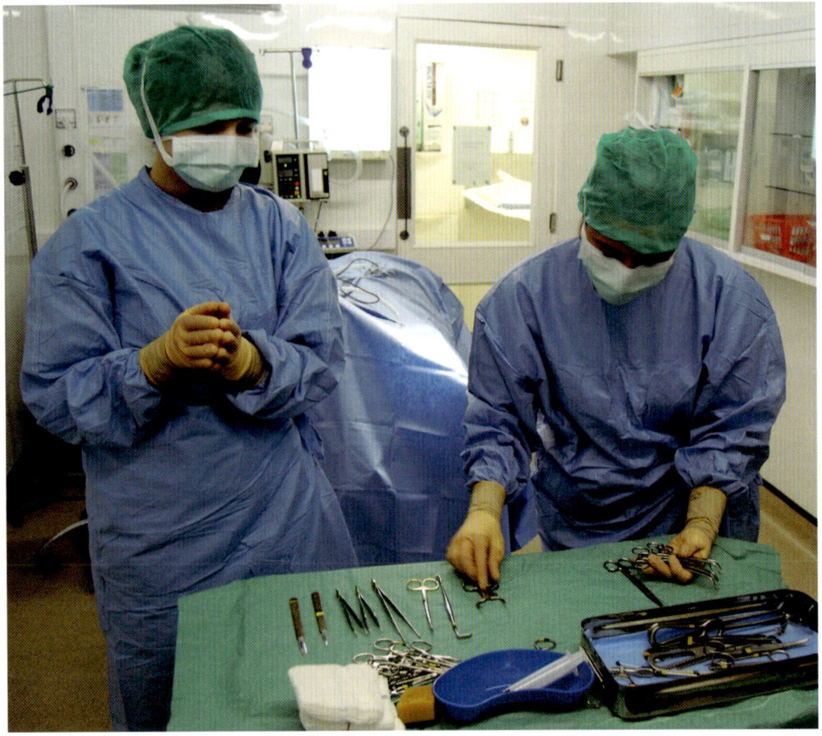

around them, including clients. It is contagious, so be enthusiastic yourself, enjoy, have fun, learn and teach, and you will be rewarded by seeing how much enthusiasm and fun at work reflects on the overall practice ambiance and working environment.

> There is truth in the protocol: see one, do one, teach one.

Staff meeting

An important moment in the clinic diary is the time when staff members are meeting to talk about practice organisation and procedures, as well as client communications, marketing, strategy and objectives – indeed, most practice management issues. This is important working time that needs to be treated as such. Certain method should be used if you wish these meetings to be successful for everyone. For example, during such meetings, make sure people are isolated from work and can concentrate on the meeting. Effective methodology includes switching off cell phones, and not allowing any interruptions. These staff meetings are expected and even appreciated by employees, and are certainly rewarding and productive when they are well prepared and conducted. In order to reach such a result and be efficient, there are rules and methodology to follow. It requires rigor and some discipline to keep staff motivated and participating to maximise such meetings.

General principles for staff meetings

- **Fix a date, a schedule, and stick to it.**

For example, this can be every first Tuesday of the month. Plan for an alternative date in case of conflict with the normal calendar.

- **Select a good location and an adapted time.**

In our experience, after trying several systems and timing, the best solution is a staff lunch meeting, when feasible, at the clinic site (if you have a suitable place for such a meeting, where there will be sufficient privacy, and yet no disturbance by the practice functions). A good practical idea is to order pizzas and/or snacks and feed the team at that time to make it more convivial and avoid interruption or time wasted with lunch breaks. An advantage of this timing is that it will automatically finish when the practice regular afternoon activities restart and, therefore, the risk of having a prolonged meeting, (which all participants fear), is no longer present.

- **Prepare a short (one page or less) agenda.**

This will help everyone to stay on schedule and will help the moderator keep the conversation going and all points covered. This sort of document will also be used as the framework for the meeting minutes. If the agenda is on time, then it can be handed out to participants to prepare themselves before the meeting, thus increasing the value and efficacy of the interactions.

- **Identify a person (moderator) responsible for the meeting.**

That person often prepares the agenda, the questions and, to a certain extent, the responses. We encourage changing this person once in a while in order to avoid demotivation, and to increase everyone's involvement. It is logical the same person should take notes and then write the meeting minutes, including planned actions, in a timely fashion.

- **No criticisms and personal comments.**

This is a rule that we recommend adopting and enforcing at the beginning of each meeting. People should address the group and not the person, and avoid personal attacks and/or comments that could be interpreted as such.

- **Involve everyone.**

It is the moderator's role to make sure everyone is consulted because, in a group, you have leaders that may monopolise the attention and could potentially alienate other people. Individuals that are naturally remote should be encouraged to speak and express their opinion.

- **Write and use the minutes.**

Staff meeting notes are a potentially valuable source of information and should be used as much as possible. If a practice procedure manual is being used, then these procedures could be extracted from meetings notes and minutes. An action list, attached to the conclusions and handed to participants, means everyone can follow up their actions. Finally, these minutes can be used when the time comes to check why certain procedures and actions have or have not worked.

Staff performance: personal evaluation

Based on the business (practice) vision, mission and annual plans, individual job descriptions and standards of performance can be written and agreed with all team members. They should be reviewed at least once a year, and an annual performance meeting between the manager and the employee is a good time to achieve such a task. Once the business consists of more than three or four persons, it makes sense to consider conducting annual personal employee evaluations or appraisals. By definition, personal evaluations aim at positive feedback on each person's performance for a certain period of time (a year seems a good interval). They are conducted by the boss, or by associates when there are several managers, with alternate evaluators to avoid potentially biased interpretations of individual performances and satisfaction from the management team. In large practices, such evaluations could be delegated. For example, a non-veterinarian practice manager and practice employee could be in charge of the receptionists' annual evaluation. Well-conducted annual evaluations are beneficial and a motivation source, which encourage employees to improve their performance. If there are difficulties with certain staff members, this is the time to tell the employee that certain improvements are needed and to specify how, in an open and productive manner. A standardised staff-performance evaluation is the most efficient method, and maximises employees' understanding and appreciation.

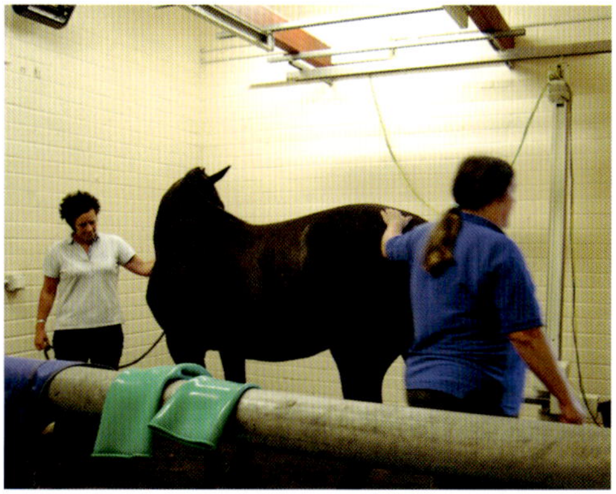

For all performance evaluations, the rule is to emphasise the good points and the positive aspects of the person's achievements.

Objectives of staff evaluation

- Improve staff communication.
- Show the team that you listen and care, and give people a chance to freely express opinions.
- Motivate employees.
- Understand and improve practice organisation.
- Share and use good ideas from staff.
- Set individual personal objectives.
- Plan management actions.
- Show staff that you care about them and their opinions.

This method show the team that he or she cares and is a fair, dedicated and responsible leader.

A proven method for good evaluations consists of providing a form for employees to complete prior to the interview. This technique allows the person to establish a self-critical evaluation of his or her performance; there is no need for the manager in charge of annual evaluations point out weaknesses or negative points, as these are often emphasised by the individual – who can be very self-critical.

Don't forget the strength of two very simple words: "thank you".

The interviewer can focus on positive points in the individual's performance, which is a rewarding experience. For all performance evaluations, the rule is to emphasise the good points and the positive aspects of the person's achievements.

Staff rewarding and empowerment

It is difficult for a soccer team to win (or even play) without certain objectives. The same is true for a clinic team. Individual and team performance is significantly influenced by rewards. Although it is often thought that financial benefits are powerful motivators, this approach has limitations. For many people, non-financial rewards can be even more powerful.

- **Acknowledging a job well done**

Don't neglect the importance and impact of acknowledging achieved objectives. The entire team should be part of the equation and participate actively in the practice mission. Acknowledging the group and all employees will motivate those who are slower or not as active. Ignoring them or criticising them may push them away or further antagonise them. When you consider quality control and service performance, everyone is involved: the nurse helping and assisting in surgery; the receptionist assisting on the phone; the kennel help; or the cleaner. It is common for clients to thank employees (because they were directly involved with patient care during, for example, a hospital stay) and to give them small gifts, flowers, thank-you cards, or pet pictures. When you receive such a letter or thank-you note, it is a good idea to share these congratulations with the team. Why not display these letters and pictures in the personal or staff lounge so everyone will see them? If the message is directed to a specific individual, you can even add your comments or outline some quotes to emphasise your involvement in thanking the team.

- **What is the best reward for your employees?**

Money is undoubtedly important as most people live on low incomes and anything extra is welcome. However, the strongest reward for employees might often be a few complimentary words to show your appreciation. Don't forget the strength of two very simple words: "thank you". There are other actions you may consider, such as giving an afternoon off, or a small gift such as tickets for a show or a good restaurant. You should tailor the personal gift to the person, thereby showing that you know his or her taste and you made a special effort. Ideas are numerous.

- **Financial reward**

A strong, direct way to interest your employees in the practice performance and results is simply to display the week's financial results (even in such detail as the days of the week). Or, make it simple and mention just the overall income, with all transactions included. You could also divide it up into categories, such as OTC sales, surgeries, examinations, diagnostic procedures and emergency service. It is essential to compare the figures with those of the previous year and to display the weekly (and monthly) total for each week alongside the same period for the previous year. It immediately provides a quick analysis of the practice's financial trend: is it growing, stagnant, or decreasing? Another parameter would be the number of transactions for each period. An increase in client numbers might be a reason for a growth in revenue; on the other hand, if there were fewer clients, then growth would be due to an increased average transaction (each client spent more money). For more details, see "Financial indicators" in **Section 6.2**.

Many colleagues don't realise the impact of this information on the team. It creates a bond because they feel part of the business and, thereby, often adopt a proactive attitude to improving balance and results. Some practitioners are afraid to show how much money they make, and how much revenue the practice generates. We believe that being transparent about these aspects of the activity is a positive feature. After all, the practice is the employees' income and their future; as employees, they often feel the practice is theirs. In addition, you will be surprised how many employees already know or have a pretty good idea of the general income of the practice – often thinking it is higher than the actual amount. By displaying the practice's financial numbers, the team embraces the need to get better results and will naturally be motivated to act accordingly. Next to such a spreadsheet, displayed in a private staff-only place (such as the staff lounge area), would be the ideal place for a permanent quote such as: "Good medicine is also good business", or "Optimal medicine requires a healthy business".

- **Specific bonuses**

There are simple methods of pleasing employees by giving bonuses related to general performance or achieved objectives. Various forms of incentives could

> By displaying the practice's financial numbers, the team embraces the need to get better results and will naturally be motivated to act accordingly.

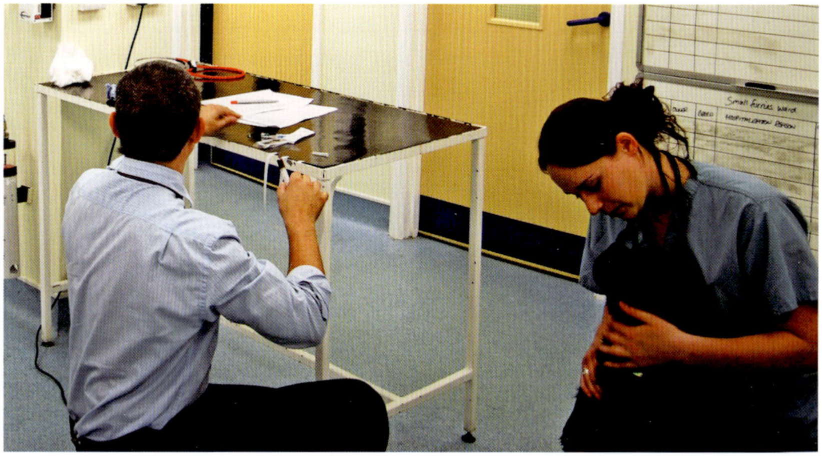

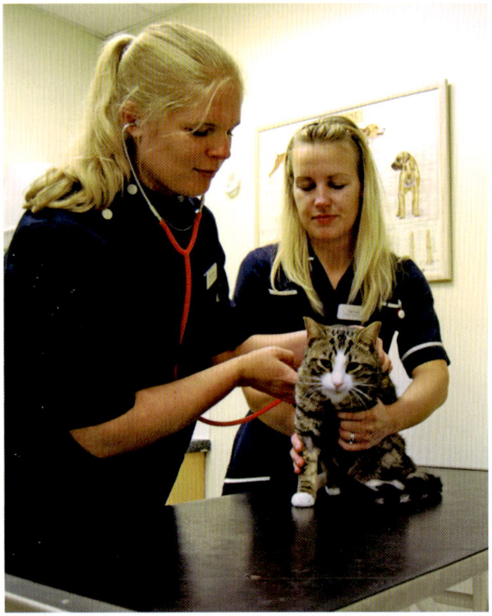

Learn to train and educate your staff and assistants – you will trust them and they will perform better.

be allocated to such a reward system. Ideally, it should not be considered or registered as an additional portion of salary, but as a bonus or incentive. The legal and fiscal regulations may vary from one country to another but, as a rule, it is better to establish a bonus system as non-permanent and performance related. In some countries there are taxes associated with such additional income, and you should ask for professional help to ascertain the legal and fiscal equation for a financial bonus. We like a system that is acceptable to the entire team, because the cleaning staff participate as much in client satisfaction and practice performance as the surgery nurse, even if some jobs may sound less noble. The reward system should be fair, transparent and easy to measure and apply, and should be the same system for everyone. The bonus system should also be linked to practice performance and calculated on continuous growth. By applying such an equation, both employees and the practice benefit, which is the purpose. Ideally, the timing for the incentive and its impact should be as near as possible to each employee's performance. For example, a bonus based on an annual performance is fine, but does not allow modifications for fluctuations during the year. In addition, if the employee's efforts were strong in March, and less effective in December, what kind of impact would you achieve if you give the annual reward at the end of the year? Finally, it is financially better for the practice to allocate bonuses each month, rather than dealing with a large total sum at the end of the year. In a small business, cashflow is often critical.

If you have adopted the formula described above you will have achieved the initial necessary step to create a fair incentive formula. The method is very simple (see panel).

Certain employers add a "personal evaluation factor" each month for each employee. This has value, because you can tailor a specific reward to a individual according to his or her personal performance that month. The major problem with such a system is that, after a while (months or years) the employers find it more and more difficult to score employees each month. The subjectivity increases and when we look at such scoring over a year it balances out and does not significantly modify the overall individual bonus. For individual actions, we recommend that you do it as they happen, on a punctual basis, and not systematically.

Summary and conclusion

This chapter reviews most aspects of staff human resource management. The veterinary team entity is described; if coordinated appropriately, a strong synergy should exist. Team performance and measurement are linked to an established level of discipline. The mission and vision of

How to create a fair incentive formula

- **First: establish a monthly piggy bank or purse.** This could be a percentage of the monthly income, or a percentage of the monthly benefit. We prefer a formula based on the month's increased total income compared to the same month the year before. By doing this, you look at the progress each month. From one year to the next, there are differences in the number of monthly working days, but if you look at the formula as an annual programme, then items that decrease one month will automatically increase the next. The monthly purse should be a percentage of that difference. In our practice, we looked at our annual benefit (which was about 28 per cent of growth) and then allocated a percentage of the total income growth to the purse (in our case, we allocated eight per cent of the growth to the incentive purse).

Example for Smith Veterinary Hospital
February 2007: c. €55,000
February 2006: c. €48,000
Growth: €7,000
We agreed to allocate eight per cent of annual growth, based on the previous year's profit.
In this example, €490 would be distributed among employees.

- **Second: divide the purse.** It is time now to distribute the purse, using a fair system that involves everyone. To do so, we looked at the hourly salary of each employee, limiting it non-veterinary staff; we believe veterinary assistants should also be linked to specific transactions such as surgeries, examinations and procedures they generate.

Multiply the hourly salary by the number of effective hours (including extra or over-time hours) each employee has worked that month. By doing so, you take into account several differentiating factors such as employee ranking in the practice (the hourly salary would reflect that aspect), full-time versus part-time work (the number of hours would reflect that aspect), absenteeism for vacations and sickness, and periods that forced the rest of the staff to work harder (the number of effective hours worked that month would reflect that aspect).

Example for Smith Veterinary Hospital
There are three full-time employees (receptionists and nurses or technicians) and one part-time cleaner and maintenance person.

Time worked in February and resulting payments

Silvia: hourly salary €9.50.
160 hours, including four hours overtime = €1,520.00

Isabelle: hourly salary €8.55.
148 hours = €1,265.40

Mary: hourly salary €8.68.
112 hours = €972.16

Michele: hourly salary €6.83
70 hours = €478.10

Sum of four salaries = €4,235.66

Sum of total hours worked = 490

Purse share for each employee:

Silvia:	€1,520.00 / €4,235.66	= 0.35886 x 490	= €175.84
Isabelle:	€1,265.40 / €4,235.66	= 0.29875 x 490	= €146.38
Mary:	€972.16 / €4,235.66	= 0.22952 x 490	= €112.46
Michele:	€478.10 / €4,235.66	= 0.11287 x 490	= €55.32

Total distributed bonus for February:
€175.84 + €146.38 + €112.46 + €55.32 = €490
(individual amounts rounded up)

the clinic should be known and shared by the team - both successes and failures. When a new member joins the team, there are simple attitudes and introductions to help make initiation easy and effective. The new team member should also know how to adapt to the new environment and people.

Empowerment and proper delegation are two important features of human resource management. Many vets have a hard time delegating tasks. This may be an issue when planning business growth as there are only 24 hours in a day. If you don't delegate it is often because you don't trust other people, or because they are not trained. Learn to train and educate your staff and assistants – you will trust them and they will perform better.

Team communication is essential. Meetings, messages and direct individual talks, including job performance evaluations, are all important aspects of practice management. Simple and practical methods are described in this chapter. How to gratify your employees? There are some rules. A financial reward programme is detailed. The most effective system is not necessary a financial reward – the manager's attitude with staff is as important.

You can be the best veterinary surgeon, and yet fail to satisfy your clients if the people working with you – the staff – are not working in phase with you and the rest of your team. Having good employees: is a treasure you should be ready to find, keep and gratify. Building your human resources is the most difficult task that any entrepreneur may face, but it is also one of the most gratifying parts of the job. In order to achieve such an objective, it is worth making the effort, dedicating time to select and train, and help your teammates and employees grow within the business.

Don't forget to treat staff well, and make sure you recognise and reward efforts and work. They are the people who contribute to your success.

Building your human resources is the most difficult task that any entrepreneur may face, but it is also one of the most gratifying parts of the job.

Time management 5.2

Introduction

TIME MANAGEMENT COURSES are among the most popular junior management courses in the corporate world. Ask people nowadays how they are doing and it is very likely the answer will be "busy, busy, busy". It seems many young people have a problem coping with all the perceived responsibilities, obligations and opportunities with which they are presented. Consequently, they find it hard to make the right choices, and then be happy with those choices.

The same applies in veterinary practice. Most vets are constantly running behind schedule and wasting valuable client time, which often results in working late and overtime. Consequently, the work/life balance is a big issue in veterinary practice. An increasing number of younger colleagues and their families suffer significant consequences to their health from stress and work overload, and end up with burnout. Psychological problems, depression and suicide are at alarmingly high levels among young vet professionals in absolute numbers compared to other starting professionals. So what is going on?

The world has become a smaller place, and we are exposed to more news and information via more media, including the internet and mobile phone. We are in contact with more people, from more places in the world. News of a bus accident in India reaches us in Europe the same day it happens, along with the morning news. During the evening news, we are kept updated on the actual FTSE and Wall Street stock market developments, on hurricanes in the Caribbean, and on political developments in Brazil. Not all this information is necessarily relevant news for most of us, but it is part of the constant flow of information that reaches us via digital media at an ever-increasing speed of delivery. Political systems have changed in China, the former USSR and Eastern Europe, allowing access and insights into countries that were closed to us. Our terms of reference have become more complicated overnight and old knowledge is obsolete. Daily, we hear names of countries and their capitals

"Until you value yourself, you won't value your time. Until you value your time, you will not do anything with it."

– M Scott Peck

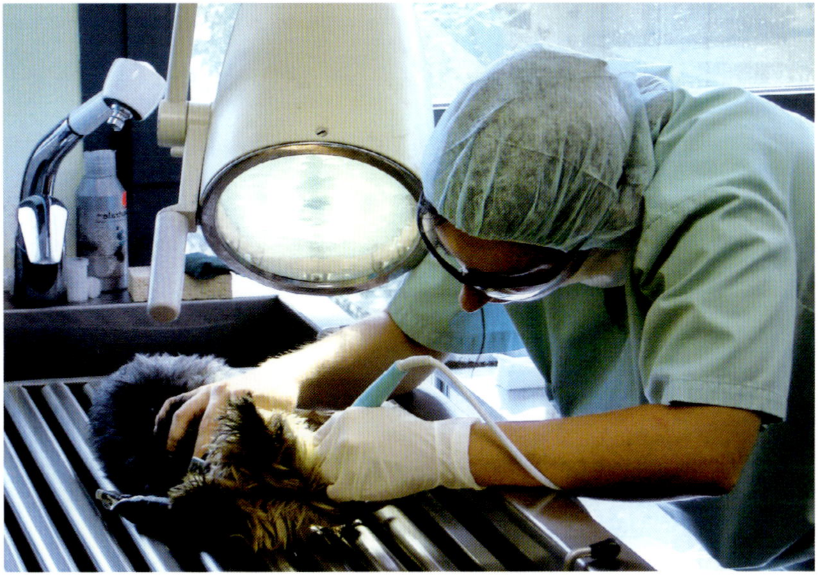

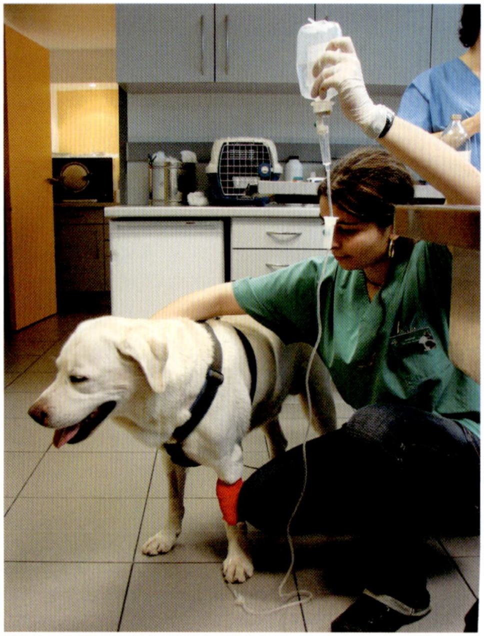

Life is becoming more complex, and while the world may seem smaller, our personal world is larger.

that we did not even know existed a few years ago; now we know what goes on in these cities as soon as it happens. World news services like CNN, BBC and TV5 Monde make sure we are the first to know.

Because of this, life is becoming more complex, and while the world may seem smaller, our personal world is larger. Knowledge and experience has gone far beyond our own family, school, business, village and town. Wherever we live, most of us have access to more than 30 television channels, and have broadband internet allowing instant updates from an increasing number of previously unimagined information sources. Many of us desperately try to keep ahead of all this new information technology. Compared to adults, teenagers seem to cope with a surfeit of high-tech input and are easily able to handle more than five peer chats while simultaneously watching television, listening to music and doing homework. However, it seems even teenagers are losing the battle and feel "busy. There is always more to accomplish than can be fitted into a 24-hour day.

Time management or task management?

Although time management is often perceived to be an issue, it is important to realise that available time has not changed. Wherever we are in the world and whoever we are, we all have only 24 hours in a day. No matter how important or unimportant our position is, no matter how rich or poor we are, we all have the same number of hours in a day. The issue is not about time management – time manages itself, and the sun and the clock keep us informed of its progress. The real issue relates to task management – to fit everything we want to do into our day. We need to take ownership of this reality and make choices. What can we do and what do we postpone or delete? It is very important to be happy with what we do and how we do it.

Selection and deselection

What makes us feel so busy? The most important factors responsible for time (in fact: task) management problems (and, therefore, a popular topic for junior managers' courses) are:

- task (over)load; and
- problems of selection and, possibly more important, deselection. In other words: what to do and what not to do?

Most of us don't have a problem in deciding, from our list of responsibilities and tasks, the important things that need to be done. We can classify items as needing doing today or in the short term. The problem starts when we have to decide what not to do. The intermediate solution of selecting what can be done or has to wait is not too difficult, but it does not solve the real issue of what should not be done at all. Time management courses have attempted to classify tasks into groups:

- A is the most important;
- B is less important, but still high priority; and
- C is unimportant.

This seems a nice tool, but in itself is not sufficient as it does not decide what should be done with the group C tasks and, more importantly, if and when they should be done. There is no problem in indicating what is important and must be done, but it can be difficult to decide what we will not do, and say no to people (family, friends and colleagues) without feeling guilty. The ABC classification does not even include the type-D tasks that are often the most pleasant ones, which can pop-up unexpectedly at any moment of the day and tend to draw our attention and time away from the As and Bs (**Figure 5.2.1**).

Figure 5.2.1

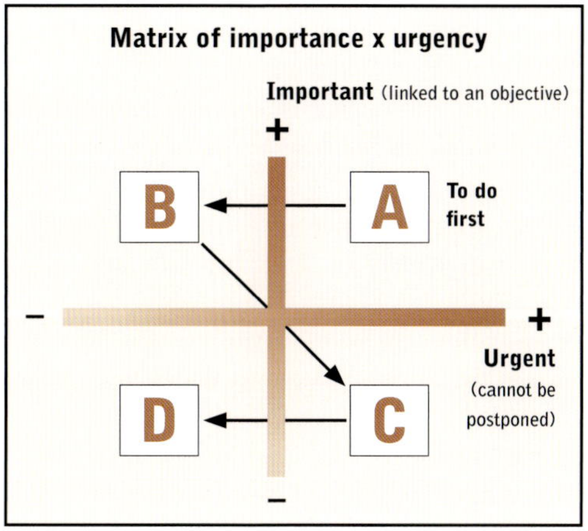

Apples and pears

Time management and the problem of being busy is not only about prioritisation. An important factor is the competition between various considerations involved in decision making – for example, work versus personal tasks and responsibilities. People who we deal with on a daily basis have their expectations of us and we have our commitments to them. Most people perceive the most critical problem with time management is when their spouse or significant other (SO) indicates there is a problem and asks for more time and attention than we (think) are able to give them. If we are fortunate, the SO manages to red-flag the issue early and gently, and only gradually increases the pressure when time goes by and nothing is done by us to deal with the issue. When all goes well, this results in an adequate rebalance and continuing happiness in good work/life balance.

But, in many cases, problems occur. The partner's wishes are not met as compliance is perceived as being detrimental to ones' career prospects. Young people, especially, feel this pressure in a highly competitive work environment (where single colleagues work even longer hours).
Another practical and valid reason is that most of us need to work to make a living and to pay the bills, and we cannot afford to work stop working, or we work part-time. The bills are the result of choices we made in the past, responsibilities and expectations we have undertaken, and they are a reality that cannot be escaped. In most cases, changing the amount of cash needed to finance our lifestyle cannot be effected in the short term. We need to manage the balance between our work and our private lives in a way that our partners find acceptable. It is not a matter of what is more important, work or the family. Of course, we all agree family is more important, but the family needs the income. The income is needed to pay for what we have become accustomed to, and for further growth. Just when you had thought you had everything, the next generation audio or digital device comes on to the market and you or your family cannot think how it was possible to live without it. Can you

We need to manage the balance between our work and our private lives in a way that our partners find acceptable.

> We should appreciate the significant other is often just the messenger, signalling our overall life is out of balance.

remember the days when there were no computers, digital cameras, iPods and mobile phones? Today, many (if not most) 12-year-olds have access to one or more these gadgets and use them on a daily basis.

Because of the consequences of work commitments on the work/life balance, family members (and especially the SOs) need to share responsibility for the choices that helped incur these bills. This includes the priority in careers for both SOs. It is easy to predict that when this is not done, one party will get the blame. Often this is the one who works most hours outside the house. Problems with the work/life balance often turn out to be problems with the work/SO balance (**Figure 5.2.2**). We should appreciate the SO is often just the messenger, signalling our overall life is out of balance. For most of us, it is a mistake to suggest work is more important than family. If we pay attention to family relationships (and other private responsibilities), invest in them and nurture them, they will remain good, grow and improve, despite work being part of the mutually agreed reality and takes (too much) time. Work can take up a lot of what should be our free quality time (evenings and weekends). Ranking work and family on the priority scale is like comparing apples with pears. Our private life is far more important than work, but there are many days when work must dominate things. This is the consequence of choices. Family commitments and work are different and cannot be measured by the same yardstick. They must exist alongside each other in harmony, respecting differences and occasional conflicts, with work supporting the overall long-term family objectives (vision and mission).

Figure 5.2.2

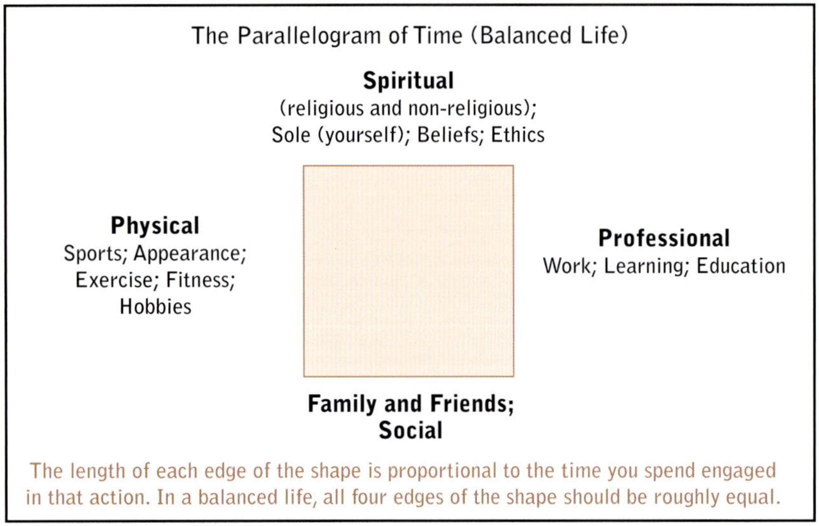

Objectives, roles and responsibilities

In order to accommodate new opportunities to allocate our available time, we need to make choices. These choices will need to be based on the nature of the tasks, projects or whatever we call the activities that keep us busy. The criteria may be importance and urgency – this is rational – but other aspects such as the appeal and fun factors are involved in the evaluation. In addition, there are real or perceived considerations of outcome and timing which also influence our decision. When these expectations are associated with people we see as important in private or work-life, this may result in them being given inappropriate priority in both time and attention.

How do we decide what is important and needs to be done, and what to reject? The classic ranking is based on importance and urgency, but this does not deal with the limited amount of available time each day, week or month. In most cases, others (boss or SO) tell us what is urgent, and request priority for themselves or their projects. Only a few people suggest their own requests are non-urgent or of lesser importance. In fact, do we ever select the "low-priority"

Figure 5.2.3

	Urgent	Not Urgent
Important	**1** Crying baby Kitchen fire Some calls	**2** Exercise Vocation Planning
Not Important	**3** Interruptions Distractions Other calls	**4** Trivia Busy work Timewasters

From: Covey S, Merrill A R, Merrill R R (1994) *First Things First: To Live, to Love, to Learn, to Leave a Legacy.* Simon and Schuster, New York.

option when sending out our own e-mails? This option could be deleted from e-mail message systems. On the other hand, the "high-priority" button is repeatedly overused. In reality, it is the receiver who needs to make the decision on importance and urgency. But based on what?

In his brilliant book *First Things First* (Simon and Schuster), best-selling author Stephen R Covey advises us to list all our life's tasks and roles, (including private, community and business), in addition to time needed for rest, sleep and vacations (**Figure 5.2.3**). Which roles and responsibilities do we have in life? They can include father, mother, spouse, partner, SO, child, neighbour, friend, society or sports club member, and so on. It is important to list all our activities and contacts that have or may have impact on our agenda because, at some point, we may need to spend time on some of them. The result of this exercise will probably be a surprisingly long list. In addition, Covey suggests we indicate how much time we plan to allocate to these roles on a daily, weekly or monthly basis. In order to make accurate judgments on time allocation, we need to be clear on our primary tasks and roles in both corporate and private life. By adding up the totals, we can get an idea of whether the allocations are realistic or not, taking into account the inflexibility of the 24-hours-a-day clock. One cannot add one second to a day.

The result of this exercise often demonstrates the impossibility of our expectations – we are unable to live up to our own perceived expectations. Unless we and our SOs jointly face up to this reality, we risk continued frustration. If the timed total exceeds the available 24 hours (don't forget to allow time for sleeping, thinking and unexpected events) it becomes obvious we need to reduce and/or delegate responsibilities. This is not easy, and requires carefully honed decisions as opposed to simply shortening all commitments until they fit. Once we have pruned the list of responsibilities and are confident with our time and agenda planning, then comes the difficult task of having to say no to some people who were on our original list. This should be done pleasantly and with confidence. We have to tell them we have insufficient time left to deal with their needs effectively. Good evaluation and planning will help us to build up the confidence to say no. By never saying no we would risk jeopardising projects that we have decided are of higher importance. There is no need to explain to others (except possibly to our boss and, of course, SO) why we need to say no, but we need to be able to explain it to ourselves and be happy with our decision. Good bosses will appreciate quality time planning and replanning based on new information. They will often help shoulder the responsibility of dropping another task to free up time. This also applies to our husband, spouse or SO.

By never saying "no", we would risk jeopardising projects that we have decided are of higher importance.

The next phase of the work plan is deciding when to schedule the allocated time. In this process it is important to consider factors such as urgency and importance, but also the amount of time that needs to be allowed for each case.

In general, it is advisable to schedule the bigger projects (procedures) first and fill up the time available with smaller commitments, especially when these are of a more flexible nature. In many cases, conflict can be avoided in a day's work by scheduling smaller, urgent and highly important projects for the following day in slots which had been left open for emergencies, enabling project deadlines to be met. Deadlines that were proposed to us, but not agreed, have limited value in most cases, (unless the deadlines were imposed on us by higher management). This can occasionally be the case, but does not often happen in modern management, as in most cases employees are responsible for their own schedule. No matter what position you are in, you most probably own at least 10 to 12 hours per day (24 minus work and minus sleep). What follows is good advice, but it does not fit in with the above.

> Knowing when to stop working on a task (or a patient) is an important element in time management.

An important part of proper planning is scheduling time for the unexpected. We know from experience that 20 per cent of our time at work each day is taken up by unexpected events. If possible, this should be moved into the category of expected, and time allocated to it. If we decide the unexpected matter is not important or urgent (Covey, box four), and does not need attention, it can be moved to the no list (group D priority). On a day when no emergencies occur, we can move tasks forward from another day to fill the slot, or just conscientiously enjoy a break. Do not forget to include some time for the unexpected, unimportant, but fun parts of life that we all come across most of the days. Often, these are the social chats and gatherings at the coffee machine. These breaks are important in another social way, being essential to stay in touch with colleagues and friends, and building networks they may even have future business or private relevance. They are in Covey boxes three and four, depending on the subject and people involved. Just plan and schedule it. Don't assume 100 per cent time efficiency, and include some downtime for a power nap or a siesta.

Execution

Time planning is not the only important aspect of quality time and task management. Effective execution is just as critical. We all are familiar with days when we had great plans to finish a project, but emergencies interfered with the planning and we ended up taking work home at night and staying up late to complete things. In retrospect, some of the day's perceived emergencies were not that important and could have been avoided by rescheduling and, in some cases, matters could have been avoided by better planning or by stating a gentle, but firm no at presentation.

We all have 24 hours every day and many people have freedom to decide what to do with a significant number of these hours, even with a 9am to 5pm job that is completely planned and scheduled by others. However, not many veterinarians are in such a position, although there are many open hours per day that we own. We manage our time, we need to make decisions, accept the consequences and communicate our decisions. If a new project comes up that potentially makes it to the list, we need to be clear on which other projects will need to be downgraded, delayed, or even deleted from the priority list.

Knowing when to stop working on a task (or a patient) is an important element in time management. Many projects do not benefit from total perfection: the difference between 95 and 100 per cent perfection may not be noticed, but the last five per cent requires significantly more time investment. An eye for detail is good – and essential in such fields as neurosurgery – but too much focus on detail may detract attention from the big picture and disrupt other tasks.

Knowing how much time is involved in each activity/task and allowing for some flexibility in the schedule is crucial to time management in a veterinary clinic. This is critical because the whole team relies on a smooth execution of the daily workload. When

the vet or the nurse is not available, other people (including pet owners) are kept waiting, and at best, are spending their time less efficiently. During the learning curve, a young veterinarian or a locum needs more time per appointment and procedure compared with an experienced veterinarian. Don't forget to schedule time for training and coaching, because if this is not done one can confidently predict agenda conflicts. For instance, when a particular appointment runs seriously over time, the veterinarian should take the initiative to allow more time when rescheduling the follow-up appointment, devoting more time to matters which had possibly been rushed in the first examination. Another way to increase flexibility in the agenda is, in suitable cases, to ask owners to leave their pets at the clinic in the morning and pick them up in the afternoon. By doing this, these cases can fill holes in the schedule. Obviously, the pet has to be ready at the designated pick-up time. Social chatting with clients can be important, but consumes valuable time and should not be overdone as it can reduce the value perception of the vet's time when he or she seems to have all the time in the world to chat. This can sometimes cause clients to question the bill.

Key accounts management

When re-evaluating and downgrading a task's urgency, it is important to recognise projects and commitments that are untouchable first priorities. These must not be at the bottom of the list, but always at the top. Typically, these are commitments to important business partners, our spouse and our children, or an important private project. These key commitments cannot be allowed to suffer under any circumstances. They have overall priority and cannot be neglected except in the most exceptional circumstances. Time management problems often turn out to be spouse management communication problems because different priority considerations compete for the

When re-evaluating and downgrading a task's urgency, it is important to recognise projects and commitments that are untouchable first priorities.

limited amount of time. Once a certain time allocation has been decided on and agreed with the key partner, this time is no longer available for other activities, whatever they are, and whenever they occur. This time slot no longer exists in the agenda, and it should be deducted from the available 24 hours per day.

A major principle of time management consists of finding and observing a balance between objectives and priorities.

- **We cannot add a minute to a day**

Of course, there should be an option for the exceptional case. However, this option should be used only with extreme care and only after cautious and quality key account management to make up for it. By definition, this can be done successfully only when practised as an exception and with genuine appreciation for the support to solve the agenda conflict. When these time-conflict cases are treated as a routine, gratitude loses its value and kills the key-account relationship. SO relationships are the foundations of our long-term happiness, health and well-being. Compromising key-account relations, whether business or private, is not an option.

The clock and the compass

Agenda planning, project scheduling and time management are part of a bigger reality – the project of our life. Before we can manage something we need to be clear on what we want, why we want it, and whether we want it now or later. In order to help answer these questions, some people decide to develop their personal mission statement.. This describes what they want to achieve in life and what is important for them, or in other words how they want to be remembered. Where do you want to go? Both in professional as well as in private life we need to have a clear idea on:

- where we are;
- where we want to go, and
- how we want to get there.

The agenda, time issues and the clock are all

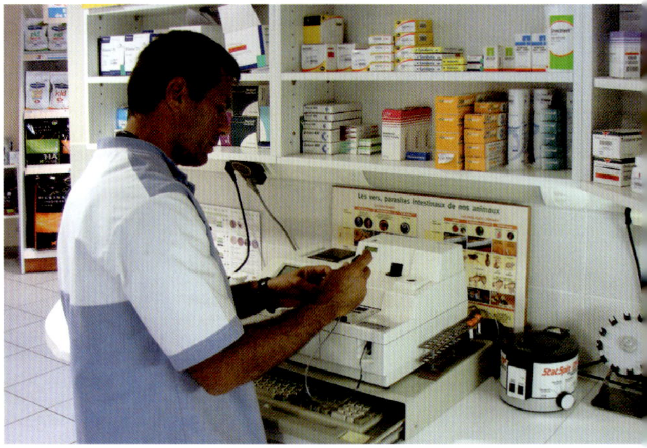

part of the third point – the first and second points comprise the important process of "where am I?" and "where do I want to go?"

A clock can partially and conditionally (as long as the position of the sun is known) help us decide direction, but only one tool can do this infallibly and that is the compass. It conveys long-term reference points (north, south, east and west) and position and goal related to known coordinates. It does not provide details of how to get there, but it does give direction. When we are directed to travel over land we can choose to walk, use a bike or a car or choose public transport. Where we need to cross water, we might decide to use a boat (when swimming is not an option). When time is pressing, we may consider a helicopter or plane (then we must consider the landing options on arrival). The car, boat and plane, are all "how" alternatives, but first we need to know "where" we are and where we want to go to. These conditions and circumstances will determine the optimal way "to get there".

It is important to keep this analogy in mind when planning and scheduling the agenda.

- Where do we want to go, and which achievements

do we want to add to our personal list?

- How do we want to be remembered?
- Is it important to always be on time and informed, or is it more important to be recognised as an open person who listens and demonstrates flexibility when it is required?

Dali's famous clock painting (The Persistence of Memory) illustrates the flexibility of time. It helps to recognise there might be times when private matters are more important. Time and task/responsibility management is about priorities and ownership of both clock and agenda while following your compass. It is about:

- taking responsibility for the part of the agenda that you control;
- being happy with your choices and decisions; and
- not hiding behind the excuse that you have or had no time.

Each of us has 24 hours per day and it is up to us to decide how to spend them. We also need to accept and appreciate that other people may, for whatever business, personal or cultural reasons, decide on a different priority ranking. Remember: there is more than one road that leads to Rome.

Time management in veterinary practice

Veterinarians and staff often work under great pressure from clients, animals and assistants. Telephones, emergencies, surgical procedures that does not run as planned, unexpected visits and problems passed on by reception or colleagues are just a few things that can make our days miserable or difficult. We should be aware that stress is a common cause of distress and is a syndrome recognised by the medical profession.

Major reasons for time-management related stress in the veterinary practice are:

- distraction from major tasks;
- not planning for the unexpected (the everyday emergency);
- waiting until the last minute;
- trying to accomplish everything at once;
- lack of preparation;
- lack of communication and staff delegation;
- lack of training;
- lack of clarity in objectives;
- absence of task priority; and
- handling non-urgent (and sometimes even non-important) tasks as urgent when under pressure from the owner or referring veterinarian.

A major principle of time management consists of finding and observing a balance between objectives and priorities (**Figure 5.2.4**).
But what is a priority? A priority is the most important action to reach an objective – in this definition, the crucial word is action.
Unfortunately, if you have a passive attitude, you are more likely to be overwhelmed by various tasks that are falling on your shoulders. Also, bear in

We should be aware that stress is a common cause of distress and is a syndrome recognised by the medical profession.

Figure 5.2.4

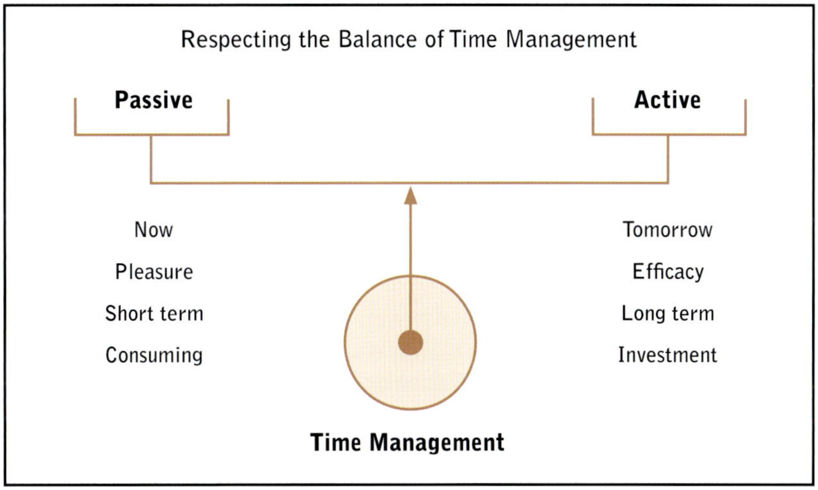

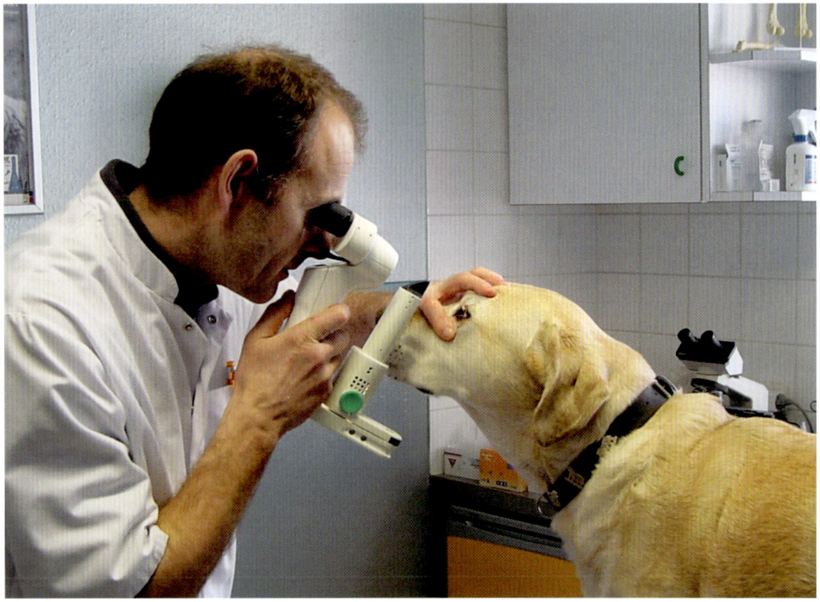

> The process of effective time management begins with accepting and taking responsibility for your personal agenda.

mind the importance of a task relates not so much to what you are doing, but why you are doing it. A good practical way to handle any situation where you question the best use of time is to simply ask: is this the best way to use my time to accomplish this task?

Delegation is a highly effective way to reduce time-related stress. However, it requires a change in attitude by many veterinarians to ask someone else to do a task. In many cases, well-trained staff do an excellent job, which often results in a high level of satisfaction for themselves and owners – all at a lower cost to the practice. After quality training and coaching, clinic staff can be a great help in managing the vets' overloaded schedule.

The principle of Pareto (or the law of 20/80) tells us to look at the results of our efforts. It is a widely accepted general principle in economics that 20 per cent of one's products correspond to 80 per cent of one's income. When striving for optimal use of resources one should, therefore, concentrate on these 20 per cent products and services as they are the core of our activity. Although veterinary practice field studies suggest this 20 per cent might, in reality, be nearer 40 per cent , the principle still holds good and demands we focus our resources to optimum advantage. Why spend time on things that are not crucial and are not within your 20/80? Everyone has his or her 20/80.

If you and your staff are well organised, you will gain a stronger professional recognition from those that come to your practice, not only from clients, but also from colleagues and suppliers (see **Section 5.3**). This will inculcate a better confidence in yourself and your team. You will work with more efficacy and improve your productivity, making your life more comfortable. At the end of the day, your self esteem and image will also be improved, increasing your and your team's job satisfaction.

Summary and conclusion

Time management is an issue for many people. It seems as if we don't have enough time to cope with all our roles and responsibilities. Information overload, ease of travel and modern communication technology increasingly leads people to feel busy, busy, busy – and still are losing the battle against the clock.

The process of effective time management begins with accepting and taking responsibility for your personal agenda. Based on your personal priorities, decide what course you sail (compass) and how much time you are happy to spend on each role and responsibility. The clock offers us all just 24 hours in a day – and not a split second more. We need to take charge and organise, manage and enjoy that time.

Organisation of the practice

5.3

Value of a good working organisation

If you and your staff are well organised, your image will improve, and you will gain better professional recognition from staff, reps, colleagues, clients and suppliers. Being better organised will help your daily working efficiency and develop your management confidence. A good organisation induces better productivity and better comfort. At the end of the day, your improved self esteem and self-image also increases your personal satisfaction.

The importance of confidence

The more people you have working together in a team, the more there is need for a certain level of organisation and discipline, and the less room for improvisation. Some may see this as the downside of a larger number of team members or human resources. However, it is also through staff expansion and development that you can provide services to your clients – simply because there are only 24 hours in a day and you cannot do it all alone. In order to reach an acceptable level of quality, and to be able to control it day after day, there is need for a good, organised practice where policies and procedures are known and applied by the entire team. Once you have reached that level of organisation, you and your staff should automatically gain confidence, and the quality of service delivery is improved. On a practical level, remember to take notes and manage details, using a practice notebook or liaison pad where you and your staff can retrieve information and communicate internally. This can be a file in paper or digital format.

Practice policies and procedures

There is a list of organisation points that you need to plan, establish, review and possibly change with time. Ideally, all these procedures should be written in a practice procedure manual, such as a ring-bound type of folder where documents are added and removed as needed. It is kept as the definitive source of internal procedure information that all staff can use to learn or review certain methods the clinic has established. Once this

The more people you have working together in a team, the more there is need for a certain level of organisation and discipline, and the less room for improvisation.

Practical organising tips

- Know where to find information: the important matter is not to remember it all, but to know where to find the answer.
- Know the internal rules: in a vet clinic, this could include issues related to appointments, pricing, news from hospitalised pets, classification, medical records, computing, cleaning, payment modes and arrival and departure formalities.
- Know the common elective procedures: elective surgeries, hospitalisation, nutrition, vaccination, identification and pet insurance policies.
- Know the calendar: by month, week, and day. This can be achieved with a reminder system for various issues such as bank deposit, accounting deadlines, taxes deadlines, cleaning, supplies ordering and mailing.
- Know how to delegate and share tasks among the team. Examples include giving one of the receptionists the responsibility for sending client reminders and for stock maintenance.

The logistics associated with an appointment system are simple, but can be tricky.

form of documentation is created (usually done progressively), it becomes a valuable information source for training new employees, temporary human resources and so on. As certain procedure (for example: documents issued for patients discharge after long-term hospitalisation) are adopted, an outline form describing the procedure is inserted in the clinic manual where everyone can find and use it. New documents should always be dated in order to know which one is the most recent version.

Questions and themes for a practice policies and procedures manual

Opening hours

- Patient admission.
- Consultations.
- Reception and OTC sales.
- Emergency services.
- Weekend services.

Appointments

For optimum management of reception areas and appointment systems, determine the average time taken for regular events.

- Hours of heavy traffic.
- Average time of regular office calls, and speciality examinations.
- Each vet's plan.
- Individual personal preferences.
- Patient discharges.
- Walk-ins.

Enquiries about hospitalised patients

Answer the following questions.

- What time is best (for the clinic and clients) for follow-up calls?
- Should clients be forced to use these specific time slots?
- Should the vet surgeon answer enquiries? If not, who should it be?
- Should the answers (news about hospitalised pets) be planned and prepared ahead of the calls?
- Should the vet surgeon call the client? At what time? Should the pet's owner's phone number be written on the hospitalisation form?
- Would it be appropriate for someone else to call the client?

Establishing payment methods

Answer the following questions.

- Should the total amount owing be divided into several payments? If so, with what frequency, and what is the paperwork linked to such a procedure?
- Should clients pay at the end of treatments?
- Should clients pay when the animal is discharged, or at the end of each office call (when there are several short visits)?

"Organisation of daily activities results in a better work and a better life, and are part of a pleasant job environment"

General comments about an appointment service

Numerous clinics still work with no client appointments or a limited access to appointments. We believe that most clients favour services where they are taken care of personally and immediately. By using limited access to appointments (or no appointments), you are not matching clients' needs and expectations. It is true that offering an appointment service takes time and effort, but when you work in a service-oriented business, such as a veterinary clinic, you should seriously consider adopting such a system. The average waiting time for clients in a practice should not exceed 15 to 20 minutes. This the longest wait level usually accepted by clients, particularly if they have an appointment. For people who made an appointment, even a 10-minute wait may be interpreted negatively. Basically, waiting for 15 minutes is a long time – just try it yourself. To initiate an appointment service, you may follow the general guidelines that refer to any new service.

Appointment management and setting up appointments

Once you (and your team) are convinced that setting up an appointment service is appropriate and will help your clients, their pets and your practice, you need to do it well. The logistics associated with such a system are simple, but can be tricky. You need to use an appointment book or log, paper or electronic. Whether you use an appointment book or a computer file set for your appointments, the same principles will apply. The appointment pages must function in a simple mode, adapted to your working day. It needs to be clear and easily visualised by any person looking at these pages. It is often beneficial to separate outpatient examinations from surgical or in-house procedures (diagnostic, or treatment), using, for example, two appointment books or pages, one for surgery and special procedures services (requiring a stay in the clinic) and one for examinations and visits as outpatients. Most veterinary practice-management software includes appointment management systems. Some even use and include the possibility for clients to set up their appointments via the practice website. Obviously, these services will help practice organisation as well as clients' access to your services.

Client convenient services = client satisfaction = client loyalty.

The in-patient appointment book (surgery, special procedures, diagnostics, hospitalisation and boarding) does not need many details. It can be divided into half days, and also by practitioner. Once the book is completed, it can be used to transfer the various pet procedures on to a wallboard where all in-house animals should be logged. Such a board is usually placed within the technical area of the clinic (treatment room, for example). Such an appointment book can also be used to insert all outside calls and visits – including those related to large animals, if you work in a mixed practice. It is better to separate the appointment book into areas that include patient and client names, patient's signalment, client phone number and, of course, the reason for the clinic stay. These details may seem superfluous and require time, but you will save time at the end and it will, therefore, be a time investment in your organisation. Sometimes you may include the tentative duration of stay (short term or long term) and the duration of the planned procedure. Other information such as the medical status of the patient or past problems with the animal (or the owner), may be also added to the book (examples may include cardiac or renal insufficiency, allergies, owner attention to details and animal temperament).

Appointment log book

The appointment log, a book or a computer file, should be practical and easy to use. It should clearly detail the days and weeks and help organise your working day, and the division of tasks among the team. It is often better to divide the pages into vertical columns (either per room, or per clinician). The horizontal lines should be placed at time intervals that divide the day into 15 or 20-minute blocks. This system is easy to adapt to any practice. For example, if you need to use 30 minutes (perhaps for a long examination) it is convenient to use two blocks of 15 minutes. Using such a system, means a quick glance is enough for you to see what your day will look like and plan accordingly; similarly for your week planner. Veterinarians' absences and special meetings can also be included on such pages (either on the side or on the top of each day or each column. We like to add a column devoted only to show-up cases, particularly

Avoid having four consecutive clients coming in every 15 minutes for an hour, and then no-one for an hour.

The average waiting time for clients in a practice should not exceed 15 to 20 minutes. This the longest wait level usually accepted by clients, particularly if they have an appointment.

if this is a consistent problem in the practice, or if a designated person is allocated to these cases.

In our experience, this system has worked quite well. It is simple, yet very efficient. We suggest adding buffer cases between appointment slots. This helps prevent major delays and allows for an important or sudden client arrival. These slots represent virtual appointments and should only be filled at the last minute, and as a last resort. A good example is when a client calls in the morning and all appointments are filled, the animal has been sick all night and the owner wishes to see someone. The receptionist knows that there are no open slots, but a virtual appointment exists at 10am. The receptionist may say in such a case: "Sorry, Mrs Smith, all our appointments are taken, but why don't you come a little before 10am and I'll arrange for a doctor to see your pet". In this way, the virtual appointment has been filled to satisfy a semi-emergency, and this is done without upsetting an already busy schedule.

These virtual slots should be spread around the day and dispatched between all examining veterinarians. In cases where no one takes the slots, this time can be used to call clients, and take care of in-house patients. When there is a busy day, and delays have accumulated, these virtual appointments help decrease overtime at the end of the day. They are time-management tools to manage the unexpected (see **Section 5.2**).

A slot box can be used for information about the patient (name, species, cause of visit) and the owner (name, phone number). By adding the pet's name, you add value to reception. People and pets can be greeted by name, and an appointment for several pets will allow time to fill a suitable number of cases or lines. Similarly, if you ask for the patient's record

number, and find out it is a first visit, then you know that such a patient deserves more time (at least two slot boxes) and you can ask them if they know how to get to the clinic. Again, time investment and detail management improves performance and makes better use of allocated time slots. The purpose of the examination should also be briefly noted in the book – such as *V* for annual vaccination healthcheck, *derm* for skin problem, or *limp* for a lameness. These details allow you to better tailor the time slots required for each case. For example, the presence of lameness in a large dog may tell you that some time-consuming radiographs will be needed. Similarly a examination for a behavioural problem will always deserve more time. Be aware of this information and schedule appointments accordingly.

A common beginner's mistake is to fill the appointments one after the other as they call in. It is better to spread the appointments as much as possible along the day and avoid having four consecutive clients coming in every 15 minutes for an hour and then no-one for an hour. To make sure you fill the appointment book according to your preferences, it is easy and practical to offer two appointment times, both of which should suit you. The client will generally pick one of these options. Example: " Mr Smith, I can propose a visit either at 11am or would you prefer this evening at 6pm?" Finally, it is important the receptionist knows and understands each practitioner's needs. It is human nature that people will have their personal preferences, and it is important to adapt the appointment scheduling to the wishes of the people in charge of receiving patients.

Appointment for patient discharges

Most practices give appointments for incoming patients, usually outpatients. Few give appointments for the release of pets (animals leaving the practice after being hospitalised for a short term). With increased use of in-house patient management and the use of half-day hospitalisation (day or external hospital), this technique is useful and should help significantly improve clinic traffic and both client and staff satisfaction. Most practices ask clients to come and pick up their pets after a certain time (usually 5pm or something of that nature), with no precise time. The result is often disastrous, because most people arrive at the same time. The resulting traffic creates a jam at the reception counter, with several animals to discharge, in addition to the regular appointments and possibly some clients coming in to buy some products such as pet food. Everyone is unhappy and stressed, and work is done in a hurry, with no time for client communication. To avoid or reduce this sort of incident, the technique is simple. You add a column on the appointment book dedicated to patient discharges (the same as incoming examinations, every 15 or 20 minutes). When a pet is hospitalised for any procedure and you know the time of discharge, then you give a firm and precise appointment to the person, instead of an approximate period: "Could you pick up Tessa at 5.45pm or do you prefer 6.20pm?" Again, two choices. In some cases (ideally) these patients' discharges will be handled by veterinarians. However, it may not always be the best use of their time, and some discharges can be done as well (or maybe even better) by receptionists or nurses. This is particularly true for conventional diagnostic or treatment procedures (identifications, bandages and cat castrations). Often, the team synergy can work best with a veterinarian coming to greet the owner of the pet being discharged, telling them briefly how the procedure was conducted and its outcome, and then referring to the nurse who will take care of explanations and practical details: "I operated on Tessa, it went well. She woke up normally. She will be tired for a day or so. Anita will bring her to you and explain some details concerning her diet and the management of the bandage. I will see you in a few days or so for the control. Please make an appointment with Anita."

Appointment via the internet

Travellers can book their airline flights and print the boarding pass directly via the internet. People are familiar with an online booking system and dentists and human doctors have adopted the system for online appointment booking – to everyone's satisfaction. Similarly, such a direct service should be considered and used by veterinary clinics. Clients can use it 24/7 without using precious staff time. Time is saved, but also efficacy and clients who have been brought up with computers are active in processing a service and are more inclined to use it.

In-house patient management

The clinic should be equipped with sufficient hospitalisation capacity (cages, runs or room and suites). It is better time management to schedule procedures on an out-patient or day hospitalisation format. This is particularly true for senior check-ups or any procedure that requires several steps (such as radiographs, blood-work, ultrasound and physical examinations) or any procedure that demands

It is not uncommon for pet owners to mention they go to a specific practice because that is where their pet's medical record is kept.

> It is better time management to schedule procedures on an out-patient or day hospitalisation format.

anaesthesia or sedation (dental work and certain imaging techniques). Some hospitalisation forms should be used and distributed to clients once such a procedure is scheduled. These forms add value to the examination or test as they describe the service and remind clients of practical details such as appointment time, and any precaution prior to hospitalisation (such as removing all food from the animal 12 hours prior to hospitalisation, bringing a urine or faecal sample). These forms may also include logistical details and remind the client to pick up the pet after or at a certain hour, to call, or to leave their phone number. On some forms, you may also include some information about additional tests on some forms, not only to suggest questions and generate additional services, but also to show clients the scope of services and diagnostic procedures For example, one may include a block of text at the bottom of the hospitalisation form, with some explanations regarding pre-anaesthesia check-ups. This information can be divided into two differentiated panel, one being the standard pre-anaesthetic panel and the second being the premium panel. Clients will ultimately ask which one you recommend, but the importance of such information is that it generates client awareness about the preventive services that you provide and recommend. If they don't proceed immediately, chances are they will in the future. You invest and communicate for a long-term client relationship.

Once this form is distributed to clients, they are asked to bring it with their pet on the day of the procedure. Hopefully, most people will remember to do that, on arrival and admission, you will gain a lot of time and be more efficient. The receptionist knows immediately why the animal is there and, when the pet is hospitalised, the form will be placed on the cage or close by. The clinician and technicians can add all pertinent information, including treatment details. On discharge, that same form can be used to prepare a prescription, medication, recommendations and invoices. We also recommend keeping these forms (particularly for long-term hospitalisation) in the patient record file, (at least for a certain period) in case there is a need to control or justify any details internally or with the owner. If there is any question, or even a dispute, it is always important and useful to refer to documents that can help you identify the source of the potential problem.

Walk-in client management

As discussed above, it is our recommendation to organise office calls using an appointment schedule. However, there will always be instances of people showing up without an appointment. This may vary from one place to another because there are some local cultural habits associated with consumer behaviour, or simply because, in the past, veterinarians were open at all times and did not use appointment systems. People showing up without an appointment may trigger turmoil and generate levels of stress and discomfort at the reception. The following suggestions on handling these walk-ins, (which should apply in most cases) will take care of the animals and owners, and yet avoid any major disorganisation in the clinic.

Some basic principles on appointments management

- **Respecting the 15 or 20 minutes planned into your book for each office call.**

As a rule, if a case needs further time, it should be either rescheduled for the second part of the diagnosis (*we will do the imaging tomorrow*) or the patient should be hospitalised (*we need to keep your pet to perform the necessary diagnosis and treatment*). Failing in such strict timing will always result in an accumulation of delays that will jeopardise smooth daily activity, including being late for all further appointments. It is crucial to find out and note the reason for the office call at the time the appointment is taken. This simple step allows you and your staff to allocate the respective appointment schedule according to the potential time that will be needed for each patient (annual health visit, behaviour problem, new client, puppy, multiple pets with a single owner or euthanasia). Owners can be informed if they need to book two slots (such as for a behaviour examination). This implicitly tells them there will, potentially, be a higher fee for this longer examination time. It remains your choice as to whether to charge for any additional time.

- **Always give priority to appointments.**

Emergency cases, by definition, should be attended to immediately and should never use the normal appointment path. If you don't have a dedicated person or system to move emergencies through a dedicated pathway, we suggest you move them towards an alternative pathway, away from the regular waiting area, even if you have noticed the patient was not in any distress and did not show any signs needing urgent actions. If there is only one vet available on duty, all clients with appointments should immediately be informed of the urgency and the possible delays. Alternatives should be offered (such as waiting, leaving the animal or setting up another appointment). If, for example, the emergency case requires further time than initially estimated, make sure these clients are kept aware of the situation. Most clients will not object to the inconvenience as long as they are treated fairly and informed about the problem.

- **If a person shows up without an appointment.**

If the situation is not urgent, there are some procedures we recommend that will help you, your staff and clients to manage the situation. The first step consists of telling the person that the clinic works with an appointment system and, in future, it would be best for them to make an appointment, except for emergencies. You could add, however, that even in the case of any urgent event, clients should call first as they will receive initial instructions, and if the animal needs to be seen, the clinic staff can prepare for the arrival of the urgent case and plan appropriate actions.

People showing up without an appointment may trigger turmoil and generate levels of stress and discomfort at reception.

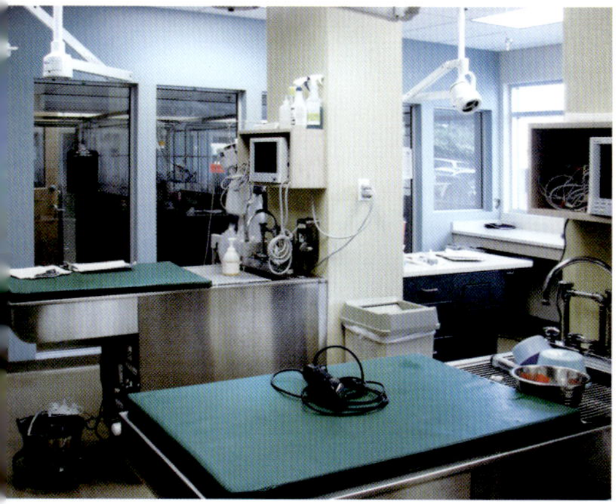

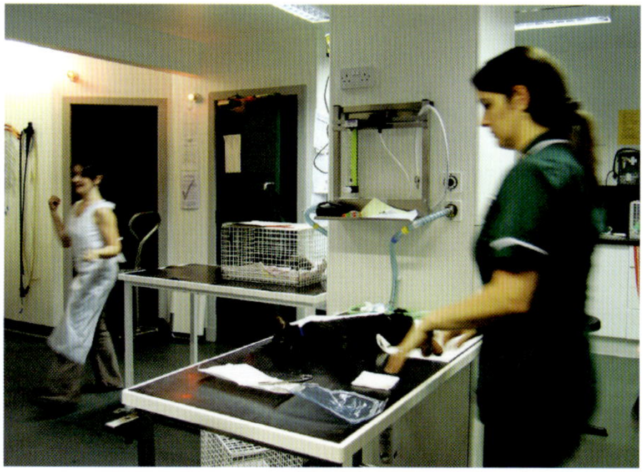

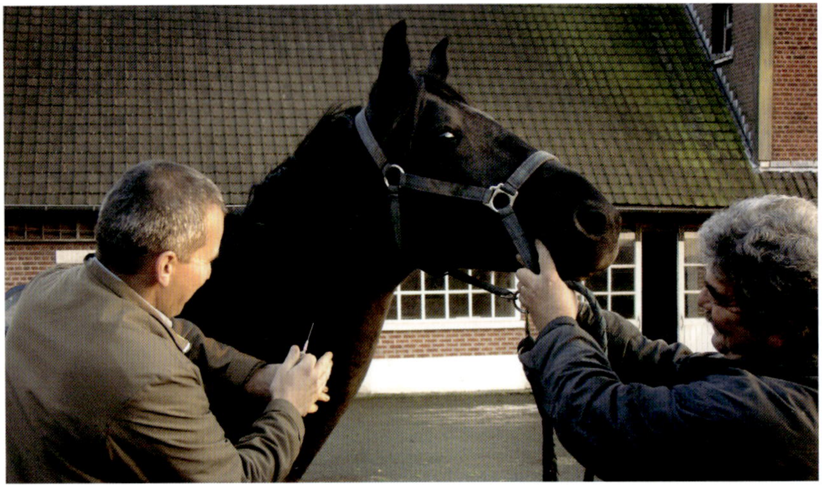

For people who made an appointment, even a 10-minute wait may be interpreted negatively.

- **The walk-in case should be given several alternatives.**

– Waiting, knowing that appointments will have priority. An estimation of the waiting time should be determined, preferably sufficiently long.
– Setting-up an appointment later in the day or the next day.
– Leaving the pet to be hospitalised (at no extra cost?) with all instructions for the office call (a questionnaire form could be used to complete basic questions for the case history). In such a case it is a good idea to write down the owner's mobile phone number, in case the veterinarian needs to contact the client about the pet's history or simply to obtain the client's authorisation to proceed with certain diagnostics or treatment.

- **Thanking the person.**

Thank them for their assistance in making the walk-in procedure easy and pleasant for everyone, and beneficial for pets and people.

Any modification of the appointment schedule and organisation requires planning and communication internally with staff, and with clients. We recommend anticipating any such changes with sufficient time (three to six months) to enable you to communicate with all clients about the future changes in your appointment system (poster within the clinic, emails and client mailing).

Client communication regarding hospitalised pets

Pet hospitalisation for diagnostic tests or treatment has triggered a new situation that many veterinarians did not expect or think of: clients will always call or need to be informed about their pet's health progress. This is normal. In many cases, the ideal method is to call the clients and be proactive. This requires time and good organisation from the staff and vets in the practice. Setting up a time slot to call clients is a method that can be used. You can also use the virtual appointment slots (see above) to make phone calls. If your website allows this feature, you can write information directly on the patient's file and clients can retrieve it. Problems occur when vet and staff try to contact clients and find they don't have the telephone number handy or get an answering machine. To reduce the chances of this happening, we recommend noting the number in the phone log or on the hospitalisation pet form, including the time when people can be reached. The few minutes spent adding this information will save a lot of time and frustration.

Another solution is to suggest to clients that they call at a certain time (that suits you), making sure the information is ready and available. For example: "News about pets in the hospital could be obtained by calling between 10am and 11am or between 4pm and 5pm." In such a case, we suggest the person in charge at reception or the front desk retrieves all information about hospitalised patients prior to these time periods and keeps it handy. A hospital information log book could be also used and placed next to the telephone. To avoid multiple log books, a single manual could be used to collect all information and messages. Another system is to use the practice management software and allocate a page for in-house hospital patients, including information and news.

Tools to improve clinic organisation

Many tools could be used to help with clinic organisation. If your clinic reaches a certain size (and even for small facilities) it is often helpful to plan an interphone or paging system. Veterinarians move throughout the hospital, often busy with a patient, or talking to a client or a colleague.

In all circumstances, it is important for the receptionist to be able to contact everyone without leaving his or her position at the front desk. Interphones (hand-free systems) and intercom pagers will allow them to contact people. Even if the veterinarian is busy and cannot take the phone or interrupt his or her present actions, these systems often allow the vet to let the front desk know briefly what action is needed and what answer can be transferred (for example: "Dr Smith asked if you could call back at 5pm", or "Can you give me your phone number and Dr Smith will call you as soon as he is finished with his current appointment").

Using such systems and tools allows for improved organisation and better client service while improving your workload. This system is also a practical way to improve time management (see **Section 5.2**) and make working life easier.

Electronic management and practice management software

The question is no longer should you install a computer system to manage your practice, but rather when will you move forward, if you have not done so already. Farm animal breeders use computers to manage their business, so your clients – including farmers – would not understand why the veterinarian continues with a manual system, using aging paper systems to manage the medical records, patients' information data, stock and financial information. Pet owners use other medical or health services (physicians, opticians and physiotherapists) and are used to seeing computers at all times. Practice management software systems are numerous and offer features to improve practice management.

The long-term value of your clientele will be directly related to your client data and the content of your patient records. This means any investment to collect and keep additional information about your clients and their pets/animals is increasing the value of your practice, in addition to helping you manage daily activities. Our recommendation is not only to use electronic data collection through a computerised practice system, but also to collect information and use computers in your examination room and enter data in the presence of clients.

This may sound quite basic for all young colleagues or veterinary undergraduates where computers have been an integral part of their education, and the use of a keyboard should not be an objection. One of the more advanced applications of computer technology in the hospital is the use of staff fingerprint recognition in medical supplies' dispensers for in the clinic. Only after the computer has registered the staff member's identity (fingerprint), pet and owner details will the machine dispatch the requested item. (Much like a Coca Cola dispenser that only releases the bottle after you have inserted coins or a debit card.) Immediate data transfer adds the items' costs to the patient's bill. This system prevents significant losses,

The long-term value of your clientele will be directly related to your client data and the content of your patient records.

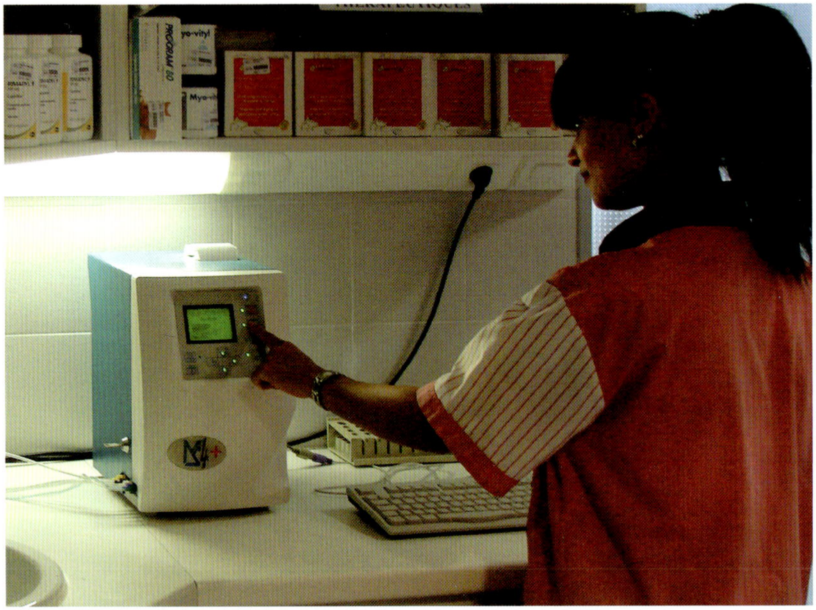

especially when dealing with emergency cases where urgency does not guarantee the team members remember and register all details.

> One of the more advanced applications of computer technology in the hospital is the use of staff fingerprint recognition in medical supplies' dispensers for in the clinic.

Practice management software should include all aspects of clinic management. Recent systems (such as Vetstreet from MediMedia) include interfaces with the practice's website that allow clients to access their pet's medical record (Pet Portal), and receive dedicated information pertinent to their need and their pet's medical condition (such as obese cat, diabetic dog). If the clients elect this option, the information is sent to them via personalised emails or SMS, including reminders and any other messages.

We recommend moving toward a paperless organisation, and even all digital where not only medical records are kept on the clinic server, but also all digital images and laboratory data received from external sources. This allows direct communication with suppliers (automated stock maintenance), clinic staff (intranet information), external consultants (such as accountant, bookkeeper and practice manager) and current and future clients (via the website). Time taken to collect the information is well worthwhile and will pay for itself, simply because this data will be the most important part of your clinic appraisal evaluation.

Clients attach increasing importance to their pet's medical record. It is not uncommon for pet owners to mention they go to a specific practice because that is where their pet's medical record is kept. All aspects of such a medical record system, including various reminders, automatic appointment system and access to their pet's medical record via the website, are all good reasons to remain loyal and value the full service provided by the practice. It is all about consumer services and convenience.

Summary and conclusion

A well-organised business is a prerequisite. It allows work efficiency and work satisfaction, a well-structured working environment is crucial in generating productive working time and it triggers a positive and professional image to clients. Organising your working place requires time and effort. It implies the setting of procedures and a certain level of discipline from the entire team. The larger the practice, the more important is such management. Various tools assist in better workplace organisation – it is our recommendation that you select and use those tools best suited to your practice needs.

6

Practice Finances

In this section:

Setting the fees

Financial indicators

Setting the fees 6.1

Introduction

THE VERY NATURE of running a business means charging an accurate price in exchange for products and services. In general, veterinarians find it hard to charge their clients, particularly for time spent in examinations and surgeries. Historically, veterinarians charged for medications and procedures, but did not charge for an examination when both the client and the vet perceived that nothing happened except a physical exam and a conversation; few vets charge clients for a telephone consultation. However, in the former instance, the result was some expert advice by the veterinarian. In many cases, the practitioner injected a medication (often antibiotics or a multivitamin cocktail) and followed up with oral medication for a week, and maybe included a dietetic pet food. This would provide a perceived reason for a reasonable charge for the examination.

Obviously, the old-fashioned approach to charging for products and services cannot be the basis for a healthy price policy in a modern practice. It dates back to when the community had only one vet and provided the practitioner's annual income. Time was not an issue; the veterinarian (and his wife) was on call 24 hours a day, and responded when he was called for help. Times have changed. Clients are aware they have various options when choosing a veterinarian, and will make the choice based on reasons that have most relevance for them. Cost is a reason, although quality is more important in the case of the strong human/pet bond. Owners are mobile and willing to drive significant distances if there is a good reason. The practice has to calculate and set prices based on sound business (marketing and sales) decisions. In general, veterinarians around the world (and their staff) continue to be surprised by the price that many owners are willing and able to pay for (perceived) high-quality pet healthcare. Owners unable to pay the price should be

In general, veterinarians find it hard to charge their clients, particularly for time spent in examinations and surgeries.

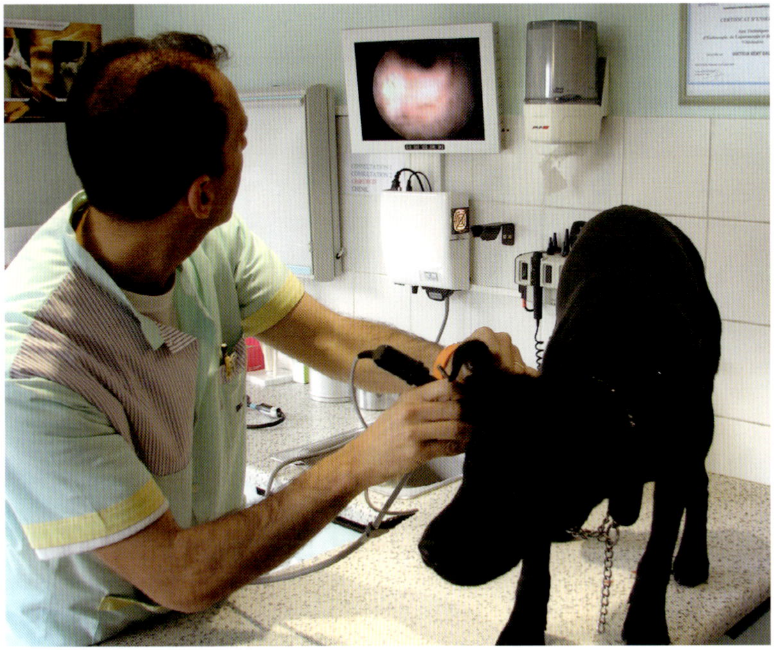

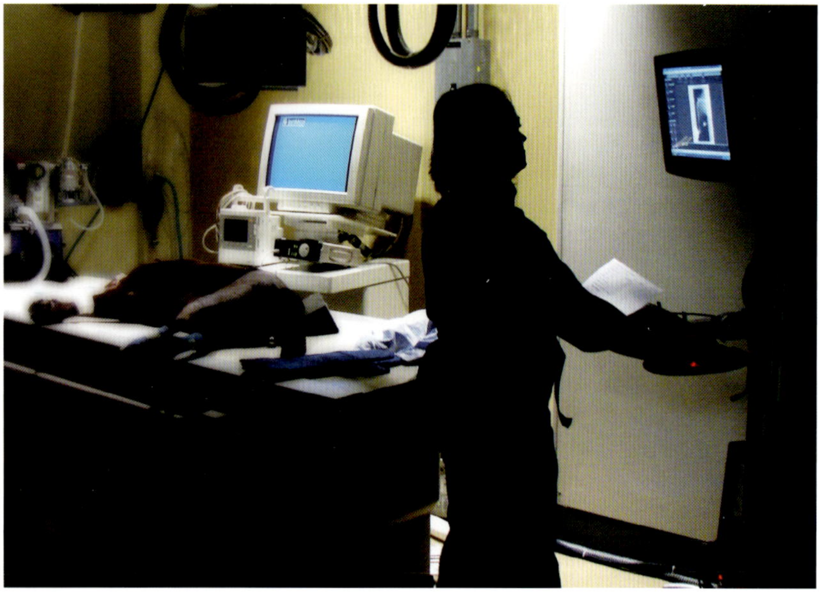

Classic learning experiences

A classic, personal learning experience was hearing the remark by a board certified surgeon (Diplomate ACVS) that his hospital was indeed very interested to know the price per procedure in all clinics in the area (and did not intend to be at the same price level). Their philosophy was that their hospital provided the best possible healthcare in the area, and they wanted to always charge at least 10 to 20 per cent more than any of the other vets. They could not keep up with the ever-increasing patient load, despite the presence of many colleagues charging significantly lower fees next door.

In a second example, a brand-new hospital in the area offered surgical services by ACVS Diplomates and did not reduce the workload for existing non-boarded surgeons, but did increase the fee they could charge for the same procedure. They enjoyed the rising tide.

Another of our friends, a board certified surgeon (Diplomate ECVS) working downtown in one of the major European capitals, had too much work and wanted to reduce the workload. He decided to increase prices by more than 30 per cent overnight and had calculated that this should not reduce his profits, even if it reduced the number of cases. It turned out that he gained more clients – despite the higher price – and ended up hiring two colleagues to satisfy the demand.

advised to look for alternative services – preferably before an acute health problem makes them visit the practice in the middle of the night. In some countries, pet health insurance provides peace of mind for both the owner and the veterinarian. Owners should be advised about the availability of such services when they first visit the practice.

General methodology principals

The client fee should have a logical basis and be transparent, because we are likely to be questioned on the fees or asked to quote a fee in advance for a routine procedure. We should be able to justify our response. Fees are charged for the provision of a service – whether it is a clinical examination, a surgical intervention or, more difficult for veterinarians than lawyers, advice given without hands-on contact. Fees do not include the sale of veterinary medicines as a part of, or in parallel to, the provision of a service. The sale of medicines and other products (for example, pet food) should be charged separately. For these products, the retail price should take into account the cost price, plus storage costs, out of date losses, broken bottles and left-from-shelf items, as well as a profit on the exercise. A dispensing fee, if charged, is for providing the service and is not linked to the value of the commodity.

Earning time

As a rule, all practice costs, other than those related to medicines, should be recovered by the fees. This could be evaluated in daily fee-earning time. To some extent, this time is outside our control, but if a practice's average working day is approximately nine hours, you will be fee earning for only four to seven hours. This excludes driving time, which is of great importance in large animal and equine work. The number of fee-earning hours is critical because, when multiplied by the number of annual working days, it provides the total number of working hours for which you can reasonably charge your clients in a year. If you know how much you need to earn for the practice (excluding VAT) in a year, then it is simple to determine what hourly rate you must apply to your fees.

Fact versus emotion

Setting the right price for a product or a service is an important part of the business in veterinary practice. Factors that influence the price level are based on facts and on emotions.

- Facts include:
  - cost of the goods; and
  - price charged by the competition.
- Emotions include:
  - perception of the price level by the client; and
  - perception of the price level by the veterinarian and the nurse.

Many practice team members (vets and nurses) are reluctant to ask the right price and are even willing to charge below the cost price – in many cases, not charging for availability, time involved and or fixed costs.

The costs of goods and services include the purchase price, taxes, stocking, damage, out-of-date provision and a percentage of the practice's total fixed costs, including human resources. The price charged by a competitor is another important element, although there can be very good reasons to charge higher fees than the competition. Other veterinary outlets may be non-comparable when it comes to quality; clients understand and appreciate that quality comes with a price, and will be happy to pay a premium for this higher level of quality healthcare if the value and quality are well communicated (marketed). In many businesses, the product price is not based on the cost of goods, but rather on what the client is willing to pay. Obviously, market and client knowledge are essential to determine the price point.

Table 6.1.1. **Fee plus 10%**

	Before	After	Change
Total sales	200,000	220,000	10%
Number of transactions	4,000	4,000	–
Average transaction fee	50	55	10%
Average variable costs	15	15	–
Total variable costs	60,000	60,000	–
Total fixed cost	75,000	75,000	–
Profit	65,000	85,000	30.8%

Table 6.1.2. **Fee plus 10%, visits minus 10%**

	Before	After	Change
Total sales	200,000	198,000	-1%
Number of transactions	4,000	3,600	-10%
Average transaction fee	50	55	10%
Average variable costs	15	15	–
Total variable costs	60,000	54,000	-10%
Total fixed cost	75,000	75,000	–
Profit	65000	69000	6.2%

Table 6.1.3. **Fee minus 10%, visits plus 17%**

	Before	After	Change
Total sales	200,000	209,970	5%
Number of transactions	4,000	4,666	16.7%
Average transaction fee	50	45	-10%
Average variable costs	15	15	–
Total variable costs	60,000	69,990	16.7%
Total fixed cost	75,000	75,000	–
Profit	65,000	64,980	–

Note that lowering the fee has a dramatic impact on profits unless there is a substantial increase in the number of visiting clients (6.1.3). However, a fee increase, despite a lower number of transactions, results in a higher profit (6.1.2).

Veterinarians continue to be surprised by the price that many owners are willing and able to pay for high-quality pet healthcare.

Competition based on (low) pricing is a very limited and risky way to compete. It restricts creativity, creates a downward business spiral and eventually kills the business.

Influence of pricing on revenues

Pricing offers a powerful tool to influence the practice's profitability. Increasing the price will significantly increase the profit if variable and fixed costs are kept at the same level, or increased at a slower pace.
For example: a five to 10 per cent price increase can result in a more than 30 per cent increase in profit (**Table 7.1.1**); even in the case of a reduced caseload (**Table 7.1.2**), profitability increases (despite a lower workload, and a healthier work/life balance). On the other hand, a price reduction of 10 per cent can only be compensated by a 15 per cent (or more) increase in caseload (**Table 7.1.3**).

The influence of competition on pricing

Competition based on (low) pricing is a very limited and risky way to compete. It restricts creativity, creates a downward business spiral and eventually kills the business –not only the individual veterinarians' business, but also overall veterinary business in an area or a country.
A healthy competitive price structure, based on a quality product and services portfolio, will allow veterinarians to earn a decent profit in order to reinvest in the practice (staff and hardware), allow growth and provide improved services. A healthy veterinary profession is in the best interest of pets and owners. Price wars among veterinarians restrict development and limit service availability.

How to decide the right price level

The baseline price will be determined by the cost of the goods or service, increased by the proper margin, followed by awareness of competitor pricing of similar products and services. Neighbouring practices may have a more healthy cost structure (less fixed costs related to the buildings and the staff) and therefore, may generate the same or better margins at a lower consumer price. Business owners should always be working on cost reduction. Any cost that can be reduced or removed should be considered for the impact on the overall result. In addition to the above factors, client price perception important. Not all clients are able and willing to spend the same budget for veterinary healthcare and products. Veterinarians have a tendency to estimate a client's spending power and offer treatment options based on that guess. These judgements based on owner impressions can be hopelessly wrong. First of all, a high income and high available family or personal budget does not guarantee that this budget will be spend on pet healthcare, while owners with a limited budget may spend it all on the pet they love. In addition, it is well known to jewellery store staff that some of the richest clients may show up very poorly dressed. The bottom line is to never judge clients based on perceived appearance, and to base product and service offering and prices on a correct business approach, leaving the choices to the owner.

The veterinarian has to provide advice and insights, but choice is the owner's responsibility. When the price of optimal treatment turns out to be too high, the veterinarian has the responsibility to explain the consequences of the second choice, if available. Where alternative treatment can result in a predictable, good result, the veterinarian has to communicate clearly with the owner, including the consequences of non-treatment. Treating the pet at a below-cost level can be offered as an exception, but cannot be a routine proposition. When clients are offered two or more treatment options, only very few will decide to take the cheapest. The pet's healthcare is the owner's responsibility; the health of the practice is the responsibility of the veterinarian and staff. Only financially healthy clinics will be able to provide reliable pet healthcare and invest in the future.

Difference between cost and price

Cost is the total amount of money necessary to buy a product or a service. Price is the estimated value of a product or a service when buying or selling.
Example: a similar surgical indication is performed using either an old technique or a new one.

	Old technique	New technique
Operating time	2 hours	1 hour
Cost of goods	€100	€50
Functional recovery	85%	95%
Side effects	5%	1%

Which one is most costly to produce?
Which one will sell higher?
In this particular example, it is obvious the new procedure has more value and could be sold at a higher price.

But would it be the same logical reasoning for every practitioner? Is it because some specialists performed some procedures faster and better that they sell those for less? Not necessarily and it is important in this context to remember the following points.

- **It is the process that determines cost:**

– time of human resources (vet, nurses, staff);
– consumable goods;
– equipment investment;
– efficacy; and
– percentage of aftercare.

- **It is the market that determines price:**

– value of the service;
– perception of the value by the client;
– market price and competition; and
– overall trend of the market.

Any cost that can be reduced or removed should be considered for the impact on the overall result.

If competition is low and demand high, the enterprise has plenty of latitude in which to set its prices. It is important to notice that, in most Western countries, the animal health market has been stagnant for the past few years. However, pet owners' needs and demand for medical services is increasing, and the premium segment in the product and services market continues to grow. There is an increasing number of people with a lot of buying power. Veterinarians should approach these (potential) top clients in a similar way to other businesses by offering high quality and high service.

CHARGES AND COST OF THE SERVICE	
•TOTAL SURGICAL TIME OF VET (30MIN @ €120/HOUR)	€ 60,00
•TOTAL SURGICAL + PREP TIME OF NURSE (60MIN @ €25/HOUR	€ 25,00
•POST-OP NURSING CARE (VETERINARY AND NURSING TIME)	€ 15,00
•COST OF GOODS (SUTURE, BANDAGES, SYRINGES)	€ 5,00
•COST OF ANAESTHESIA (ISOFLURANE)	€ 7,00
•DRUGS (PAIN, ANTIBIOTICS, DISINFECTANT)	€ 3,00
•OPERATING ROOM COST	€ 12,00
•GENERAL REPARTITION OF COSTS (RENT, INSURANCE ETC)	€ 8,00
•HOSPITALISATION (1/2 DAY)	€ 10,00
TOTAL CHARGES AND COST	€ 130,00
MARGIN (50%)	€ 65,00
PRICE OF SERVICE	€ 210 + VAT

Figure 6.1.1

Example of price setting for a spay surgery in a 15kg female dog.

Cost

The cost is the sum of financial charges necessary to obtain a final product or service. When you evaluate the total amount of financial charges of a product or a service, you should, in theory, include the initial cost of goods, but add production costs (hourly salary x time, a percentage of fixed charges such as rent or electricity) to obtain the final cost of the product or service (ready to be sold). Knowing these costs enables knowledgeable decision making, such as reducing the fixed costs (salaries, time for productions, overall expenses), abandoning a product, or developing its sales.

Examples of obvious costs include the following.

- **Salaries:** veterinary staff, support staff, technicians, nurses and part-time help. Remember to include all employer taxes associated with these salaries.
- **Motoring costs:** garage bills, car insurance, depreciation on vehicles, interest on the capital invested in vehicles and practice equipment.
- **Establishment costs:** rent, rates, water rates, building insurance, heating, lighting and maintenance of the premises.
- **Overheads:** machine rentals, postage, shipping, telephone, laboratory fees, carcase disposal, consultancy fees, accounting fees, interest, bank charges, subscriptions, courses and continuing education expenses, laundry and cleaning, stationery, bad debts losses and depreciation on instruments and equipment.
- **Notional costs:** initial capital invested in the practice properties (this will help in future planning).

Note that owner or partner salary or net profit are not included in the above points. This should not be ignored until the end of the year, nor should it be added in as an outrageous figure. About 1.5 x an assistant's salary, adding the equivalent

taxes and employer wages, is a reasonable owner or a partner income. The final cost is a profit margin – over and above everything else. It acts as a buffer if costs escalate or work diminishes. The margin could be 10 per cent of other costs.

Calculation based on margin

Generally, it is simple to calculate the cost of a product. Its retail price will be determined according to the margin you want for that class of product. Both direct cost (buying price from the wholesaler, for example) and indirect costs (time and salary of people involved in the transaction, cost of merchandising and product turnover) should be considered. It is important to include discounts, free goods' bonuses, rebates, and other benefits that will impact the cost. Calculating the cost of a service is more complicated, and involves calculating the time taken by each employee and veterinarian involved in the transaction, then adding the hourly salary to this time. How much would you charge for your time? We suggest you look at what is usually done for similar professions to establish an hourly valuation of your time. For example, in most Western European countries, veterinarians (general practitioners) should value their time at a minimum €100-120 per hour. Look at the hourly rate of your local plumber and you will feel better when you charge more than €100 per hour; even more so when you compare the evening and weekend rates. Consumables and other goods involved in the service (direct charges) should be added, followed by indirect charges. A percentage of these charges could be charged to different services in your practice (such as rent, building cost, equipment amortisation, insurances and taxes).

Total Charges = Direct Charges (no repartition)
+ Indirect Charges (repartition between services)

Once the services' total charges are established, you may look at the desired margin (as a rule, we encourage a minimum margin of 50 per cent) and establish your retail price accordingly. If you are higher than the market price, something may be wrong and the equation may need re-evaluation, such as reducing some fixed cost or decreasing your margin. On the contrary, if you are lower, either your profit on that service will be higher or you may consider reducing the retail price in order to remain competitive.

For most routine procedures, we consider it important to create a spreadsheet of all activities associated with each service, showing each unit of cost for that service, including time, human resources involved, rechecks and consumables.

The veterinarian has to provide advice and insights, but choice is the owner's responsibility.

It is important for practitioners and his or her team members to understand the impact of price levels on the practice's financial results.

Only financially healthy clinics will be able to provide reliable pet healthcare and invest in the future.

Summary and conclusion

It is important for practitioners and his or her team members to understand the impact of price levels on the practice's financial results. This includes understanding how working at marginal price levels will decrease opportunities to grow and develop the business. Veterinarians need to establish their financial strategy related to retailing products and services. As in other small businesses, such price setting should follow certain rules and guidelines, and fit with local or regional realities. Consulting an accountant will ensure no major errors are introduced in your financial process. The objective is to run a financially healthy business. By helping clients to perceive the value of their purchase, the practice makes a profit, which allows for further investment in improved services.

Financial indicators 6.2

Introduction

FOR HEALTHY AND efficient management, it is necessary to measure and control business performance. This is true for all businesses, including micro corporations or small businesses such as veterinary clinics. To ignore these methods and work without any objective measurement of services and products is to take a serious risk with long-term practice health. It can be compared to navigating without instruments.

As the professional medical veterinarian relies on correct diagnostics (to prescribe relevant medical treatments, give appropriate prognoses and make correct decisions), so the professional managing veterinarian should rely on financial indicators to determine appropriate decisions related to practice business. Indicators must be useful and utilised, which means their use must be simple, rapid, efficient, objective and a true evaluation (a sort of barometer) of the practice health. It is a true diagnostic tool of basic practice management. Here are some indicators we believe are relevant for veterinary practitioners. Some are general, while others are more specifically dedicated to the veterinary practice economical environment.

Conventional indicators

Pure finance people will consult the classic tables and reports, including annual company reports, business summaries, and general accounting. This includes basic gross revenue reports. Daily, weekly and monthly gross income can be analysed and compared it to the previous year's results for similar periods. Some variable costs can also be determined, allowing a better evaluation of the margin. Once this is done, deduction of fixed costs will show profit prior to taxes. After deduction of all taxes, you can obtain your

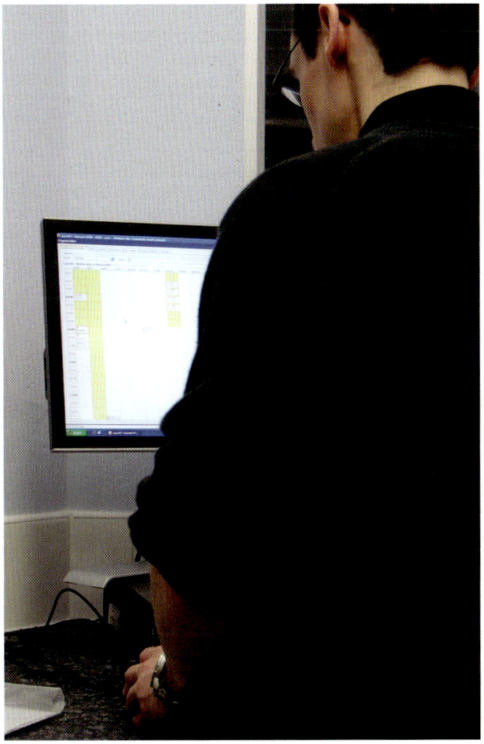

Even with a computerised practice, many practitioners do not regularly examine the practice statistics, looking for trends that could signal trouble.

Statistics can prove anything!

A practitioner was happy to report that his practice was up six per cent in March compared to the year before. When asked about fee increases, he proudly added that they raised fees by eight per cent at the beginning of the year. It was clear this veterinarian had no idea he was losing ground. If he had monitored all the numbers, not just those for monthly production, he probably would have noticed that the number of monthly invoices, active clients, and annual visits per client had decreased.

profit after taxes. Even with a computerised practice, many practitioners do not regularly examine the practice statistics, looking for trends that could signal trouble. Keep in mind that graphs and other visual images of the results will make it easier to recognise financial results. We have listed some important statistics that should be monitored in the practice, along with methods of making graphs for useful analysis. Thanks to modern technology, such graphs are easy to create and modify with spreadsheet software such as Microsoft Excel and Lotus), which will meet the needs of most veterinary practices.

Simple, but critical and fundamental statistics include:

- monthly production;
- monthly invoice numbers;
- register average transaction fee;
- veterinarian's average transaction fee;
- new client numbers;
- active client numbers;
- annual visits per client;
- production by category or classes of products;
- percentage of pets under one year of age.

The annual trend (increase/decline) indicates the trend for future business.

Another popular management parameter is net income per veterinarian. If you own a mixed practice, you should include statistics for production by species. Once you have selected which statistics to evaluate, you can chart and graph the numbers from existing monthly reports on to the spreadsheets; then use the spreadsheets to produce monthly and annual comparison graphs. If needed, ask your practice management software service company to help you with the retrieval of data and its conversion into a spreadsheet and graph format.

> A practical system is to raise fees regularly until the invoice numbers flatten, then back off for a while until they catch up.

Gross revenues or general productions.

In a service business, such as a veterinary practice, it is important to understand that sales of services and products drive the business, and that costs usually follow in proportion according to the revenues generated. Costs can, therefore, be estimated and are, to a certain extent, easy to control. For example, daily revenues can be determined as the number of clients x average transaction/client. Variation in results can, therefore, be explained by a fluctuation in client numbers and the average transaction/client. Monthly production statistics are an old standby for determining how the practice is doing. However, you need to put this figure into proper perspective – if you don't, it can give you a false sense of security.

The monthly invoice numbers provide a more accurate measure of practice activity than monthly production, but they're also the most sensitive to fee changes. Regular, small increments in fees barely affect the number of invoices. Be aware, however, that any sudden massive price raise, exceeding what the market will bear, may have negative consequences and lead your clients to seek veterinary services elsewhere. A practical system is to raise fees regularly until the invoice numbers flatten, then back off for a while until they catch up. A bar graph is a good way to track the monthly invoice numbers.

Number of clients.

It is interesting to evaluate this measurement and the way this parameter changes with time. For example, annual numbers might show the following:

Initial clients (at beginning of fiscal year)	5,000
New clients	750
Clients that did not return or clients owning an animal that died	350
Final clients (at end of fiscal year)	5,400

Several interesting indicators can be evaluated from this data:

- **Growth percentage.**
Final clients minus initial clients divided by initial clients:

$$\frac{(5{,}400 - 5{,}000)}{5{,}000} = 8 \text{ per cent}$$

- **Renewal percentage.** New clients divided by initial clients:

$$\frac{750}{5{,}000} = 15 \text{ per cent}$$

- **Lost percentage.**
Lost clients divided by initial clients:

$$\frac{350}{5{,}000} = 7 \text{ per cent}$$

- **Retention percentage.**
Retained clients (initial minus lost) divided by initial clients, or

$$\frac{(5{,}000 - 350)}{5{,}000} = 93 \text{ per cent}$$

These numbers tell the story of a growing practice.

Figure 6.2.1 illustrates a sudden drop in new client numbers. By using a bar graph to identify such a trend, you can react immediately to correct the problem rather than waiting months or years to learn you have a problem.

- **Mean transaction.**
This is the gross revenue for the period divided by the number of transactions for the same period. A transaction is determined by an invoice number. To facilitate criteria evaluation, take all the transactions that do not have a dedicated invoice and group them under one invoice and one virtual client. These may include sales of services versus sales of products, OTC product sales or pet food. The average transaction fee is an important and practical indicator to monitor. Declines may be due to economic recessions, employee theft, poor retail sales or lack of staff commitment to offer clients full pet services. To explore each individual performance, one tool is the veterinarian's average transaction fee. To arrive at this indicator, simply divide each veterinarian's production by the number of invoices he or she produced for the period. Some practitioners produce the same overall income with fewer clients, and their average transaction fees are more important than others. In such a case, matching production reports may aid better understanding of services and features some associates may have overlooked. For example, for every 100 examinations you perform 10 dental scaling procedures while your associate performs two. Bringing such a finding to the associate's attention, by discussing the number of missed cases of periodontal disease, is more likely to achieve a positive response from a conscientious veterinarian, and improve his or her quality of medical care far better than a blasting attack on the colleague's financial productivity.

If needed, ask your practice management software service company to help you with the retrieval of data and its conversion into a spreadsheet and graph format.

Figure 6.2.1

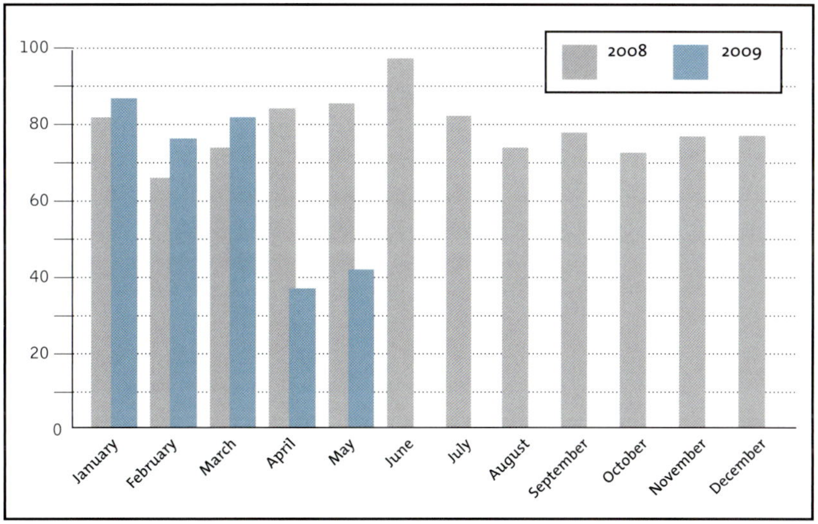

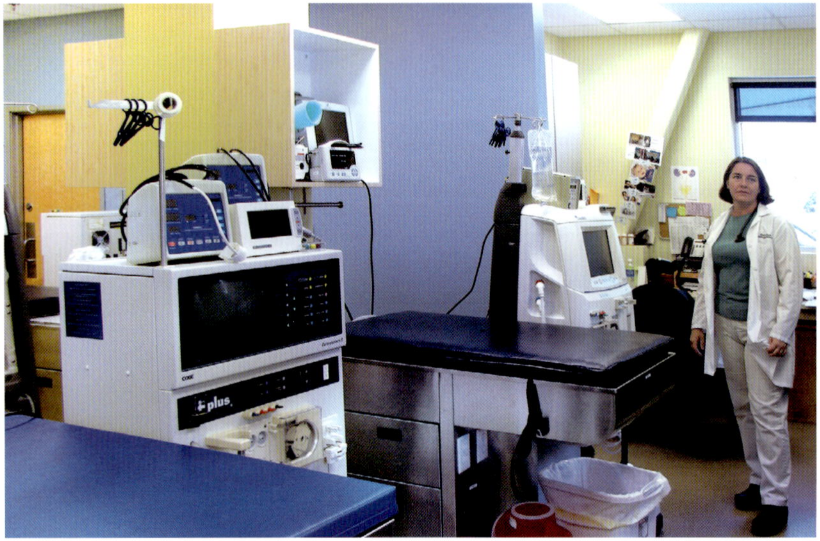

It is not unusual to see practices generating between 15 and 20 per cent of their total gross revenue through retailing pet food.

- **Client loyalty (number of transactions per client).**

This is the number of transactions divided by the number of clients for the time period. It is a good parameter to estimate clients' loyalty to the practice and should be measured on a monthly basis.
The active-client ratio is an interesting parameter: run two reports each month – one for clients who have visited your practice in the past 12 months and another for those who have visited in the past 24 hours. To generate the ratio, divide the number of clients for the 12-month period by the number of clients for the 24-hour period and add these together for the monthly period. A line graph from a spreadsheet works well here. If you live in an urban area and a client has not visited your practice in the past year, the odds are that he or she will not come back. The annual-visits-per-client statistic indicates how well your practice promotes total pet services and, to a certain extent, how loyal your clients are. Identifying your gold clients or key accounts is also useful. Once you list the 100 best clients and look at the overall production generated by this small number of regular clients, you will be surprising how much these people contribute to general practice production. The well-known marketing analysis, which says that 20 per cent of clients produce 80 per cent of income, applies equally to the veterinary enterprise.

- **Growth.**

Growth can be represented by the percentage of variability between two periods. The purist manager will choose a time period in which the number of days when the practice is open is quite similar (the year versus the month). A monthly indicator has the advantage of allowing prompt reactivity towards an event such as a sudden growth slowdown.

- **Fixed costs.**

These are costs unrelated to the number of services and to gross revenue. In a clinic, they cover rent, insurance policies and maintenance costs (electricity, heat). It is usually estimated these expenses should not be more than 20 per cent of gross income.

- **Variable costs.**

In a well-managed veterinary practice, variable costs of goods include the stock, salaries and wages. If the stock is not monitored it is no longer a variable, it becomes an expense that penalises clinic profitability. In a well-managed clinic, variable costs should not be much more than 40 per cent of overall income.

- **Profit.**

Whatever remains after deducting paid bills, variable costs, salaries and fixed costs, is the profit before income tax. It is preferable if this is more than 20 per cent of the gross income.

- **Costs and sales of retail products (drugs and food).**

It is important (even if this sounds basic) that sales are higher than the cost of products. Some small animal practices are highly dependant on the retail aspect of their business. This is particularly true as some premium pet foods or veterinary diets are available only through the veterinary channel. It is not unusual to see practices generating between 15 and 20 per cent of their total gross revenue through retailing pet food. There might be an upper limit to the percentage of turnover generated by pet food and other pet products sales. However, that upper limit should be decided by the clients and not by the veterinarian. In some countries, owners receive very high levels of sales generated in the practice. Clients appreciate the one-stop healthcare shopping convenience in a place they trust: the veterinary healthcare centre.

Less conventional indicators

- **The diagnostic ratio.**

This is the total gross revenue of services (excluding all OTC sales and non-medical revenues such as grooming or boarding), divided by the diagnostic services revenues entered through ancillary diagnostic procedures (laboratory, ultrasound, radiology and endoscopy). In the US, it is usually preferable to keep this ratio to less than five. If this not the case, it could reveal the practice is not using diagnostic resources as it should and relying too much on empirical diagnostic methods.

- **Vaccination ratio.**

Vaccines are, historically, an important part of veterinary practice income. However, it is dangerous to rely too much on these services, and veterinarians should diversify their services as much as possible to avoid being dependant on a clinic service that may decrease in revenues. There is a threat that vaccines may become either less prescribed or performed by veterinarians and/or would be performed by other professionals or by the owners. New vaccines are also proven to protect longer. Some data seem

There might be an upper limit to the percentage of turnover generated by pet food and other pet products sales. However, that upper limit should be decided by the clients and not by the veterinarian.

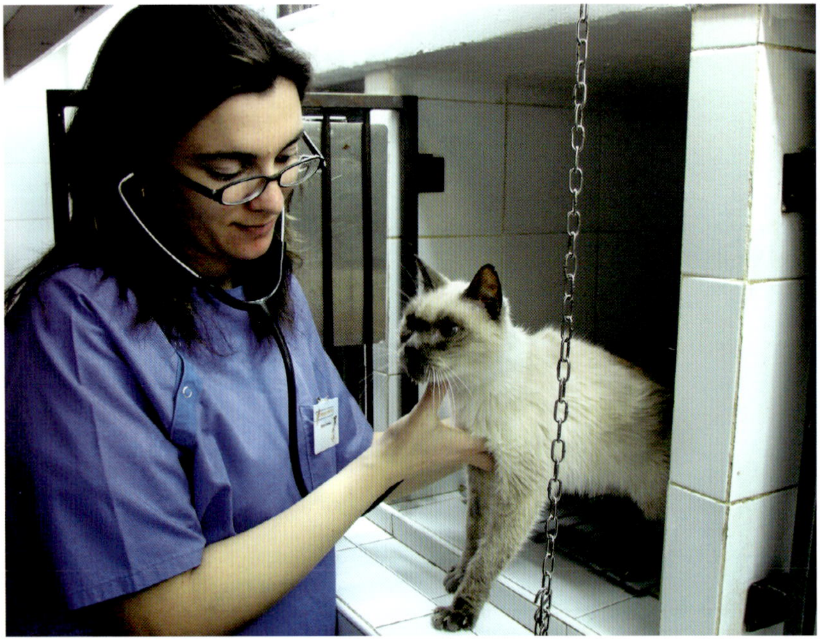

Veterinarians should diversify their services as much as possible to avoid being dependant on a clinic service that may decrease in revenues.

to suggest that scientists may recommend less vaccination. All these reasons are sufficient to advise veterinarians not to be vaccine dependant.
To calculate this ratio, multiply the number of client-purchased vaccines by the clinic examination fee (unless the computer data details such services automatically), thereby calculating the income. Next, divide the vaccine examination income by the gross revenue of services (GRS), but excluding all OTC sales and non-medical revenues such as grooming or boarding). One can also simply divide the GRS by the number of vaccines used for the period. This ratio is a good indicator of clinical services. Medical and surgical services require investments, which increase clinical variable costs, which in turn increase the ratio (GRS:vaccines) per prescribed vaccine. A progressive clinic should demonstrate high revenues per vaccine (independence from vaccines). It is not unusual to see practices generate more than 20 per cent of revenues from the annual vaccination examination. For an economically healthy practice, we recommend that vaccine-associated services remain under 20 per cent.

- **Hourly income per veterinarian.**

This is a measure of veterinarian activity and income. To obtain such an indicator, divide the gross income produced by each veterinarian by the number of each vet's work hours for that period. This parameter will show each practitioner his or her relative profitability compared to the working time (time-related efficiency).

- **Client surveys.**

You should always listen to your clients. The best source of information and an excellent form of "audit" is a survey obtained from your own clientele. It is also better to repeat this exercise regularly (once a year) to observe the variance. If this is done well, it is an excellent source of quality control.

Summary and conclusion

Many indicators can be used, depending on the practice, clients and imagination of each veterinarian. It is remarkable how computers contribute to data mining and allow leveraging of this accumulated information. Some practice owners remain reluctant to embrace the computer to develop their business; this resistance results in a competitive disadvantage. Additionally, purchasing a practice (or part of) without access to these critical business indicators creates a risk for the new owner (or co-owner). Certain criteria used in conventional businesses can easily be adapted to the veterinary practice, while non-conventional indicators are interesting, because they look beyond the factual numbers and help analyse the trends of our professional activity.

7

Conclusion

In this section:

Epilogue and Conclusion

Further reading

Acknowledgement

Epilogue and Conclusion 7.1

"VETERINARY MEDICINE IS a profession that could be compared with a boat that the veterinarian moves with two paddles. One represents the scientific and technical features, the other the business features. If you wish to move fast and keep on moving forward, you need to paddle equally on both sides of the boat – otherwise, you will only make nice circles."

The veterinary profession has changed considerably during the past 25 years. Dogs, cats and other companion animals have moved into our houses, and have become members of our families. There will be additional changes in our future. We believe small pets, such as cats, but including rodents, will increase in number, and clients will look for practices providing "specialised services". Don't expect your experience – or that of your family – to be the standard one to use in your professional future. Veterinarians and clients in other villages, towns, cities and countries prove, day in and day out, that there are fantastic opportunities for the development of the veterinary professional business.

The pet industry is a very big market and veterinarians are only a small part of it. For example, it is estimated that 85 per cent of pet healthcare purchases are made outside the veterinary practice. This means there is a tremendous opportunity for the profession to improve and grow its share for services to pet owners. Veterinarians who visualise and adapt their way of practising to our society, and fully embrace and emphasise the importance of the family/pet bond, will be more successful.

It is clear that owners no longer visit their veterinarian for therapeutic services. They expect total healthcare, and they want to trust the veterinarian and his or her staff to optimally care for their pets health. We believe owners are looking for an "optimal healthcare experience" when they visit their vet. Remember, it is not what customers receive (the facts, the science), but more what they perceive (how do they feel when they leave your practice?).

Veterinarians who consider their practice as a total service, directed towards the needs of pets and pet owners, will be successful. In other words, keep in mind that the services you provide, the products you sell and the people you sell to will determine

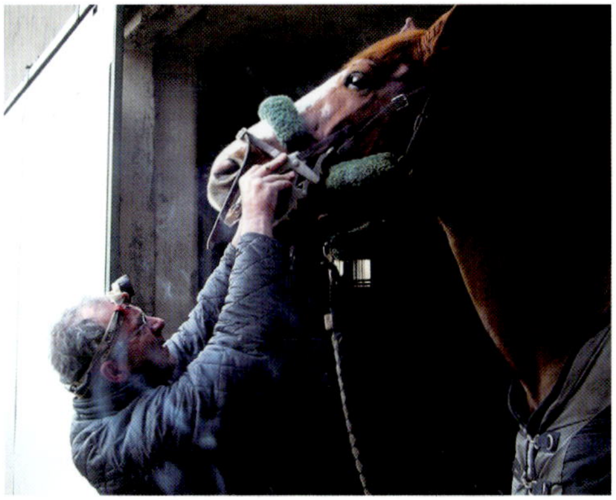

Veterinarians who visualise and adapt their way of practising to our society, and fully embrace and emphasise the importance of the family/pet bond, will be more successful.

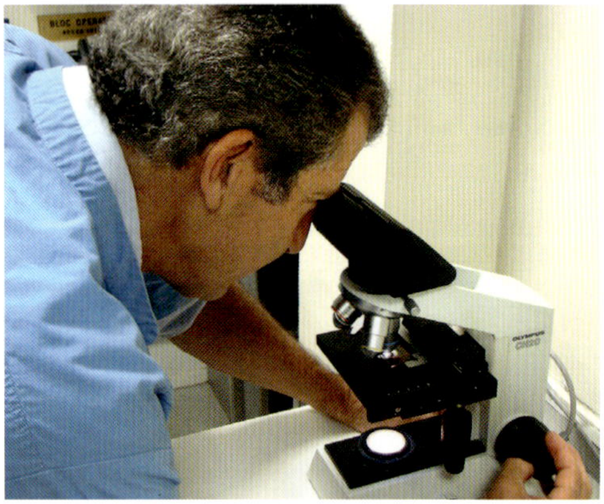

All the indicators are that the pet industry is very profitable and will become more so in the foreseeable future.

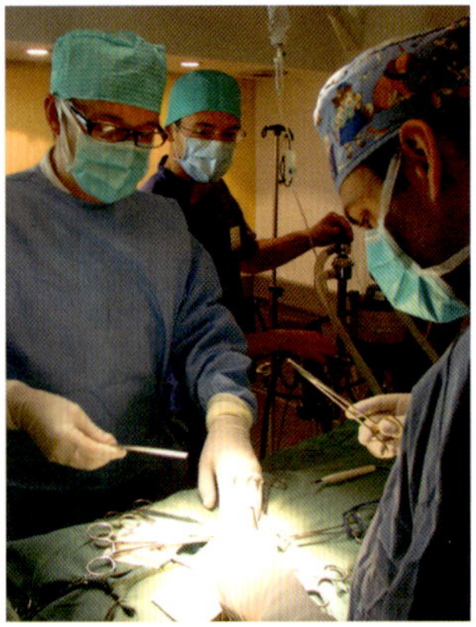

this success. It is your choice whether you wish to retail in your practice. But we feel that as long as you sell products in line with the vision and mission of your practice – products you feel comfortable recommending – and as long you retail these items in a professional manner, then they can only be beneficial for the practice.

All the indicators are that the pet industry is very profitable and will become more so in the foreseeable future. Many experts concur with this view. Are you ready for the future? Are you ready to anticipate and service your clients' needs and expectations? The future will be promising for those who will be ready to make the appropriate changes.

Across the world, the proportion of female vets is increasing. In certain veterinary schools, females represent more than 80 per cent of the student population. This has and will continue to impact on the profession, and it is a trend we all need to consider. Young vets are now often looking for part-time jobs, and also prefer an employee status, working with groups versus the classical "independent", single-handed vet who does it all alone. The birth of corporate practice 20 years ago in the USA has also provided new opportunities for young graduates, and will no doubt continue to do so in the future. Franchises such as Banfield Veterinary Hospitals in the US, or corporate group practices representing large public companies such as VCA (Veterinary Clinics of America) in the US, or CVS (UK) Ltd in the UK, are offering a new approach to pet healthcare. We are convinced these groups (and others to come) will increase the size of the market and help to move it forward, rather than lowering the standard of care and revenues for the profession. A large proportion of pet owners will prefer the "more personal, family-orientated approach" of the local practice rather than the "anonymous" aspect of the standardised chain hospital. As the vet population is ageing, the large proportion of vets from the baby-boomer generation who qualified in the 1960s are also happy to find such corporate groups to buy them out when the time comes to retire – particularly when young vets are not eager to invest in buying established veterinary hospitals and may prefer to work as vet employees, or start a practice from scratch.

In Europe, the EU Services Directive is scheduled for full implementation at the end of 2009, and will also trigger some changes in many professions, including the so-called regulated professions such as veterinarians. It may take some time in certain countries, but vets will be able to communicate and market their services and products in a much more open way. It will be interesting to observe how our profession is taking advantage of this European liberalisation, and we hope some positive initiatives will take place to help veterinary clients have access to more and better services for the benefit of all.

Facing such a potentially "open market", it will be our role – and our political representatives' challenge – to secure some of the profession's assets, such as the distribution of veterinary drugs by veterinarians. Should such distribution be limited solely to pharmacists in the future, it could not only jeopardise the easy access to medications for animals, but also an important source of income for vets. On the other hand, opening up the retailing of drugs to non-veterinarians could also have some significant, negative consequences. Vets should remain the animal health experts who guarantee the proper dispensing and prescription of medications. When one realises that vets are closely related to the safety of food, with all the public health-related aspects of medicines given to animals and the control of drug residues in large animals, it would be a nonsense to let non-veterinarians deliver certain drugs. However, the profession needs to be cautious and aware of these potential threats, as politicians are sometimes influenced by consumer needs, or blinded by some professional groups that may be strong and could lobby to obtain some favours.

Technology will continue to influence our lives and also our profession. The internet is present everywhere and impacts our clients and our practices. It is not only products that are available on the internet; DIY diagnosis is as well. Clients come to the hospital with a pre-diagnostic approach found on their favourite pet portal, and even ask you to write the prescription for the drug suggested on the web page. Communities and social internet groups such as Facebook, Twitter, MySpace, Hyves, LinkedIn and others will also create easy and friendly access to information. Vets need to be prepared for these new clients (or consumers) and adapt rather than react. Shouldn't we anticipate and create our own community, rather than wait to let others take the initiative? Some scientific and professional information is already available for vets (VIN, IVIS, etc), but the trend is to open our communication to client communities. What about internet sales of drugs, pet foods and other pet and animal-related products? Shouldn't we create our own delivery service, or join a veterinary-dedicated delivery service for our clients, rather than wait to let others drive these services and revenues away from our control?

The influence of technology will continue to be seen daily – one only needs to look at the influence of cell phones and the likes of the iPhone, BlackBerry and other smart tools coming to the market. Vets could be talking to their client on his or her cell phone, and clients could even show their pet's skin lesion using their smartphone. The vet could send an e-mail within minutes with a prescription attached to the foot of the message. It's a good thing there will still be a need for physical exams and diagnostic work-ups. Again, success will be closely related to your ability to adapt.

The electronic world will continue to influence our education processes. Many classes are now given online. What about the continuing education services, so important, essential, and more and

Clients could even show the vet their pet's skin lesion using their smartphone.

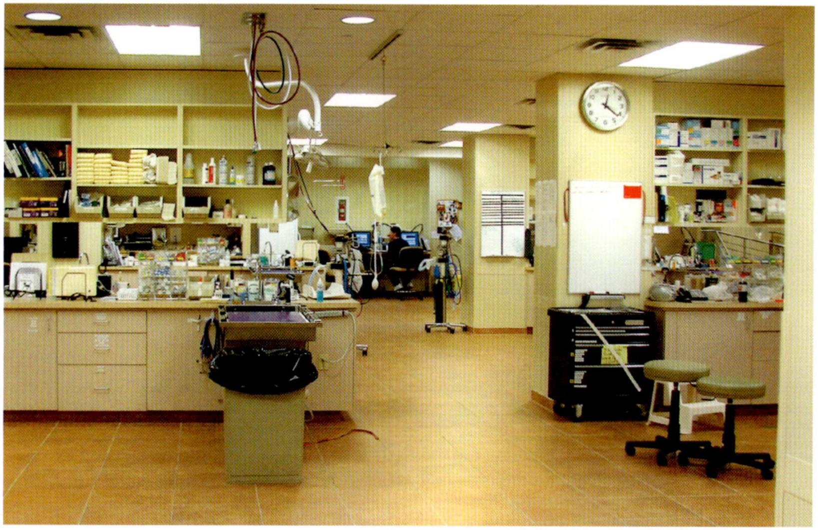

more required for the renewal of the licence to practise? Distance learning will certainly play a role; however, there will always be room for "hands-on" and interactive, face-to-face educational events. Practice management software will also evolve, not limiting its features to a client and animal database, but bringing some additional online features, such as diagnostic aids and instant data analysis relevant to the area, and the results of the initial examination and ancillary diagnostic tests.

Veterinarians should stop assuming they know what is working based on historical data. Instead, they should find out what is working in an ever-changing environment.

The human/pet bond grows stronger every day, and our clients are often more willing to pay for our services than we are to charge for them. Consumer surveys show that clients want value, choices, convenient locations, extended hours, one-stop shopping, no waiting, friendly staff members and a pleasant environment. To be successful, don't focus on the present, but include the future in your plans. Practices must assess clients' needs on an ongoing basis and provide what they expect. They should develop products and services that fit with the highest standards of healthcare for family members and make the clients aware of their availability.

Even if some of us question the new turns our profession is taking, there are tremendously exciting perspectives for our future. Among our clients, we vets are highly valued and respected for our knowledge, our compassion, our honesty, and our intelligence. We are loved and trusted as a profession, and, in many instances, respected above our human medicine counterparts. As Lawrence Peter "Yogi" Berra once said: "The future ain't what it used to be." Veterinarians should stop assuming they know what is working based on historical data. Instead, they should find out what is working in an ever-changing environment.

Veterinarians are facing a new era; a new opportunity to grow as a profession and to shape their future for the better. As a profession, we were once able to prosper with little competition or threat to our livelihood. Knowledge and doing our best used to be enough. Those days are gone. As Dr Michael Paul, AAHA president for 1999-2000, said recently: "We must now develop communication skills, business skills, and innovative attitudes if we are to continue the vision of what we all want this profession to be – an opportunity to serve and provide as we prosper."

We trust that *Essentials of Veterinary Practice* will contribute to this exciting and challenging exercise.

Success to you, your teams, your families and your friends!